The Continuity of Linguistic Change

Studies in Language Variation (SILV)
ISSN 1872-9592

The series aims to include empirical studies of linguistic variation as well as its description, explanation and interpretation in structural, social and cognitive terms. The series covers any relevant subdiscipline: sociolinguistics, contact linguistics, dialectology, historical linguistics, anthropology/anthropological linguistics. The emphasis will be on linguistic aspects and on the interaction between linguistic and extralinguistic aspects – not on extralinguistic aspects (including language ideology, policy etc.) as such.

For an overview of all books published in this series, please see *benjamins.com/catalog/silv*

Editors

Peter Auer
Universität Freiburg

Frans Hinskens
Meertens Instituut &
Radboud Universiteit
Nijmegen

Paul Kerswill
University of York

Editorial Board

Suzanne Aalberse
Universiteit van Amsterdam

Arto Anttila
Stanford University

Gaetano Berruto
Università di Torino

Jenny Cheshire
University of London

Katie Drager
University of Hawai'i at Mānoa

Katarzyna Dziubalska-Kołaczyk
Adam Mickiewicz University in Poznań

Jürg Fleischer
Philipps-Universität Marburg

Peter Gilles
University of Luxembourg

Brian D. Joseph
The Ohio State University

Johannes Kabatek
Universität Zürich

Pia Quist
University of Copenhagen

Anne-Catherine Simon
Université catholique de Louvain

Sali A. Tagliamonte
University of Toronto

Øystein Alexander Vangsnes
UiT The Arctic University of Norway

Juan A. Villena Ponsoda
Universidad de Málaga

Volume 31

The Continuity of Linguistic Change
Selected papers in honour of Juan Andrés Villena-Ponsoda
Edited by Matilde Vida-Castro and Antonio Manuel Ávila-Muñoz

The Continuity
of Linguistic Change

Selected papers in honour
of Juan Andrés Villena-Ponsoda

Edited by

Matilde Vida-Castro
Antonio Manuel Ávila-Muñoz
University of Malaga

John Benjamins Publishing Company
Amsterdam / Philadelphia

The paper used in this publication meets the minimum requirements of the American National Standard for Information Sciences – Permanence of Paper for Printed Library Materials, ANSI Z39.48-1984.

DOI 10.1075/silv.31

Cataloging-in-Publication Data available from Library of Congress:
LCCN 2023048260 (PRINT) / 2023048261 (E-BOOK)

ISBN 978 90 272 1448 5 (HB)
ISBN 978 90 272 4728 5 (E-BOOK)

© 2024 – John Benjamins B.V.
No part of this book may be reproduced in any form, by print, photoprint, microfilm, or any other means, without written permission from the publisher.

John Benjamins Publishing Company · https://benjamins.com

Table of contents

Preface *Frans Hinskens*	VII
Introduction *Matilde Vida-Castro & Antonio Ávila-Muñoz*	1
CHAPTER 1. Cognitive attributes of preclassical phonology *Francisco Moreno-Fernández*	15
CHAPTER 2. A Swedish merger: Production and perception of the short vowels /œ/ and /ɵ/ *Lena Wenner*	36
CHAPTER 3. Social patterns in s-palatalisation in Moroccan and Turkish ethnolectal Dutch: One half of a sociolinguistic study *Frans Hinskens & Etske Ooijevaar*	56
CHAPTER 4. Coronalisation in the German multi-ethnolect: Evidence for regional differentiation? *Peter Auer & Daniel Duran*	79
CHAPTER 5. Sociophonetic variation in a context of dialect contact: Standardisation and semi-standardisation in Canarian Spanish *Manuel Almeida & Juan M. Hernández-Campoy*	100
CHAPTER 6. Nuclear pitch accents in the assertive speech prosody of Acapulco, Mexico: Between lowland and highland Spanish *Pedro Martín-Butragueño*	119
CHAPTER 7. Little words, small moves: Clitic placement and syntactic change *Stavroula Tsiplakou*	140
CHAPTER 8. After dialectalisation: An overview of ongoing processes of convergence in Italian *Massimo Cerruti*	164
Juan Andrés Villena-Ponsoda's publications	183
Index	193

Preface

Frans Hinskens
Meertens Instituut | Radboud Universiteit Nijmegen, Netherlands

One gratifying aspect of my job is that it has given me ample opportunity to meet colleagues and students from numerous countries across the world. And many of them turned out to be not only interesting to talk to and sometimes work with, but also pleasant people. The combination of complementing each other's skills and insights on the one hand and enjoying the time spent together on the other (something I was lucky to experience already as a student) has led to valuable new ideas and collaborative projects. In a few cases, this combination has also yielded a lifelong friendship.

One of the first names that comes to mind in this regard is that of *mi querido amigo*, the unsurpassed Juan Andrés Villena-Ponsoda. Not only is he one of the most gentle and loyal people I know, he is also a brilliant and versatile linguist. He has always been highly regarded by his students and colleagues, has supervised outstanding PhD dissertations and has gathered excellent fellow researchers and professors around him in his department over the years.

In addition, he has been one of the driving forces behind PRESEEA, an exemplary, corpus-based research project on European and American varieties of Spanish about which we will undoubtedly hear a lot more in future. (Matilde Vida-Castro and Antonio Manuel Ávila-Muñoz describe the project in their Introduction to this volume.) However, this is not the only reason why Juan may be called one of the main ambassadors of the study of language variation in Spain. Like no other, through his work he has opened the doors to colleagues from the outside world, including the non-Spanish-speaking outside world. This work has included his role as the Spanish representative at the European Science Foundation Network on Social Dialectology "The Convergence and Divergence of Dialects in a Changing Europe" (1995–1998), as one of the founders and members of the Scientific Committee of the International Conference on Language Variation in Europe (ICLaVE, 2001–present), and as a loyal and most reliable member of the Editorial Board of the Benjamins' book series Studies in Language Variation. (It is only fair that the volume you now hold in your hands has been published in this series, for which this book is a worthy enrichment.)

On top of all this, Juan has also consistently managed to find the time to conduct excellent and innovative socio-dialectological and socio-phonetic research and present it at international forums. Few sociolinguists have conducted such in-depth research into social networks and language variation, and Juan Villena is not one to stop when the complex facts have been disentangled and brought to light. In this respect, his work is reminiscent of the words of the French mathematician Henri Poincaré in his Science et Méthode (1908): "On fait la science avec des faits comme une maison avec des pierres; mais une accumulation de faits n'est pas plus une science qu'un tas de pierres n'est une maison." ('Science is built of facts the way a house is built of bricks; but an accumulation of facts is no more science than a pile of bricks is a house.')

Juan Villena truly deserves to be honoured with a selection of thoroughly reviewed and revised papers, consisting of contributions by a group of linguists from a range of countries and language areas in Europe and Mexico and on a range of interrelated themes. Each theme and research question addressed reflects an aspect of Juan Villena's diverse, extensive and thorough oeuvre. I can only hope that, after his retirement, he will enjoy a well-deserved rest, but will not stop his excellent research altogether, so that his colleagues may continue to be provided with new ideas to chew over as well as just as many excuses to meet with him again.

This preface is far too short to do justice to Juan Villena's many qualities both as a linguist and friend. By way of conclusion (and at the risk of being dismissed as a pushy francophile), I would therefore like to join Voltaire, who wrote in a letter (dated 8 March 1732) to his friend M. de Cideville: "Courtes lettres et longues amitiés, tel est ma devise." ('Short letters and long friendships, that's my motto.')

Frans Hinskens

joined by numerous colleagues from the field who want to convey their appreciation and best wishes:

Suzanne Aalberse, Manuel Almeida, Arto Anttila, Álvaro Arias Cabal, Rosario Arias Doblas, Peter Auer, Antonio Manuel Ávila Muñoz, Marta Concepción Ayala Castro, María del Carmen Ayora Esteban, Enrique Baena Peña, Francisco Báez de Aguilar González, Isaac Barba Redondo, Karen B. Beaman, Antonio Benítez Burraco, Gaetano Berruto, Joan Borras-Comes, David Britain, Yvette Bürki, Raúl Caballero Sánchez, Miguel Calderón Campos, María Luisa Calero Vaquera, Javier Calle Martín, Rafael Cano Aguilar, Giovanni Caprara, Rocío Caravedo Barrios, Pedro Carbonero Cano, Inés Carrasco Cantos, Pilar Carrasco Cantos, Francisco Carriscondo Esquivel, Miguel Casas Gómez, María Auxiliadora Castillo Carballo, María del Carmen Cazorla Vivas, Massimo Cerruti, Ana María Cestero Mancera, Irene Checa García, Godsuno Chela Flores, Jenny Cheshire, Jael Correa Correa,

Luis Cortés Rodríguez, Franciso Javier Cuevas Alzuguren, Inmaculada Cuevas Molina, Francisco Díaz Montesinos, María Tadea Díaz Hormigo, Raúl Díaz Rosales, Katarzyna Dziubalska, Josefa Dorta Luis, Daniel Duran, Wendy Elvira-García, José María Enguita Utrilla, Luis Escoriza Morera, María Clara von Essen, Diana Esteba Ramos, Inés Fernández Ordóñez, Mauro Andrés Fernández Rodríguez, Manuel Galeote-López, María Pilar Garcés Gómez, Livia Cristina García Aguiar, María Teresa García Godoy, Francisco Joaquín García Marcos, Pilar García Mouton, Josefa García Naranjo, Juan Manuel García Platero, Juan Gavilán Macías, Rafael Gobernado Arribas, José Ramón Gómez Molina, Silvana Guerrero González, Gloria Guerrero Ramos, Susana Guerrero Salazar, Gregory R. Guy, Juan Manuel Hernández Campoy, Roeland van Hout, Antonio Jiménez Millán, José Jiménez Ruiz, Juan Luis Jiménez Ruiz, Johannes Kabatek, Paul Kerswill, María de la Cruz Lasarte Cervantes, Ángel López García, Pilar López Mora, Juan de Dios Luque Durán, Lucía Luque Nadal, Luis Luque Toro, Irania Malaver Arguinzones, Antonio Manjón-Cabeza Cruz, Pedro Martín Butragueño, María Antonia Martín Zorraquino, Eugenio Martínez Celdrán, María Antonia Martínez Núñez, Álvaro Molina García, Belén Molina Huete, Isabel Molina Martos, Ángel Luis Montilla Martos, Esteban Montoro del Arco, Francisco Moreno Fernández, David Moreno Olalla, Ignacio Moreno-Torres Sánchez, Esther Morillas García, Ramón Morillo-Velarde Pérez, Juan Antonio Moya Corral, Antonio Narbona Jiménez, Etske Ooijevaar, Antonio Pamies Bertrán, Susana Pastor Cesteros, Florentino Paredes García, Salvador Peláez Santamaría, Inmaculada Penadés Martínez, Chantal Pérez Hernández, Aurelio Pérez Jiménez, Manuel Fernando Pérez Lagos, Celia María Pérez Marqués, Juan Antonio Perles Rochel, Amparo Quiles Faz, Doina Repede, Brendan Regan, María Francisca Ribeiro de Araujo Santo Orcero, Sara Robles Ávila, Marcos Rodríguez Espinosa, Guillermo Rojo Sánchez, Lourdes Romera Barrios, Paolo Roseano, Assumpció Rost Bagudanch, Unn Røyneland, Engracia Rubio Perea, Daniel Moisés Sáez Rivera, Ventura Salazar García, Marta Samper Hernández, Marta Sánchez-Saus Laserna, José María Sánchez Sáez, María Sancho Pascual, Juana Santana Marrero, Inmaculada Clotilde Santos Díaz, Stephan Schmid, Beat Siebenhaar, Yorgos Sionakidis, Marcin Sosinski, Eivind Nessa Torgersen, Mats Thelander, Blanca Torres Bitter, Peter Trudgill, Stavroula Tsiplakou, Hans Van de Velde, Fabiola Varela García, Carmen Varo Varo, María Victoria Vázquez Rozas, Agustín Vera Luján, Matilde Vida Castro, Lena Wenner, Juan Jesús Zaro Vera, Sanja Zmijanac, and, of course, all those who made this volume possible.

Introduction

Matilde Vida-Castro & Antonio Manuel Ávila-Muñoz
Universidad de Málaga, Spain

> [...] en aquel mismo instante supe que ya había elegido el libro que iba a
> adoptar. O quizá debiera decir el libro que me iba a adoptar a mí.
> *La Sombra del Viento*, Carlos Ruiz Zafón

> [...] at that precise moment I knew I had already chosen
> the book I was going to adopt, or that was going to adopt me.
> *The Shadow of the Wind*, Carlos Ruiz Zafón

This volume presents a collection of selected papers in honour of Professor Juan Andrés Villena-Ponsoda, motivated by his recent retirement. The essays revolve around a common theme: linguistic variation, specifically sociophonetic variation and the analysis of the processes that promote linguistic change, a field to which Professor Villena-Ponsoda has dedicated so many years of research and to which he continues to contribute.

With his curiosity and intelligence, Villena-Ponsoda could have chosen any discipline, and no matter the subject, his contributions would have been just as valuable as they have been in the area he ultimately chose: the study of language and languages. He may have sensed in some way that philological knowledge would open the gates to new, limitless fields of knowledge. It is also possible that the reverse was the case, that, just as happened to Daniel Sempere, the protagonist in the novel by Ruiz Zafón, *The Shadow of the Wind*, it wasn't Villena-Ponsoda who chose to study philology, but philology and sociolinguistics that chose Villena-Ponsoda.

Juan Andrés Villena-Ponsoda, professor of general linguistics at the University of Malaga, is one of the Spanish researchers whose work has contributed the most to the development of the study of European Spanish varieties. This field has been transformed from being merely descriptive to providing explanatory value relating to the nature of linguistic change and the behaviour of speakers. Villena-Ponsoda's contribution to this development has, without doubt, been through his ability to recognise the lines and directions of international research most appropriate for the purpose, and through his determination to incorporate the theoretical and methodological foundations of these international currents into his own

https://doi.org/10.1075/silv.31.intro
© 2024 John Benjamins Publishing Company

research. To a certain degree, this tribute is one of the results of his effort, since the contributions are by some of the researchers with whom he has been able to work closely thanks to his ability, and with whom he has developed not only academic ties, but also bonds of sincere friendship.

Villena-Ponsoda's ability to recognise and incorporate the theoretical models and the methodologies most suitable for understanding linguistic behaviour derives from the successive layers of education he has acquired since his first years as a university student. First, we should point to his solid philological background, gained through his studies in Romance philology at the University of Granada. A profound understanding of the comparative grammar of the Romance languages and of the works of the German school of dialectology (Rohlfs 1966), among many others, began to shape him into a researcher capable of pursuing projects that would be innovative, but always rooted in solid philological foundations and in the rigorous approaches of the classical schools, a characteristic that would allow him to always choose the appropriate path when proposing working hypotheses or interpreting results. This is where we meet the philologist Villena-Ponsoda, the prudent and reflective Villena-Ponsoda who always finds a classical antecedent to seemingly new interpretations, but above all, the bold and creative Villena-Ponsoda who knows how to build on well-established foundations. This is also where we meet a young researcher who has an extensive education in dialectology and who writes his licentiate thesis on the palatalisation of /-a/[1] in Andalusian Spanish. This is the academic who, having found an interest in linguistic variation, set off along a path that would determine his subsequent career.

With his knowledge of the Romance languages and philology as the basis, Villena-Ponsoda took advantage of his years living outside of Spain, while working as a visiting lecturer in Spanish at the University of Bordeaux III, to focus on the detailed study of a broad series of works that, with their various traditions and approaches, had formed a relatively new discipline: the socially oriented approach to linguistics. This could thus be described as the time when Villena-Ponsoda added an education in sociolinguistics to his thorough knowledge of philology and dialectology, an education that was at the same time profound, meticulous and broad and that gave him an understanding of the multifaceted nature of both sociolinguistics and linguistics as a whole.

The results of so many years of study and thought are reflected in his dissertation, presented in 1982 and published later in his book *Fundamentos del pensamiento social sobre el lenguaje* 'The fundamentals of social thought in the field of language' (Villena-Ponsoda 1992). With impressive foresight and departing from

---

1. The fronting and raising of the central open Spanish vowel /a/, which is frequently realized as [ɛ] in Eastern Andalusian Spanish.

an exhaustive literature review, he proposed the principal demarcation criteria for the characterisation and, to a certain extent, the delimitation of a field of research that is multidisciplinary in essence, while at the same time describing the origin of sociolinguistics and defining the theoretical foundations of the field. That book is a magnificent essay that covers all the points of contact between linguistic systems and the social, cultural, historical and human environment in which they develop, by examining the various ways in which these points of contact have been reflected upon by the different authors, both in Europe and the Americas. Here we find again a researcher who based his entire subsequent academic career on a thorough understanding of the sources of a discipline that, despite being new, had a preceding tradition at its foundations, rooted in the nineteenth century (Humboldt 1822, 1827; 1836; Rousselot 1891; Durkheim 1895; etc.) and developed via multiple avenues throughout the twentieth century (Bakhtin 1929; Fishman 1966, 1968; Gumperz & Hymes 1972; Lambert 1972; Weinreich, Labov & Herzog 1968; etc.).

Shortly after the 1992 book, Villena-Ponsoda wisely added a second line of research that gave him access to a natural source of linguistic data for direct analysis. That line of research led to one of his best-known publications, *La ciudad lingüística: Fundamentos críticos de la sociolingüística urbana* 'The linguistic city: Crucial foundations of urban sociolinguistics' (1994), which was published following the formation, in 1993, of the research team that he has led throughout his academic career. The research team Vernáculo Urbano Malagueño 'Urban Vernacular of Malaga' (VUM) focuses on the study of the system of vernacular varieties used in the city of Malaga, and it has promoted the implementation of practices that, despite being well known in sociolinguistic research, could still be considered emergent in Spanish academia at the time when the team was established. Within this framework, Villena-Ponsoda (a) conducted an in-depth study on the city of Malaga, which he saw as an ideal "laboratory" in which to study language variation and change because of its particular sociodemographic characteristics; (b) performed a detailed analysis of the structure and organisation of Andalusian Spanish (the system of varieties); and (c) developed a methodology that considers ethnography, based on the observation of intermediate social structures (social networks), inspired by the works of Milroy (1980, 1982, 1987, etc.) and the quantitative analysis of data (Labov 1966, 1972a, etc.).

The initiative soon began to bear its first fruits. The attention and exactitude that went into its design allowed the research team to test (and prove) that the dynamism of the system of varieties of Andalusian, as well as the processes of change affecting this system, were equivalent to those of other languages to which these research methods were already being applied. In connection with the analysis of these first data, there began to grow an active collaboration with some of the researchers studying linguistic change, whose work Villena-Ponsoda, by now appointed to a professorship, had always followed so closely. In 1996, Villena-Ponsoda published the article *Convergence and divergence of dialects in a standard-dialect continuum. Networks and individuals in Malaga*, in the journal *Sociolinguistica* (in an issue edited by Peter Auer, Frans Hinskens and Klaus J. Mattheier), in which he demonstrated the external factors that promote processes of dialect convergence and divergence (Villena-Ponsoda 1996). This was the first of a long list of studies on linguistic variation in Europe produced in collaboration with an impressive array of researchers, some of whom have participated in this book.

It must be mentioned that this collaboration not only resulted in an interesting collection of publications, but also in a series of projects that, particularly in Europe, have served to raise interest among and encourage many young researchers to enter the field and pursue an academic career in linguistic variation. The first of these initiatives, organised in collaboration with colleagues such as Frans Hinskens, Peter Auer and Paul Kerswill, consisted of running the *Summer School on Social Dialectology "Convergence and divergence of dialects in a changing Europe"*. With the support of the European Science Foundation (ESF), it was hosted at the University of Malaga in November 1998. This was not only the first meeting point for many researchers who were beginning to develop their dissertations in this area, but the project also planted the seed for the *International Conference of Language Variation in Europe* (ICLaVE), which was first held in the year 2000 at the Pompeu Fabra University in Barcelona and is now, after 22 years and 11 editions, considered by many to be the main European research forum on linguistic variation.

In addition to the collaboration with this productive network of researchers, interested in the mechanisms of variation and change in the European languages, came the integration into a promising and ambitious pan-Hispanic project, *Proyecto para el Estudio Sociolingüístico del Español de España y América* 'Project for the sociolinguistic study of Spanish in Spain and The Americas' (PRESEEA). The idea was first proposed in 1993 and the project established in 1996, by Carmen Silva-Corvalán, Humberto López-Morales and Francisco Moreno-Fernández (Moreno-Fernández 1993, 1996). The project integrates more than 40 research teams from universities in Spain and the Americas, and the objective is to obtain a macro corpus of spoken language that consists of oral material from the main cities in the Hispanic world, collected using a common methodology, to allow for a comparative analysis of the diverse varieties of Spanish (Molina-Martos, Paredes-García & Cestero-Mancera 2020, Cestero-Mancera & Moreno-Fernández 2023). The fact that Professor Villena-Ponsoda and his team joined this project – which has been running today for more than 25 years – at such an early stage, means that they have been able to add to their historical sources a large corpus of the speech spoken in the city of Malaga, consisting of two sets of data obtained in two synchronic studies conducted 20 years apart (Vida-Castro 2007; Ávila-Muñoz, Lasarte-Cervantes & Villena-Ponsoda 2008; Lasarte-Cervantes, Sánchez Saez, Ávila-Muñoz & Villena-Ponsoda 2009; Vida-Castro 2022; Vida-Castro forthcoming).

During the same time, based on the empirical analysis of the data obtained via the ethnographic methodology he had previously developed, Villena-Ponsoda linked the study of processes of variation to the research into the history of the Spanish language, and in 2001, published *La continuidad del cambio lingüístico. Tendencias conservadoras e innovadoras en la fonología del español a la luz de la investigación sociolingüística urbana* 'The continuity of linguistic change. Innovative and conservative tendencies of Spanish phonology considered through the lens of urban sociolinguistic research' (Villena-Ponsoda 2001). This work was an utter innovation; it combined the quantitative analysis of synchronic data with the study of historical processes affecting the Spanish consonant system from the Middle Ages through to our time. In this work, Villena-Ponsoda shows himself to be at once a conscientious philologist, an outstanding dialectologist and a bold sociolinguist, who, as he himself acknowledges, seeks to link the contributions of important Spanish philologists, such as his own supervisor and mentor, José Mondéjar (1991), as well as those of many others, such as López-García (1992), Frago (1993) and Ariza (1994), with the theoretical and methodological assumptions of Labov's variationist sociolinguistics (1994) and the current European developments centred on sociolectal research (Auer & Hinskens 1996).

One of Villena-Ponsoda's principal contributions over the course of his publishing history has been the presentation of evidence that, in southern Spanish, the phonetic distinction between the phonemes /s/ and /θ/ is becoming increasingly frequent, particularly among young speakers with a medium or high educational level. This distinction, typical of Standard Spanish, is replacing the variable realisation of the single category of voiceless dental fricatives /θˢ/, present in the traditional varieties of Andalusian Spanish (deriving from a previous merger and with different allophonic realisations used by speakers depending on their geographic and social origin). This is a remarkable case of a split, to which Villena-Ponsoda and some of those who have followed in his footsteps have dedicated many years of work, and that seems to be the main feature of a hypothetical variety that became the focus of one of Villena-Ponsoda's most recent lines of research: the development of a potential intermediate variety that consistently combines the acquisition of Standard European Spanish features with traditional Andalusian features. It began to emerge during the 1970s, seemingly encouraged by the political, economic, demographic and social changes that took place at the time, and reflecting a mixed identity: an urban, modern and cosmopolitan speaker who continues to be committed to certain Andalusian cultural traditions. This conclusion is also the result of Villena-Ponsoda's career-long ability, described at the beginning of this portrayal, to incorporate and never abandon appropriate practices, namely methods for data collection and analysis always closely related to the ethnographic line of research (that Villena-Ponsoda (1994) could already recognise in the first contributions of Labov (1963, 1972b) and that has been revisited today by the so-called third wave in linguistic research; Eckert 2012). Ethnographic and interpretative analysis are the undertakings that gave him an in-depth, comprehensive and detailed understanding of the individual characteristics of those who kindly offered to contribute to the different speech corpora created, and that allow him to speak now of a proactive speaker, capable of assigning and producing the social significance of the variants they decide to use in their linguistic interactions (Villena-Ponsoda, Vida-Castro & Molina-García 2022: 249–254).

Villena-Ponsoda focuses on the study of the development of koine varieties, which have emerged across Europe following the various demographic and social changes that have occurred in recent history, and who therefore links this development to European research on sociolinguistics. To do so, Villena-Ponsoda departed from a detailed analysis of the description of the different patterns of pronunciation that have emerged in the Andalusian Spanish variation continuum (in the vernacular–standard continuum). which he shared in his article *Sociolinguistic patterns of Andalusian Spanish*, published in 2008 in the *International Journal of the Sociology of Language* (Villena-Ponsoda 2008). This analysis subsequently resulted in three principal lines of research, reflected in different works, of which most were published in collaboration with some of his colleagues and friends. These consisted of, first, the detailed study of the variety spoken in Malaga, based on the different levels of linguistic analysis (Ávila-Muñoz & Villena-Ponsoda 2010; Villena-Ponsoda & Ávila-Muñoz 2012); second, the stability of the traditional patterns of pronunciation, fostered by the local loyalty associated with covert prestige (Hernández-Campoy & Villena-Ponsoda 2009; Villena-Ponsoda & Ávila-Muñoz 2014); and third, the development of the intermediate Andalusian variety (Villena-Ponsoda & Vida-Castro 2017, 2020; Villena-Ponsoda et al. 2022)

As captured in these pages, Juan Andrés Villena-Ponsoda's character is defined primarily by a profound knowledge of the fields in which he has worked throughout his research career, and by an ability to quietly reflect on his analysis and interpretations for the required amount of time and without undue haste. The outstanding quality of the results that he has achieved through these traits is beyond question. However, a further important group of qualities can also be observed in all his academic and personal actions, lending him an unquestionable human touch. We have already mentioned his intelligence and curiosity, his creativity, intuition, perseverance and enthusiasm. To these qualities, we must now add his tremendous generosity, from which those of us who have followed in his footsteps as well as his colleagues have benefited, and his unwavering honesty and sincerity that, together with his prudence and integrity, have allowed him to surround himself with a circle of friends – one that includes the individuals who have participated in this tribute – who appreciate, admire and respect him, and who hope that he is going to produce many more contributions that are sure to enrich and progress our discipline, and who, above all, look forward to many more hours of enjoyable conversation and shared experiences.

Contents of this volume

This volume is a compilation of a series of papers on different topics that, as mentioned above, relate to the area that has defined the research career of Juan Andrés Villena-Ponsoda: the study of linguistic variation and of the mechanisms and processes associated with linguistic change. The authors are researchers of renowned international prestige who have made significant contributions in this field and who wanted to pay a well-deserved tribute to a respected colleague, but above all to a dear friend by whose side they have walked during many years of fascinating work.

The contribution of **Francisco Moreno-Fernández** is a bridge that connects classical, structuralist phonology with the more advanced concepts of cognitive phonology. Moreno-Fernández examines the proposals made for the concept of phoneme between the years 1889 and 1921, with an emphasis on those put forward by Edward Sapir and, particularly, by Jan Baudouin de Courtenay. Although more than a century has passed, the author presents evidence showing that ideas as recent as those of mental representation, social use and frequency, among others, considered today as innovations of cognitive linguistics, were already present in those early formulations, whether in more or less evident form. This chapter by Moreno-Fernández constitutes an appropriate prologue for a book focused on phonetic variation, but it also directly links to one of the facets of Villena-Ponsoda, that of the philologist who, in addition to being aware of the most current developments in linguistic research, has never renounced the teachings of those who preceded us.

The chapter by **Lena Wenner** is a perfect example of how most recent research on sociophonetics is making an ever-increasing use of the new (or not so new, as observed in the previous paragraph) concepts of cognitive phonology. The author analyses a phonetic change in progress in the region of Uppland

(Sweden), which consists of the merging of two Swedish vowels. For this purpose, she has conducted three different tests with the same group of informants: a production test, a perception test, and an attitudinal test to evaluate linguistic attitudes towards this specific change. One of the most significant results is that the informants who pronounce both vowels in a similar manner (those who "merge" the most) are, in fact, also the listeners who differentiate most easily between the two sounds. Wenner's study is an inevitable reminder of all the work that Villena-Ponsoda himself has dedicated to researching historical processes of the merger and subsequent split of coronal consonants in Andalusian Spanish. In such a process, one can observe how external factors can reverse phonological changes that, once complete, are considered irreversible simply by linguistic means (Garde's Principle, Labov 1994: 311), and how cognitive factors prove to be of particular importance.

The work of **Frans Hinskens** and **Etske Ooijevaar** follows one of the most recent lines pursued in the research of European sociolects and promises to provide valuable information on linguistic change induced by language contact. The authors present the preliminary findings of a contribution to the *Roots of Ethnolects* project (Muysken 2013; Hinskens 2019), which studies the development of composite varieties that derive from the international flows of migration seen over the last few decades. The main long-term objective of the project is to try to determine to what extent the characteristics of ethnolects are rooted in substrates, in processes stemming from second language acquisition, and in internal variation within the languages involved. In addition to this main aim, there are also certain secondary objectives, such as identifying the indexicality of the new features and how they spread to other speaker groups. Hinskens and Ooijevaar's study focuses on the process of palatalisation of /s-/ in the Dutch used by two second-generation migrant groups – one of Turkish descent (where the palatal fricative phoneme /ʃ/ exists) and the other of Moroccan descent (where this phoneme does not exist) – in two different dialect areas of the Netherlands (Amsterdam and Nijmegen). Although the study has not yet been concluded, the data display the influence of the substrate and dialect area on the process of palatalisation of /s-/ in the ethnolects of the two Dutch varieties under study.

The chapter by **Peter Auer** and **Daniel Duran** also analyses a phonetic feature occurring in an ethnolectal variety. In this case, it is the merger of the palatal fricative consonant /ç/ with the alveopalatal /ʃ/, a phenomenon that can be frequently observed among young people of migrant (mainly Turkish) background in the German city of Berlin. The authors perform acoustic analyses on the productions of these two phonemes by speakers with a migrant background from the city of Stuttgart. They observe that, in their own data, there is a great acoustic distance between the two realisations, meaning that one cannot speak of a merger between the two consonants in the region analysed. Among the possible interpretations of this regional difference with regard to the coronalisation of /ç/, the authors place a certain degree of emphasis on the different social meanings that this feature can convey in the areas compared, since it seems to represent a stereotype in Stuttgart, whereas it is unmarked in Berlin.

The contribution of **Manuel Almeida** and **Juan Manuel Hernández-Campoy** similarly addresses the effect of the contact between linguistic varieties on socio-phonetic changes. Almeida and Hernández-Campoy analyse two features characteristic of Canarian Spanish (Spain), which coexist with interdialectal and standard variants due to the contact between the local vernacular and Standard Spanish, contact with the latter being via the media. The speech sample for this study was obtained from recordings of local radio programmes broadcast between 2006 and 2010, and it includes different speakers categorised by the authors according to their gender and degree of active participation in the programmes (*degree of public contact*). The results seem to indicate that, although it is the vernacular variants that are used most often in the media and the use of innovative variants (both hybrid and standard) can be observed more frequently among women than men, the behaviour of the two features differs when observing their distribution according to degree of participation. In the case of the first feature analysed, (c), the predominant form is the vernacular, and no significant differences between the groups come to light. However, in the second feature, (h), the innovative forms seem to show a positive correlation with a higher degree of speaker participation. This paper is not only a link to one of the principal lines of research of Villena-Ponsoda, namely linguistic changes that derive from the development of intermediate varieties, but it also focuses on one of the varieties of Spanish that, together with Andalusian, presents innovative features as compared to the northern varieties, which form the basis of Standard European Spanish.

The object of study of the chapter presented by **Pedro Martín-Butragueño** is the prosody of the Spanish of Acapulco (Mexico), a variety of Latin American Spanish. This author focuses on the intonational patterns in a large set of assertive (declarative) statements,[2] extracted from a collection of sociolinguistic interviews from the *Corpus oral del español de México* 'Oral corpus of Mexican Spanish'. The interviews are with 10 informants stratified by gender, age and educational level. One of the objectives of this work is to confirm the results obtained in a previous study based on a set of more limited data, consisting of the responses provided by informants during a discourse completion task. These previous results indicate that the Spanish of Acapulco presents similar patterns to those appearing

---

2. The author uses the term *assertive* instead of *declarative* to avoid the confluence with Searle's declarative speech acts (1975).

in central Mexican varieties. The analysis provided in this chapter by Martín-Butragueño shows that the variables influencing the distribution of the different pitch accents are (a) the informative structure of the segment in which the nuclear syllable occurs, and (b) the age of the informants. In connection with the latter, the analysis shows that the more prominent pitch accents occur least frequently among younger speakers, as also appears to be the case in central Mexico.

The chapter by **Stavroula Tsiplakou** also addresses the influence of the standard on traditional varieties. In this case, the study focuses on the change in placement observed for clitic pronouns in Cypriot Greek, where, in certain contexts, when the pronoun would usually appear in second position in the clause, it frequently appears to the left of the verb instead, thus following the structure typical of Standard Greek. The author reviews various studies conducted in the field of sociolinguistics that broadly confirm that this change in placement is produced and accepted to a greater extent by educated young women. It also explores in detail the possible explanations of this phenomenon, drawing on (a) the presence of two competing grammars within a single variety, the Cypriot koine, one belonging to Standard Greek and the other to the local variety, and (b) the Interface Hypothesis. The proposal put forward by Tsiplakou, based on a profound knowledge of grammatical behaviour, represents a direct link to the spirit underlying the research of Villena-Ponsoda: to explain linguistic processes through the detailed study of systems and their behaviour.

The book closes with a contribution by **Massimo Cerruti**. This paper takes a broader view and analyses the processes of vertical and horizontal convergence affecting the Italian language. Following a description of the complex mosaic of varieties that has developed due to the coexistence of the Italo-Romance dialects and the national standard over the past two centuries, Cerruti focuses on the regional varieties and, with the help of examples for all linguistic levels, extracted from different corpora, shows that the characteristics that distinguish the regional varieties are becoming considerably less pronounced. On the one hand, processes of vertical convergence, which can take place both "upward" and "downward", are resulting in (a) the diffusion of features marked regionally as part of the regional standard ("downward" convergence), and (b) the loss of dialect features among young speakers with high educational levels ("upward" convergence). On the other hand, horizontal convergence between varieties has resulted in the supra-regional diffusion of features originating from regional varieties. An interesting fact concerning horizontal convergence, which tends to affect the younger generations, is that the indexicality of such features changes, as they shift from being markers of origin to being markers of social identity. The chapter by Cerruti is certainly an appropriate culmination of this tribute, since it not only links to one of the subjects to which Villena-Ponsoda has also dedicated a good part of his research career, namely processes of dialect convergence, but it also reflects many of his academic qualities, such as a profound knowledge of the Romance languages and of the behaviour of speakers.

It now remains for us, as the editors of this volume, to extend our sincere gratitude to the editors of the series *Studies in Language Variation*, Peter Auer, Frans Hinskens and Paul Kerswill, for their belief in this project from its beginning, for their kindness and generosity in offering this space for the publication of this tribute, and for the support they have provided. We would also like to thank the anonymous reviewers for dedicating their time and knowledge to evaluating the manuscripts, and Zahra-Claire Bahrani-Peacock for her professionalism in performing the stylistic revision of these works, in ensuring that the editorial guidelines were adhered to, and in maintaining internal coherence throughout the volume. Lastly, we would like to express our deepest appreciation to the authors who contributed to this tribute dedicated to our dear *maestro* and colleague, not only for putting so much of their effort and time into providing contributions of excellent quality, but also for the great care they have shown throughout the process, which doubtlessly reflects the extent of the respect and affection that Juan Andrés Villena-Ponsoda has earned.

References

Ariza, Manuel. 1994. *Sobre fonética histórica del español* [On the historical phonetics of Spanish]. Madrid: Arco/Libros.

Auer, Peter & Frans Hinskens (eds.). 1996. Convergence and divergence of dialects in Europe. *Sociolinguistica* 10. 1–30.

Ávila-Muñoz, Antonio Manuel, Lasarte-Cervantes, María de la Cruz & Villena-Ponsoda, Juan Andrés (eds.). 2008. *El español hablado en Málaga II. Corpus oral para su estudio sociolingüístico. Nivel de estudios medio* [The Spanish spoken in Malaga II. An oral corpus for sociolinguistic research. Medium educational level]. Malaga: Sarriá.

Ávila-Muñoz, Antonio Manuel & Juan Andrés Villena-Ponsoda (eds.). 2010. *Variación social del léxico disponible en la ciudad de Málaga. Diccionario y análisis* [Social variation in the available vocabulary of the city of Malaga. Dictionary and analysis]. Malaga: Sarriá.

Bakhtin, Mikhail (N.V. Volochinov). 1977 [1929]. *Le marxisme et la philosophie du langage. Essai d'application de la méthode sociologique en linguistique* [Marxism and philosophy of language. The application of the sociologic method on linguistics]. Paris: Minuit.

Cestero-Mancera, Ana María & Moreno-Fernández, Francisco (eds). 2023. Patrones sociolingüísticos y geolectales del español. Estudios sobre el corpus PRESEEA [Sociolinguistic and geolectal patterns in Spanish. Studies on the PRESEEA corpus]. *Círculo de Lingüística Aplicada a la Comunicación* 94. Special Issue.

Durkheim, Émile. 1895. *Les regles de la méthode sociologique* [The rules of sociological method]. Paris: Les Presses universitaires de France.

Eckert, Penelope. 2012. Three waves of variation study: The emergence of meaning in the study of sociolinguistic variation. *Annual Review of Anthropology* 41(1). 87–100.

Fishman, Joshua. 1966. *Language loyalty in the United States*. The Hague: Mouton.

Fishman, Joshua (ed.). 1968. *Readings in the sociology of language*. The Hague: Mouton.

Frago, Juan Antonio. 1993. *Historia de las hablas andaluzas* [A history of Andalusian speech]. Madrid: Arco/Libros.

Gumperz, John & Hymes, Dell (eds.). 1972. *Directions in Sociolinguistics. The ethnography of communication*. New York: Holt, Rinehatt & Winston.

Hernández-Campoy, Juan Manuel & Juan Andrés Villena-Ponsoda. 2009. Standardness and non-standardness in Spain: Dialect attrition and revitalization of regional dialects of Spanish. *International Journal of the Sociology of Language* 196–197. 181–214.

Hinskens, Frans. 2019. Ethnolects: Where language contact, language acquisition and dialect variation meet. *7th International Conference on Modern Greek Dialects and Linguistic Theory (MGDLT7)*. 1–27.

Humboldt, Wilhelm von. 1972 [1822, 1827]. *Sobre el origen de las formas gramaticales y sobre su influencia en el desarrollo de las ideas* [On the origin of grammatical forms and on their influence on the development of ideas] (1822) & *Carta a M. Abel Rémusat sobre la naturaleza de las formas gramaticales en general y sobre el genio de la lengua china en particular* [A letter to M. Abel Rémusat on the nature of grammatical forms in general and on the genius of the Chinese language in particular] (1827). Barcelona: Anagrama.

Humboldt, Wilhelm von. 1990 [1836]. *Sobre la diversidad de la estructura del lenguaje humano y su influencia sobre el desarrollo espiritual de la humanidad* [On the diversity of the structure of human language and its influence on the spiritual development of humanity]. Barcelona: Anthropos.

Labov, William. 1963. The Social Motivation of a Sound Change, *WORD*, 19:3, 273 309,

Labov, William. 1966. *The social stratification of English in New York City*. Washington, DC: Center for Applied Linguistics.

Labov, William. 1972a. *Sociolinguistic patterns*. Philadelphia, PA: University of Pennsylvania.

Labov, William. 1972b. Language in the inner city. *Studies in the Black English Vernacular*. Philadelphia: University of Pennsylvania Press.

Labov, William. 1994. *Principles of linguistic change: Internal factors*. Oxford: Blackwell.

Lambert, Wallace. 1972. *Language, psychology and culture*. Stanford: Stanford University Press.

Lasarte-Cervantes, María de la Cruz, Sánchez-Sáez, José María, Ávila-Muñoz, Antonio Manuel & Villena-Ponsoda, Juan Andrés (eds.). 2009. *El español hablado en Málaga III. Corpus oral para su estudio sociolingüístico. Nivel de estudios alto* [The Spanish spoken in Malaga III. An oral corpus for sociolinguistic research. High educational level]. Malaga: Sarriá.

López-García, Ángel. 1992. Los reajustes fonológicos del español a la luz de una teoría del cambio [The phonological readjustments of Spanish considered through the lens of a theory of change]. In José Antonio Bartol-Hernández, Javier de Santiago-Guervós & Juan Felipe García-Santos (eds.), *Estudios filológicos en homenaje a Eugenio de Bustos Tovar*, vol. 2, 519–530. Salamanca: Universidad de Salamanca.

Milroy, Lesley. 1980. *Language and social networks*. Oxford: Blackwell.

Milroy, Lesley. 1982. Social network and linguistic focusing. In Suzanne Romaine (ed.), *Sociolinguistic variation in speech communities*. 141–143. London: E. Arnold.

Milroy, Lesley. 1987. *Observing and analyzing natural language*. Oxford: Blackwell.

Molina-Martos, Isabel, Paredes-García, Florentino & Cestero-Mancera, Ana María (eds.). 2020. Sociolinguistic patterns and processes of convergence and divergence in Spanish. *Spanish in Context*, 17/2. Special Issue.

Mondéjar, José. 1991. *Dialectología andaluza. Estudios* [Andalusian dialectology. Studies]. Granada: Editorial Don Quijote.

Moreno-Fernández, Francisco. 1993. Proyecto para el Estudio Sociolingüístico de España y América (PRESEEA) [Project for the sociolinguistic study of Spanish in Spain and America (PRESEEA)], *Lingüística* 5. 268–271.

Moreno-Fernández, Francisco. 1996. Metodología del 'Proyecto para el Estudio Sociolingüístico de España y América' (PRESEEA) [Methodology of the "Project for the sociolinguistic study of Spanish in Spain and America" (PRESEEA)], *Lingüística* 8. 257–287.

Muysken, Pieter. 2013. Ethnolects of Dutch. In Frans Hinskens & Johan Taeldeman (eds.), *Language and space: Dutch*, 739–761. Berlin & Boston, MA: De Gruyter Mouton.

Rohlfs, Gerhard. 1966. *Lengua y cultura. Estudios lingüísticos y folklóricos* [Language and culture. Linguistic and folkloric studies]. Madrid: Ediciones Alcalá.

Rousselot, Jean-Pierre 1891. *Les modifications phonétiques du langage dans le patois d'une famille de Cellefrouin (Charente)* [Phonetic modifications in language studied in the dialect of a family of Cellefrouin (Charente)]. Paris: H. Welter.

Searle, John R. 1975. A taxonomy of illocutionary acts. In Keith Gunderson (ed.), *Language, Mind and Knowledge*. 344–369. Minneapolis: University of Minnesota Press.

Vida-Castro, Matilde (ed.). 2007. *El español hablado en Málaga. Corpus oral para su estudio sociolingüístico, I. Nivel de estudios bajo* [The Spanish spoken in Malaga. An oral corpus for sociolinguistic research, I. Basic educational level]. Malaga: Sarriá.

Vida-Castro, Matilde. 2022. On competing indexicalities in southern Peninsular Spanish. A sociophonetic and perceptual analysis of affricate [ts] through time. *Language Variation and Change*, 34(2), 137 163.

Vida-Castro, Matilde (ed.). Forthcoming. Segundo corpus PRESEEA-MÁLAGA. Nuevos datos para su estudio sociolingüístico [Second corpus PRESEEA-MALAGA. New data for sociolinguistic studies].

Villena-Ponsoda, Juan Andrés. 1992. *Fundamentos del pensamiento social sobre el lenguaje. Constitución y crítica de la sociolingüística* [The fundamentals of social thought in the field of language. Constitution and criticism of sociolinguistics]. Malaga: Ágora.

Villena-Ponsoda, Juan Andrés. 1994. *La ciudad lingüística: Fundamentos críticos de la sociolingüística urbana* [The linguistic city: Crucial foundations of urban sociolinguistics]. Granada: Universidad de Granada.

Villena-Ponsoda, Juan Andrés. 1996. Convergence and divergence of dialects in a standard-dialect continuum. Networks and individuals in Malaga. *Sociolinguistica* 10. 112–137.

Villena-Ponsoda, Juan Andrés. 2001. *La continuidad del cambio lingüístico. Tendencias conservadoras e innovadoras en la fonología del español a la luz de la investigación sociolingüística urbana* [The continuity of linguistic change. Innovative and conservative tendencies of Spanish phonology considered through the lens of urban sociolinguistic research]. Granada: Universidad de Granada.

Villena-Ponsoda, Juan Andrés. 2008. Sociolinguistic patterns of Andalusian Spanish. *International Journal of the Sociology of Language* 193–194. 139–60.

Villena-Ponsoda, Juan Andrés & Antonio Manuel Ávila-Muñoz (eds.). 2012. *Estudios sobre el español de Málaga. Pronunciación, vocabulario y sintaxis* [Studies on the Spanish of Malaga. Pronunciation, vocabulary, syntax]. Malaga: Sarriá.

Villena-Ponsoda, Juan Andrés & Antonio Manuel Ávila-Muñoz. 2014. Dialect stability and divergence in southern Spain. Social and personal motivations. In Kurt Braunmüller, Steffen Höder & Karoline Kühl (eds.), *Stability and divergence in language contact. Factors and mechanisms*, 207–38. Amsterdam: John Benjamins.

Villena-Ponsoda, Juan Andrés & Matilde Vida-Castro. 2017. Between local and standard varieties. Horizontal and vertical convergence and divergence of dialects in Southern Spain. In Isabelle Buchstaller & Beat Siebenhaar (eds.), *Language Variation – European Perspectives VI. Selected papers from the Eighth International Conference on Language Variation in Europe (ICLaVE 8)*, 125–40. Amsterdam: John Benjamins.

Villena-Ponsoda, Juan Andrés & Matilde Vida-Castro. 2020. Variation, identity and indexicality in southern Spanish. On the emergence of a new intermediate variety in urban Andalusia. In Massimo Cerruti & Stavroula Tsiplakou (eds.), *Intermediate language varieties. Koinai and regional standards in Europe*, 150–83. Amsterdam: John Benjamins.

Villena-Ponsoda, Juan Andrés, Matilde Vida-Castro & Álvaro Molina-García. 2022. Coherence in a levelled variety. The case of Andalusian. In Karen B. Beaman & Gregory R. Guy (eds.) *The coherence of linguistic communities. Orderly heterogeneity and social meaning.* 239–257. New York, NY: Routledge.

Weinreich, Uriel, Labov, William & Herzog, Marvin I. 1968. Empirical foundations for a theory of language change. In Winfred P. Lehmann & Yakob Malkiel (eds.) *Directions for Historical Linguistics: A symposium.* 95 195. Texas: University of Texas Press.

CHAPTER 1

Cognitive attributes
of preclassical phonology

Francisco Moreno-Fernández
Universität Heidelberg, Germany | Universidad de Alcalá, Spain

Cognitive phonology, as a development of cognitive linguistics, is one of the
most interesting fields of research in the twenty-first century. It is often
opposed to so-called "classical phonology", since the latter mainly builds on
structuralist foundations. This chapter considers the proposals made
between 1889 and 1921 concerning the concept of "phoneme", which
coincide in many basic assumptions with contemporary cognitive
phonology. Among these proposals, those of Jan Baudouin de Courtenay
are especially relevant, together with those of Edward Sapir. Basic concepts
of cognitivism, such as mental representation, similarity, social use and
frequency, can be found in them, both explicitly and implicitly.

Keywords: phoneme, phonology, phonetics, cognitivism, mental
representation, usage, frequency

1.   Introduction

The intention of these pages is to reflect on a series of proposals and arguments
made between 1889, the date of publication of a work by the Polish linguist Jan
Baudouin de Courtenay on the tasks of linguistics, and 1921, the date of publication of Edward Sapir's *Language*. These arguments concern the nature of language and phonology, and in them, mental representations of phonic units are
given a clear priority and are explained from a psychological perspective. The
concept of reference in this respect is that of "phoneme", the origins and contents
of which have been long discussed and also negated in one case (see the approach
by British linguists, below).

The hypothesis put forward in this chapter is that the thinking and analysis
of Baudouin and Sapir, as well as that of other linguists of so-called "preclassical
phonology", is fully compatible with the foundations of contemporary cognitive
phonology. They are clear antecedents and precursors of current cognitivism

https://doi.org/10.1075/silv.31.01mor
© 2024 John Benjamins Publishing Company

because of the importance they attribute to the psychological element of the phonic field and the use of language in social interaction. For cognitive linguistics, sounds move between the space of production and that of perception, and the latter is decisive in explaining how languages vary and change and how speakers organise those sounds in their competences.

The first section of this chapter presents the main ways in which the concept of phoneme has been explained, especially in the preclassical period, prior to structuralism and, therefore, to the general diffusion of its functional and distinctive dimensions. The foundations of cognitive phonology are then summarised in order to offer a basis for comparison with the preclassical proposals and present Baudouin's comments concerning his view of languages and their phonology, relating them to various aspects of cognitivism. In the following sections, other preclassical proposals are explained in which singular relevance is given to the psychological perspective and mental representations. Special attention is paid here to Sapir's proposals as well as to the social dimension in general of oral productions and perceptions. The chapter concludes with a discussion of the extent to which preclassical phonology is a clear antecedent of cognitive phonology.

2. The history of the phoneme concept

The history of phonology is closely linked to the history of the word "phoneme" (adopted from the Greek word *phoneme*, meaning 'a sound uttered'. Fr. *phóneme*, Ger. *Phonem*, Sp. *fonema*) (Havet 1876; Jones 1957; Godel 1957; Jakobson 1958, 1971; Albrow 1981; Clark et al. 2007; Mugdan 2011). However, beyond the concrete origin of the term, linguistic historiography has been interested in the definitions given to the concept itself and the way in which these have emerged and succeeded each other. The first uses of phoneme referred either simply to speech sound or to the set of consonants and vowels, but these are not the meanings that most interest phonology. The modern term was undoubtedly born from a clear desire to distinguish the sound itself (Fr. *son du langage*, Ger. *Laut* or *Sprechlaut*, Sp. *sonido articulado*) from a reality differentiated from the phonetic fact regarding how sounds were valued or interpreted by speakers and listeners. For Koerner (1972), it was precisely an observation by Baudouin in 1895 about the use of the term *phoneme* in contrast to *sound* that led many scholars to believe that the Polish linguist created the term, when in fact Nikolaj Kruszewsky (1897), his student, was the first in Kazan to apply the concept as Saussure did in his *Mémoire* on primitive Indo-European vowels (Anderson 2021: 81)

In the history of the concept of phoneme, there is still much discussion about the interplay of influences between linguists of the late nineteenth and early twentieth centuries in relation to the first use of the term (Sweet 1877; Saussure 1915; Vinogradov 1962; Robins 1967; Mugdan 1985). The existence of such a great number of meticulous disquisitions makes it advisable to focus on the clearly established definitions for the concept of phoneme, without going into biographical detail. The numerous and diverse definitions given have been the subject of various classifications, proposed mainly by William Freeman Twaddell (1935), Roman Jakobson (1960) and Jirí Krámsky (1974), and reiterated in reference publications (Anderson 1985; Quilis 1993; Clark et al. 2007). In general terms, the definitions were coined differently depending on whether the phoneme was understood as a mental and psychological unit, as a physical fact, or as an abstract reality (Twaddell 1935). To this classification should be added the interpretation of the phoneme as an algebraic reality (Quilis 1993: 27), as proposed by Louis Hjelmslev, who abstracted from the phonic nature of language to define its units not in terms of substance but of form and relation. For this reason, he preferred to speak of "cenemes", understood as empty units devoid of meaning (Hjelmslev 1943a; Alarcos-Llorach 1977).

The unenthusiastic reaction to the mental and psychological reality of the phoneme of Britain's two schools of phonetics, led by Daniel Jones and John Rupert Firth respectively, deserves a separate note given their long and rich tradition in the applied dimensions of the discipline to the neglect of the theoretical. Although there are neither cognitive attributes nor clear parallelism with American structuralism in their work, this significant reaction must be explained when reviewing the life cycle of the phoneme. Their predominantly practical attitude – an important influence on Jones was Henry Sweet and his works (1877, among others) – led to achievements unattained by American structuralists in the areas of phonetic transcription, pronunciation dictionaries (Jones 1917), foreign language teaching, and in the devising of writing systems and extensive dialect descriptions (Wells 1982). The phoneme was defined by Jones as a "*family* of sounds" whose realisations were contextual products (1950, 1957), paying lip service only to the mental definition. The best introduction to general phonetics was written by Abercrombie (1967), a Jones disciple. The anti-mentalist Firth led the second school and strongly denied the universality of the phoneme, arguing, for example, that there were many syllabic scripts in various cultures, in the same way that Kohler (1966) denied the syllable. Firth introduced the concept of "prosodies" (1948), which exerted significant influence on later American linguistics: "long components" (Harris 1951) and autosegmental phonology (Goldsmith 1990). Relevantly, Ogden and Local (1994) attempted to disentangle prosodies from autosegments.

The aforementioned lines of definition of the phoneme have some exemplary representatives who form an essential part of the history of phonology (Dresher

2011). The most visible representatives of the conception of the phoneme as a mental unit are Jan Baudouin de Courtenay (1894, 1895) and his disciple Nikolaj Kruszewsky (1881), especially the former, although Baudouin himself did praise the contribution of his disciple, with whom he shared many views, such as on the importance of analogy or on phonetic change (Stankiewicz 1972).

Regarding the interpretation of the phoneme as an abstract unit, its representation corresponds above all to William Freeman Twaddell (1935), who, after pointing out the weaknesses of the other approaches, chose to consider the phoneme as a fiction without reality or linguistic autonomy (Twaddell 1935:34). What is interesting about these two proposals, as analysed by Twaddell himself, is that they are more closely related than is evident from each statement.

Other important linguists and their respective schools adopt lines of thought related to the concept of phoneme, though not exactly like Twaddell and not always in acceptance of the concept (Firth 1934; Halle 1962; Chomsky & Halle 1968:5, 9; Hara 1968; Eddington 1995; Senis 2016). However, where the concept of phoneme, as well as phonology itself, have found their maximum development has been within the structuralist currents: from Ferdinand de Saussure to the American structuralists and behaviourists, passing through the Copenhagen and Prague circles, with Roman Jakobson and Nikolai Trubetzkoy at the head. Such has been the extent and intensity of structuralist phonology that its concepts and theories continue to be studied and applied in diverse ways on a daily basis in current research.

The importance of structuralist-based phonology appears in its consideration as "classical phonology" (Vachek 1964). For Mompeán (2012), at least the following four features characterise classical phonology:

–   the use of an Aristotelian system of categorisation and classification;
–   little attention to the phonetic motivation of phonological categories;
–   little attention to the social component and contextualised use of language; and
–   little attention to the empirical analysis of its object of study.

In structuralist phonology, the concept of phoneme is crucial, understood as a "functional" and "distinctive" element within the linguistic structure (Vachek 1933:82). The concepts of "system", "phonological opposition", "neutralisation", "archiphoneme", "correlation", "commutation", "allophone" and "distinctive feature", although compatible with other theoretical formulations, acquire in structuralism their full measure and meaning, both for synchronic and diachronic descriptions.

The theoretical framework of structuralism is thus built on a series of key concepts that hold explanatory capacity even outside this line of study, which explains to a large extent its applicability and durability over time. In fact, it can be said that structuralism ordered a whole constellation of classical concepts, many defined at the end of the nineteenth century, around the notion of structure, just as other later phonological proposals have also relied on structuralist concepts and terms. Therefore, it was not until the emergence of Langacker's cognitivism (1987) produced a loophole strengthened by use/usage linguistics (Bybee 2001, 2010) that cognitive phonology took a belated and significant qualitative step in its evolution. This step involved breaking with some of the fundamental concepts of structuralism and reorienting them towards perception, categorisation and use, to the point of a reinterpretation of the very concept of phoneme.

3. Theoretical foundations of cognitive phonology

The theoretical foundations for cognitive phonology reside, as stated above, in the foundational work of Ronald Wayne Langacker (1987), in which reflections on sounds, their perception and categorisation are proposed. However, it must be pointed out that phonology initially played a poor role in cognitivism, perhaps because of the tendency to understand "cognitive" to refer "exclusively to meaning and conceptualisation" (Taylor 2017: 1–2).

According to the cognitivist perspective, the sounds of language are not perceived in the same way by all speakers and, in fact, some of them even go unnoticed, so that phonic variants can occur on both conscious and unconscious levels. Likewise, sounds can be considered as samples, or "exemplars", based on the possibilities of variation and the factors that condition this. These phonic variants, or exemplars, make it possible to form complex entities through a process of categorisation, and the complex categories can be internally ordered at various levels of abstraction (Geeraerts 2006).

Cognitive phonology provides valuable information about how phonic features are perceived, categorised and stored by speakers. Speakers, as listeners, sort the features perceived as acoustically relevant into discrete phonetic categories, prioritising information about categorial identity and diluting information about the specific acoustic form (Nathan 1986). In this way, structural categories are constructed by taking "core" or "best-exemplar" samples or elements as reference.

We see then that the concepts of "exemplar" and "schema" are fundamental in cognitivism. The schema is an abstract reality constructed from exemplars or concrete manifestations that are fully compatible with all the members of the category that defines them. Schemas are emergent realities and are not given by a system, meaning they can arise and disappear gradually. Related to schemas are "prototypes", which are typical examples of a given category, so that other elements can be assimilated to the general category depending on their perceived similarity to the prototype. Prototypes, as perceptual phonic categories, are sets of close variants that are grouped by their degrees of "similarity"; each variant is a relevant manifestation in a given context, and all variants are manifested in the word domain, which is why their storage is linked to that of lexical units. If one starts from a model of the exemplar, all variants of the word will be stored in a categorised form and linked to their contexts of occurrence. If one starts from a prototype model, what is stored is an abstract representation of each word constructed from a series of specific cases that, once the prototype emerges, are no longer relevant and are valued to the extent that they are established in its periphery.

The concepts briefly recalled so far justify the importance that the line of research called "use-based linguistics" (or "usage", Bybee 2001, 2010) has had within cognitive phonology. Linguistic use – ignored at the basis of structuralism and generativism – helps to shape the form and content of phonic systems. The frequency with which words, word chunks or sequences are used and with which certain patterns recur in language affect both the mental representation and the phonic form of words. Language "use" refers not only to the mere linguistic process, but also to "usage", the social (and *habitual*) interactive environments to which language is exposed (Moreno-Fernández 2017). The frequency with which certain words, phrases or sequences are used ultimately affects their phonological structure.

Bybee (2001) has proposed a usage-based phonology that is built on the following principles:

1. Experience influences the representation of linguistic phenomena in the memory of speakers.
2. Representations of linguistic objects possess the same properties as mental representations as they do as objects.
3. Categorisations are based on the concepts of identity and similarity and make possible an adequate storage of phonological percepts.
4. Generalisations are not independent of stored representations but arise from them.

Usage-based phonology accepts the conclusions of psycholinguists that more frequent linguistic elements (usually words) are more accessible to the speaker than those less frequent, which would explain why forms apparently foreign to the system, such as those often labelled irregular, can maintain a high level of use. Linguistic structures are created and consolidated by processes of repetition, whether more individual or collective, i.e. conventional. Likewise, it is frequency that makes possible the creation of schematic representations, or schemas, constructed from a high number of cases referring to the same pattern or model. In the phonic domain, since the physiological configuration of human articulation is so involved that the practice of traits is necessary, repetition and articulatory habit simply become essential.

Thus, in the establishment of categories and their prototypes, the frequency of phonic facts known to the speaker as well as the similarity of perceived features is crucial. When we think of exemplars rather than prototypes, the perceived features are categorised and stored in such a way as to create categories that directly reflect the possibilities of variation. In this way, exemplars, originating from different social and contextual conditions, are grouped together in the same conceptual space, which allows for their joint categorisation.

4. Baudouin de Courtenay, cognitivist phonologist *avant la lettre*

The purpose of this paper is, on the one hand, to argue that the notional foundations of cognitive phonology are traceable in the phonologists and phoneticians who published their studies between 1870 and 1920. On the other, it argues that phonology, as a linguistic discipline, finds in cognitivism its most solid base, to the point that phonology should be interpreted as a cognitive discipline; otherwise, it ceases to be phonology properly speaking.

Beyond the earliest terminological and conceptual dabbling, the first solid proposal of the concept of phoneme is that originating from the University of Kazan around the figure of Baudouin de Courtenay, introducer of other basic concepts in linguistics including even those used today, such as "morpheme", "grapheme", "syntagm" and "distinctive feature" (Stankiewicz 1972: 7). It is therefore worthwhile dwelling on the thoughts and writings of this Polish linguist, together with those of his disciple Kruszewski (1881). The texts by Baudouin to which we will pay special attention are *On the Tasks of Linguistics* (1889; vid. Stankiewicz 1972: 7) and *An Attempt at a Theory of Phonetic Alternations: A Chapter from Psychophonetics* (1894). These were accessed thanks to Edward Stankiewicz's translation and edition published in English in 1972. This author includes a long chapter on Baudouin's life and work and presents it as a prelude to structural linguistics. These pages claim that Baudouin's proposals can also be considered a prelude to cognitive phonology.

Twaddell includes Baudouin among the advocates of a mentalist or psychologically based concept of phoneme. This means that the phoneme is no more (or less) than a mental reality that includes both the intention of the speaker and the impression or perception of the listener. The speaker's intention is to produce the sound, while the listener's impression aims to hear the same sound. Baudouin called these intentions and impressions "psychophonic" realities, while to speak of the sounds actually produced Baudouin referred to "anthropophonic" realisations or varieties.

However, Baudouin's interpretation of the phonic domain should be understood in coherence with his interpretation of linguistics (Häusler 1976). In this respect, he clearly states that the basis of language is purely psychological and that linguistics is therefore a branch of the psychological sciences. Nowadays, to this fundamental idea the no less important one is added that linguistics is a socio-psychological science, since language exists in society and psychological development of man is only possible through interpersonal interaction. All this concludes as one of Baudouin's best-known statements:

> Linguistics is throughout a socio-psychological science.
> (Baudouin de Courtenay 1889)

This psychological interpretation of language finds an immediate relationship with the cognitivism of generative linguistics, but almost as immediately moves away to approach Langacker's cognitive grammar and, most especially, the usage-based linguistics of Bybee (2010), an integral part of contemporary cognitivism. Baudouin saw the potential of linguistics in the field of cognition:

> Linguistics is one of the sciences of human mental phenomena, [...] and in the future a linguistic mode of knowledge will take its place alongside the 'intuitive-artistic' and 'analytic-scientific' modes of cognition.
> (Baudouin de Courtenay 1909)

From this point on, the parallelism between numerous reflections put forward by Baudouin and those proposed by cognitivism and use-based linguistics is unlikely to seem strange. Thus, for example, cognitivism uses the concept of exemplar in reference to units of linguistic experience associated with similar experiences that are stored as such in episodic memory. Baudouin's phonology speaks of "divergences" to refer to purely phonetic (anthropophonic) differences between sounds, whether they are alternating or not. In these divergences, there is both the necessary adaptation to phonetic conditions and the unconscious memory of individual sounds. It is not difficult, therefore, to relate to the alternating phonetic forms and their divergence as exemplars. Moreover, Baudouin considers these divergences as appropriate to the phoneme itself.

As far as Baudouin's concept of phoneme is concerned, the cognitivist concept of schema clearly corresponds. Indeed, phonemes may be interpreted as schemas or sets of elements stored and categorised from a process of generalisation of linguistic units carried out by speakers. Cognitive linguists (Langacker 1987; Taylor 1990, 2003, 2006) believe that speakers can abstract schemas that arise from their ability to recognise common features among allophonic members of a category.

For Baudouin, the phoneme is a unified and discrete sound, the result of an "abstraction" or a "phonetic generalisation" understood as a sum of generalised phonetic (anthropophonic) properties. The concept of phoneme is thus associated with a sum of individual phonetic representations that are articulatory on the one hand, i.e. realised or likely to be realised by physiological actions, and acoustic on the other, i.e. effects of these physiological actions that are heard or likely to be heard. For Bybee, "experience affects representation. The use of forms and patterns both in production and perception affects their representation in memory" (Bybee 2001: 6).

The parallel between preclassical and cognitive phonology can also be traced in other postulates. One of the basic tenets of the use-based cognitivist model holds that categorisation occurs because of perceived phonic elements (Bybee 2001: 7). For Baudouin, the phoneme is reached by purging it of the accident of the divergence of its phonetic manifestations, which makes an abstraction or phonetic generalisation possible. On the other hand, for cognitivism, categorisation is based on identity or similarity, just as in Baudouin there is a tendency to group the variants of a phoneme according to their presumed psychological similarity: "although the Russian *i* and *y* are pronounced differently, they are psychologically closer to each other than they are to other sounds" (1903; vid. Stankiewicz 1972: 29). This is undoubtedly associated with the Wittgensteinian idea of "family resemblance". Moreover, if for Langacker (1987) the sounds of a language are not limited to being ordered in a closed list of phonemes but affect suprasegmental levels, Baudouin had already commented in his *An Outline of the History of the Polish Language* (1922; vid. Stankiewicz 1972: 332) that syllabic and non-syllabic phonemes have, in addition to quantity, a changing accent. That is, they have different degrees of stress and intonation.

In cognitive linguistics, likewise, the perception of phonic reality supposes the possibility of non-perception, while for Baudouin there are also imperceptible differences between phonemes, which he interprets as embryonic alternations. Furthermore, in the field of phonic differences, cognitivism highlights the importance of linguistic changes motivated not only by articulatory reasons but by perceptual ones as well (Bybee 2001: 82), while Baudouin stated that changes could occur and would be caused by psychological differences (1894; vid. Stankiewicz 1972: 196).

A further interesting aspect regarding the parallelism between preclassical and cognitive phonology is that the mental representations of phoneme, schema, are explained in direct and close relation to units of a higher degree of abstraction or generality. Bybee states that units such as morpheme, segment or syllable are emergent in the sense that they arise from the identity and similarity that makes representations possible (Bybee 2001: 7). For his part, Baudouin states that the similarity of alternating phonemes is in many cases neither accidental nor arbitrary but repeated in morphemes that comprise, at least partially, the same phonemes that are historically or etymologically related. Baudouin proposes the term "correlation" to refer to an alternation of phonemes in which the phonetic difference is connected or associated with some psychological difference between forms and words, that is, with some morphological or semasiological difference. This being so, the alternation would not affect isolated phonemes but whole morphemes or even words. Cognitivism identifies in this relationship the key to storage, which is organised precisely by means of a system of lexical connections based on phonic and semantic features. In addition, when words are related through phonic and semantic connections, the relations can also be morphological. More than one contemporary cognitivist would probably be willing to sign statements such as the following:

> A word, or a sentence, once uttered, disappears at the moment of its utterance. There is no physical connection between utterances. What links the separate speech acts – be they sounds, phonetic words, or utterances (that are heard and perceived by the ear) – are representations, or images of the memory, which during the utterance itself serve as a stimulus to set the speech organs into appropriate motion. (Baudouin de Courtenay 1894; vid. Stankiewicz 1972:158)

In contrast to these cases of stored representations, there are phonetic variants conditioned by their immediate context that are not committed to memory.

As is clear from Baudouin's view of linguistics, laws without exceptions do not explain the phonetics of languages – as was the tendency during his time – but individual thought and social interaction. This is possible according to psychological (association, perception, emotion, etc.), physiological (reflexes, mechanical behaviour, etc.) and physical (acoustic, mechanical, optical, etc.) "laws". Moreover, one cannot forget that individual states and social conditions affect the psychological-receptive base of communication. The transmission of representations based on articulation and perception habits is thus governed by uniformity and regularity. In the eyes of usage-based cognitive linguistics none of the above-mentioned elements can be foreign, including regularity, the basis of frequency and the foundation of repetition processes (Bybee 2001:28). According to Baudouin de Courtenay (1910; vid. Stankiewicz 1972:41), uniformity and regularity characterise both the stability of combinations of articulatory and auditory elements as well as their fluctuations and changes, and they should be interpreted as a statistical constant of coincidence of phonetic facts in given discourse conditions (Stankiewicz 1972:269–271). Following this line of reasoning, "phonetic laws" proper would only be possible if the existence of individuals, collectivity, social life and discourse were ignored. This argument, while bringing preclassi-

Chapter 1. Cognitive attributes of preclassical phonology   **25**

cal phonology closer to cognitive phonology, distances it from Chomskyan cognitivism.

The criticisms that Baudouin's mentalist position provoked throughout the twentieth century were abundant. One of the reasons may lie in the early and at the same time long-lived development first of structuralist linguistics and later of generativist linguistics. Only cognitive linguistics and the usage-based model have left a loophole for the recovery of proposals that, while still of old, contain thoughts that deserve to be acknowledged. William Freeman Twaddell (1935) formulated the most forceful criticism at the time. For this author, the concept of phoneme in its mentalist formulation does not meet the requirement of a minimum methodological viability, given that it is not possible to access (or guess) the functioning of the mind and that mentalist conjectures do not offer any advantage over other more phonetic or functionalist approaches. The only information available about the "mind" is derived from the behaviour of the individual, meaning the activity of the mind did not exist in the eyes of the scientific method of the time. Thus, in relation to "mental phonemes", the one scientific and valid matter was the observation of the sounds a speaker produces and a listener's reaction to those sounds.

In the struggle between mental and physical matter, there was no lack of proposals that aspired to the conjugation of both. For Graff (1935), for example, the constituents of a phoneme are physical, but its constitution is mental. For Jespersen (1923), on the other hand, a family of sounds may be made up of objectively distinct elements, but speakers of a given language may naturally feel them to be identical. Finally, for Marouzeau (1933), articulatory movements result in an auditory impression. These definitions, however, were not radically different from Baudouin's, who went so far as to define the phoneme also as a phonetically indivisible unit from the point of view of the comparability of the phonetic parts of speech (Baudouin de Courtenay 1881; vid. Stankiewicz 1972: 24–25; Heaman 1984). Likewise, these definitions did not overcome the mentalist obstacle that Twaddell (1935) denounced, although this author, by proposing as an alternative a conception of the phoneme as a "fictitious" and "abstract" entity, not only does not radically move away from the mentalist concept, but also falls into the error of despising abstraction as a mechanism required by many scientific notions. In this way, he fell into the easy opposition between realism and nominalism (Lepschy 1971).

In the first decades of the twentieth century, there were other attempts to overcome the inaccessibility of the mind. One was the proposal made by Edward Sapir (1921), which gave value to the judgment of non-expert speakers or to the way in which they proceed to interpret and graphically represent certain sounds. Yet it was not until several decades later that the methodological procedures adequate for the study of mental representations were validated. The development of acoustic phonetics and perceptual phonetics (Quilis 1981; Johnson 2010) undoubtedly contributed to the field, but cognitive linguistics has been largely responsible for the theoretical and qualitative advances. In this way, the contributions that science seemed to have marginalised due to their deficiencies now acquire new meaning, and it is fair to recognise the merit of daring thought that was, to a large extent, born against the tide (Mompeán 2006).

5. Other precognitive proposals

One of the areas shared by both preclassical and structuralist phonology was, in fact, that of the concept of phoneme, since both the Prague and Copenhagen circles characterise it as a mental reality, as the fruit of the speaker's intention and the listener's perception (Vachek 1933; Trubetzkoy 1939; Jakobson 1962; Stankiewicz 1972; Heaman 1984). The second thesis of the Prague Circle (Durnovo et al. 1929; Trnka et al. 1929) specified that it is the acoustic image and not the motor image that is perceived by the speaker and argued the need to distinguish sound as an objective physical fact, as a representation, and as an element of the functional system. Likewise, José Antonio Mompeán (2012) argues that the linguistic concept of "mark", developed by the Prague Circle and later widely used, can be likened to the cognitivists' concept of "prototypicality" or "representativeness". For his part, Louis Hjelmslev (1943b; 1972), after distinguishing between "schema", "norm" and "use" – attention to terminology –, points out that the "acoustic image" of which Saussure speaks in his *Course* is the psychic translation of a material fact. Likewise, when Hjelmslev speaks of the form of expression to refer to the phonological or "cenematic" plane, he is proposing a mental notion that is reflected in the concept of ceneme, which Hjelmslev himself links to the phoneme.

Nevertheless, one of the linguists whose reflections on the concept of phoneme have undoubtedly had the greatest repercussions has been Edward Sapir (1921). In this author, we also discover, *mutatis mutandis*, an antecedent of current cognitive phonology insofar as he insists on the psychological value of phonetic elements. For Sapir, sounds are not linguistic elements, but behind them there must exist a more limited internal or ideal system which, although unconscious to the non-linguistic speaker, can reveal itself in consciousness as a well-defined configuration of a psychological mechanism reflecting "linguistic intuitions". There is, therefore, an "ideal" system of sounds that is real and of great importance in the life of language (Sapir 1921, 1925). These ideas have led Sapir to be considered one of the founders of phonology (Mathesius 1929) and the only one to notice the need to justify the adscription of reality to mental units and phonic patterns (Twaddell 1935: 10).

Closely related to cognitivism are also the reflections that establish a direct and close link between phonology and writing. These reflections can be traced back a long way and bear the signature of "preclassical authors" such as Sapir and Firth. In Sapir's case, writing is one of the means by which non-expert speakers can express their phonetic intuitions; it is not in vain that he accumulated a great deal of experience in writing indigenous American languages (Pike 1947). In this respect, the fragment that exemplifies this is well known:

> In watching my Nootka interpreter write his language, I often had the curious feeling that he was transcribing an ideal flow of phonetic elements which he heard, inadequately from a purely objective standpoint, as the intention of the actual rumble of speech. (Sapir 1921:58)

Likewise, Taylor (2002:149) and Nathan (2007) state that alphabetic writing systems are based on the "salience" of the phonemic level and never represent sub-phonemic variants by means of distinct symbols. The phoneme is the basis of alphabetic writing systems, which is why a parallel term to the phoneme is needed in the graphic or visual sphere to designate the idealised representation of sounds. Baudouin himself realised this need and used the term "grapheme". The social scope of these systems of representation is part of the history of humanity and its cultures, which is why phonetic intuitions embodied in writing are fundamental in the teaching and literacy processes.

The fact that most writing systems are alphabetic does not mean, however, that the psychological mechanism that associates phoneme to grapheme is universal. Firth himself denounced the non-universality of phonemes in order to reject them as a concept, arguing the existence of syllabic scripts in many cultures, although Kohler (1966) denied also the universality of the syllable by the same reasoning. The physiological basis of syllabic abstraction is obtained, for example, in the notions of "diphoneme" and "triphoneme", which speech synthesis engineering has come to emphasise since the 1990s. The acoustic unit that starts in the middle of the stable zone of a phoneme and ends in the middle of the stable zone of the following phoneme is called diphoneme or triphoneme (Duxans-Barrobés & Ruiz Costa-Jussà 2020). These are not syllables, then, but percepts not associated with a single phonemic element. The use-based model of phonology itself explains that rather than assuming that languages have segments, it is necessary to explain why languages have structures that can be described as segments. This implies that phonetic signals can evolve over time to facilitate both production and perception (Bybee 2001:197). Lindblom (1992) proposed a simulation experiment of a model that produces a classification of CV syllables using both production and perceptual criteria.

In addition to writing, the concept of phoneme also acquires a social dimension when related to dialectal and multi-dialectal realities, that is, to aspects linked to populations. These aspects lead back to Baudouin (1889), who posed the question of what features of language as a whole, as an ideal model, linguistics considers. His answer referred to a fortuitous average cross-section of individuals in a given speech community, which would amount to the intelligible sum of dialects and idiolects in the overall community. This led Perry (1974) to propose the concept of "supralect", understood as the averaged sum of intelligible idiolects in the community. Such conjugation of the individual and the collective, of the idiolectal and the common, is directly related to the value that cognitive phonology gives to the notion of frequency and use, the social dimension of which is evident and one of the characteristics of the usage-based model.

6. Discussion

The roots of cognitive linguistics have been recognised and explained in different works, as have their derivations and the interests that gave rise to them (Bybee 2001: 11–12; Ruiz de Mendoza & Peña Cervel 2005: 17–21). In relation to cognitive phonology, Bybee includes in her list of precursors from the grammatical studies of Givón (1979) and Li (1976) to the pioneers of current cognitivism, such as Langacker (1987) and Croft (2001), as well as sociolinguists (Labov 1966, 1994) and experts in corpus linguistics (Sinclair 1991). Psychological studies on cognition (Rosch 1975) are often also included in such works.

Among the precursors or antecedents of cognitive phonology, the cultivators of this type of work make no mention of the linguistics of the first half of the twentieth century, nor of that of the end of the nineteenth century. The causes of this absence may be diverse, but two may be the most probable: ignorance or lack of recognition. Regarding the lack of recognition of pre–1921 contributions, it is true that there is no direct relation between cognitive and preclassical phonology. Besides, it is evident that the conceptual series *phoneme-psychophonetic, realisation-anthropophonetic, realisation-divergence-correlation* of the preclassical era is not parallel to the *schema-prototype-exemplar* series of cognitivism. The categorisation into basic, superordinate and subordinate elements likewise does not reflect a similar hierarchy in the early twentieth century.

Yet this lack of parallelism is no obstacle to recognising the conceptual coincidences and the similarities of many aspects of the two theoretical perspectives, as shown above. One cannot ignore the frequency with which Baudouin refers to "categories" or the importance he gives to "similarities" or to the combined processes of production and perception, just as one cannot dismiss the concept of mental representation or the decisive importance of the relationship between phoneme and morpheme in word storage or evolution. This includes the embodiment of variants in interaction and social use, wherefrom frequency and repetition arise. All these ideas, so decisive for the cognitivist model, already appear, with greater or lesser coincidence, in preclassical phonology. Several experts have considered preclassical phonology as pre-structuralist phonology. The arguments presented above also allow preclassical phonology to be considered as precognitive phonology.

Certainly, between the phonology of Jan Baudouin de Courtenay and Edward Sapir and that of Joan Bybee there is a bridge that crosses decades of more structuralist and generativist roots. In this transition, the contributions of natural phonology (Stampe 1969; Donegan and Stampe 1979; Dressler 1984) should be considered, for which phonological representation is a type and not a level of representation, given that the language is governed by the same cognitive principles as other abilities. Likewise, it must be considered here that generativist cognitivism clearly departs from preclassical proto-cognitivism to the same extent that it departs from cognitive linguistics, or rather, the latter from the former. Structuralism, for its part, ultimately showed its most serious fissures in the treatment given to fundamental questions such as those raised by preclassical phonology, which are also raised in the present day: the relationship between mental representation and sounds, the dynamics between the constant and the variable, the weight of social use in the organisation and evolution of phonic elements, and frequency as a decisive factor in phonology. As already mentioned, phonology, if not cognitivist, is ultimately diluted in the chimera of idealised models. It is perhaps for this very reason that other currents of phonology, in principle outside the hard core of cognitivism, do not hesitate to incorporate cognitive elements into their models (Kohler 2004; Strauss 1982; Ohala 1986; Goldsmith 1990; Kenstowicz 1994; Pierrehumbert et al. 2000; Gil 2015).

7. Conclusion

Structuralist linguistics has generated such an attraction in the field of phonology that it has created a vacuum around itself that has clearly existed from 1930 to 2000. This historic weight has led to the interpretation of phonology prior to the Prague Circle as pre-structuralist, without attending to its similarities to other theoretical perspectives. Cognitive phonology and the use-based linguistic model have had the capacity to weaken the structuralist position, to the point of creating a new current with important advances in both the field of theoretical foundation and methodology.

The establishment of cognitive phonology as a linguistic discipline has opened the door to a historiographical reconsideration from outside structuralism, meaning so-called preclassical phonology can now be re-read from a cognitivist perspective. From this perspective, both the vision of linguistics adopted by Baudouin and his interpretation of phonological facts could be regarded as an antecedent of cognitive phonology. This ancestry is not necessarily a direct influence on contemporary thought, but it is indeed a set of proposals that is highly compatible with current cognitivism.

Cognitive phonology is characterised (Mompeán 2012) by operating with a non-Aristotelian or classical system of categorisation, by its attention to the phonetic motivation of the categories, and by its growing attention to the social component and use of language, traditionally disregarded by classical phonology. Preclassical phonology, particularly that of Baudouin, shows, if not an absolute identity of criteria, then a clearly related and compatible approach to cognitive phonology. On the other hand, Baudouin's proposal is complementary to proposals made in the United States, where Sapir sought to bring the abstract nature of the linguistic intuitions behind the concept of phoneme to the realm of facts.

Acknowledgements

I thank the reviewers of this work for their thorough comments and suggestions, which I am pleased to accept. The references to Baudouin are from the abridged English version prepared by Stankiewicz (1972). However, the original texts are cited in the references (Baudouin 1894, 1895).

References

Abercrombie, David. 1967. *Elements of general phonetics*. Edinburgh: Edinburgh University Press.

Alarcos-Llorach, Emilio. 1977. *Gramática estructural (según la Escuela de Copenhague y con especial atención a la lengua española)* [Structural grammar (according to the Copenhagen School and with particular focus on the Spanish language)]. Madrid: Gredos.

Albrow, Kenneth H. 1981. The Kazan School and the London School. In Ronald E. Asher & Eugenie J.A. Henderson (eds.), *Towards a history of phonetics*. Edinburgh: Edinburgh University Press.

Anderson, Stephen R. 1985. *Phonology in the twentieth century: Theories of rules and theories of representations*. Chicago, IL: Chicago University Press.

Anderson, Stephen R. 2021. *Twentieth century phonology: Second edition revised and expanded*. Berlin: Language Science Press.

Baudouin de Courtenay, Jan. 1881. On Pathology and Embryology of Language. In
E. Stankiewicz (ed.), *A Baudouin de Courtenay Anthology: The Beginnings of Structural Linguistics*, 121-124. Bloomington: Indiana University Press.

Baudouin de Courtenay, Jan. 1889. On the Tasks of Linguistics. In E. Stankiewicz (ed.), *A Baudouin de Courtenay Anthology: The Beginnings of Structural Linguistics*, 125-43. Bloomington: Indiana University Press.

Baudouin de Courtenay, Jan. 1894. *Próba teorij alternacyj fonetycznych* [An attempt at a theory of phonetic alternations]. Kraków.

Baudouin de Courtenay, Jan. 1895. *Versuch einer Theorie phonetischer Alternationen* [An attempt at a theory of phonetic alternations]. Strassburg: Truebner.

Baudouin de Courtenay, Jan. 1909. The Classification of Languages. In E. Stankiewicz (ed.), *A Baudouin de Courtenay Anthology: The Beginnings of Structural Linguistics*, 155-159. Bloomington: Indiana University Press.

Baudouin de Courtenay, Jan. 1910. Phonetic Laws. In E. Stankiewicz (ed.), *A Baudouin de Courtenay Anthology: The Beginnings of Structural Linguistics*, 160-177. Bloomington: Indiana University Press.

Bybee, Joan. 2001. *Phonology and language use*. Cambridge: Cambridge University Press.

Bybee, Joan. 2010. *Language, usage and cognition*. Cambridge: Cambridge University Press.

Chomsky, Noam & Morris Halle. 1968. *The sound pattern of English*. Cambridge, MA: The MIT Press.

Clark, John, Colin Yallop & Janet Fletcher. 2007. *An introduction to phonetics and phonology*, 3rd edn. Oxford: Blackwell.

Croft, William. 2001. *Radical construction grammar: Syntactic theory in typological perspective*. Oxford: Oxford University Press.

Donegan, Patricia & David Stampe. 1979. The study of Natural Phonology. In D.A. Dinnnsen (Ed.), *Current approaches to phonological theory*. 126 173. Bloomington: Indiana University Press.

Dresher, B. Elan. 2011. The phoneme. In Marc van Oostendorp, Colin J. Ewen, Elizabeth Hume & Keren Rice (eds.), *The Blackwell companion to phonology*. Oxford: Blackwell. . (15 December, 2021.)

Durnovo, Nikolaj, Bohislav Havránek, Roman Jakobson, Vilém Mathesius, Jan Mukařovský, Nikolaj Trubeckoj, Bohumil Trnka. 1929. Thèses présentées au Premier Congrès des philologues slaves [Theses presented at the First Congress of Slavic Philologists]. In *Mélanges linguistiques dédiés au Premier Congrès des Philologues Slaves*, 5-29. Praha: Jednota Československých Matematiků a Fysiků.

Dressler, Wolfgang. 1984. Explaining Natural Phonology. *Phonology*, 1, 29-51.

Duxans-Barrobés, Helenca & Marta Ruiz Costa-Jussà. 2020. *Introducción al habla* [Introduction to speech]. Barcelona: UOC.

Eddington, David. 1995. Psychological status of phonological analysis. *Hispania* 8. 873–884.

Firth, John. 1934. ðə wəːd "founiːm" [The word phoneme]. *Le Maître Phonétique* 12(49), no. 46. 44–46.

Firth, John. 1948. Sounds and prosodies. *Transactions of the Philological Society* 47. 127–152.

Geeraerts, Dirk (ed.). 2006. *Cognitive linguistics: Basic readings*. Berlin: Mouton de Gruyter.

Gil, Juana (ed.). 2015. Nuevas aportaciones al estudio de la percepción del habla [New contributions to the study of speech perception]. *Revista Española de Lingüística* 45(1). 7–24.

Givón, Talmy. 1979. *On understanding grammar*. New York, NY: Academic Press.

Godel, Robert. 1957. *Les sources manuscrites du cours de linguistique générale de F. de Saussure* [The manuscript sources of the Course in General Linguistics by F. de Saussure]. Geneva: E. Droz.

Goldsmith, John A. 1990. *Autosegmental and metrical phonology*. Oxford: Blackwell.

Graff, Willem L. 1935. Remarks on the phoneme. *American Speech* 10(2). 83–87.

Halle, Morris. 1962. Phonology in generative grammar. *Word* 18. 54–72.

Hara, Makoto. 1968. En defensa del concepto 'fonema' contra la fonología generativa de la escuela de Chomsky [In defence of the concept 'phoneme' against the generative phonology of the school of Chomsky]. In Carlos Magis (ed.), *Actas del III Congreso de la Asociación Internacional de Hispanistas*, 435–442. Mexico City: El Colegio de México.

Harris, Zellig. 1951. *Methods in structural linguistics*. Chicago, IL: Chicago University Press.

Häusler, Frank. 1976. *Das Problem Phonetik und Phonologie bei Baudouin de Courtenay und in seiner Nachfolge* [The problem of phonetics and phonology in Baudouin de Courtenay and his succession]. Halle: Max Niemeyer Verlag.

Havet, Louis. 1967 [1876]. *The phoneme*, 3rd edn. Cambridge: Cambridge University Press.

Heaman, Isabel M. 1984. Baudouin de Courtenay – a pioneer of structural linguistics. *Working Papers of the Linguistic Circle of the University of Victoria* 4(1). 23–40.

Hjelmslev, Louis. 1943b. Langue et parole [Language and speech]. *Cahiers Ferdinand de Saussure* 2. 29–44.

Hjelmslev, Louis. 1972. Sprogsystem og sprogforandring [Linguistic system and language change]. *Travaux du Cercle Linguistique de Copenhague* XV(6). 48–54.

Hjelmslev, Louis. 1974 [1943a]. *Prolegómenos a una teoría del lenguaje* [Prefaces to a theory of language]. Madrid: Gredos.

Jakobson, Roman. 1958. Powstanie pojęcia fonemu w lingwistyce polskiej i światowej [The origin of the notion of the phoneme in Polish and international linguistics]. *Polska Akademia Nauk, Sprawozdania z prac naukowych wydziału nauk społecznych* 1(6). 48–54.

Jakobson, Roman. 1962. *Selected writings: Word and language*, vol. 1. The Hague: Mouton.

Jakobson, Roman. 1971 [1960]. The Kazan's School of Polish linguistics and its place in the international development of phonology. In Roman Jakobson, *Selected writings: Word and language*, vol. 2, 394–428. The Hague: Mouton.

Jakobson, Roman. 1972 [1929]. *El círculo de Praga* [The Prague Circle]. Barcelona: Anagrama.

Jespersen, Otto. 1923. *Language*. London: Allen & Unwin.

Johnson, Keith. 2010. *Acoustic and auditory phonetics*, 3rd edn. Oxford: Blackwell.

Jones, Daniel. 1917. *Everyman's English pronouncing dictionary*. London: Everyman's Reference Library.

Jones, Daniel. 1950. *The phoneme: Its nature and use*. Cambridge: W. Heffer & Sons.

Jones, Daniel. 1957. The history and meaning of the term 'phoneme'. *Le Maître Phonétique* 35(72). 1–20.

Kenstowicz, Michael. 1994. *Phonology in generative grammar*. Oxford: Blackwell.

Koerner, Ernst F. K. 1972. Jan Baudouin de Courtenay: His place in the history of linguistic science. *Canadian Slavonic Papers / Revue Canadienne des Slavistes* 14(4). 663–683.

Kohler, Klaus. 1966. Is the syllable a phonological universal? *Journal of Linguistics* 2. 207–208.

Kohler, Klaus. 2004. Categorical speech perception revisited. *Clinical Linguistics & Phonetics* 27(5). 339–54 https://www.rle.mit.edu/soundtosense/conference/pdfs/fulltext /Saturday%20Posters/SB-Kohler-STS.pdf. (17 May, 2022.)

Krámsky, Jiří. 1974. *The phoneme: Introduction to the history and theories of a concept.* Munich: Wilhelm Fink.

Kruszewski, Nikolaj. 1881. *Über die Lautabwechslung* [On sound alternation]. Kasan: Universitätbruchdruckerei.

Labov, William. 1966. *The social stratification of English in New York City.* Washington, DC: Center for Applied Linguistics.

Labov, William. 1994. *Principles of linguistic change. Internal factors.* Oxford: Blackwell.

Langacker, Ronald Wayne. 1987. *Foundations of cognitive grammar. Volume I: Theoretical Prerequisites.* Stanford, CA: Stanford University Press.

Lepschy, Giulio. 1971 [1966]. *La lingüística estructural* [Structural linguistics]. Barcelona: Anagrama. Torino: Giulio Einaudi.

Li, Charles. 1976. *Subject and topic.* New York, NY: Academic Press.

Lindblom, Bjorn. 1992. Phonological units as adaptive emergents of lexical development. In Charles A. Ferguson, Lise Menn & Carol Stoel-Gammon (eds.), *Phonological development: Models, research, implications*, 131–163. Timonium, MD: York Press.

Marouzeau, Jules. 1933. *Lexique de la terminologie linguistique.* Paris: Paul Geuthner.

Mathesius, Vilém. 1929. Ziele und Aufgaben der vergleichenden Phonologie [The aims and tasks of comparative phonology]. *Xenia Pragensia.* 432–435.

Mompeán, José Antonio. 2006. The phoneme as a basic-level category: Experimental evidence from English. *International Journal of English Studies* 6. 141–172.

Mompeán, José Antonio. 2012. La fonología cognitiva [Cognitive phonology]. In Iraide Iberretxe & Javier Valenzuela (eds.), *Lingüística cognitiva*, 305–326. Barcelona: Anthropos.

Moreno-Fernández, Francisco. 2017. *A framework for cognitive sociolinguistics.* London: Routledge.

Mugdan Joachim. 1985. The origin of the phoneme: Farewell to a myth. *Lingua Posnaniensis* 28. 137–150.

Mugdan, Joachim. 2011. On the origins of the term phoneme. *Historiographia Linguistica* 38(1–2). 85–110.

Nathan, Geoffrey. 1986. Phonemes as mental categories. *Proceedings of the Annual Meeting of the Berkeley Linguistics Society (BLS).* 212–223.

Nathan, Geoffrey. 2007. Where is the natural phonology phoneme? In Jürgen Trouvain (ed.), *Proceedings of the 16th International Congress of Phonetic Sciences ICPhS XVI, 6–10 August 2007, Saarbrücken, Germany*, 93–98. Saarbrücken: Universität des Saarlandes. http:// www.icphs2007.de/conference/Papers/1752/1752.pdf. (15 December, 2021.)

Ogden, Richard & John K. Local. 1994. Disentangling prosodies from autosegments. A note on a misplaced research tradition. *Journal of Linguistics* 30(2). 477–498.

Ohala, John J. 1986. Consumer's guide to evidence in phonology. *Phonology Yearbook* 3. 3–26.

Perry, Joseph A. 1974. Phoneme and supralect. *Journal of the International Phonetic Association* 4(1). 13–19.

Pierrehumbert, Janet, Mary E. Beckham & Robert Ladd. 2000. Conceptual foundations of phonology as a laboratory science. In Noel Burton-Roberts, Philip Carr & Gerard Docherty (eds.), *Phonological knowledge*, 273–304. Oxford: Oxford University Press.

Pike, Kenneth L. 1947. *Phonemics: A technique for reducing languages to writing*. Ann Arbor, MI: University of Michigan Press.

Quilis, Antonio. 1981. *Fonética acústica de la lengua española* [Acoustic phonetics of the Spanish language]. Madrid: Gredos.

Quilis, Antonio. 1993. *Tratado de fonología y fonética españolas* [Treatise on Spanish phonology and phonetics]. Madrid: Gredos.

Robins, Robert. 1967. *A short history of linguistics*. London: Longmans.

Rosch, Eleanor. 1975. Cognitive representations of semantic categories. *Journal of Experimental Psychology General* 104. 192–233.

Ruiz de Mendoza, Francisco J. & M. Sandra Peña Cervel (eds.). 2005. *Cognitive linguistics. Internal dynamics and interdisciplinary interaction*. Berlin & New York, NY: Mouton de Gruyter.

Sapir, Edward. 1921. *Language*. New York, NY: Harcourt, Brace & Co.

Sapir, Edward. 1925. Sound patterns of language. *Language* 1. 37–51.

Saussure, Ferdinand de. 1879. *Mémoire sur le système primitif des voyelles dans les langues indo-européennes* [Memoir on the primitive system of vowels in Indo-European languages]. Leipzig: Teubner.

Saussure, Ferdinand de. 1915. *Cours de linguistique générale* [Course in general linguistics]. Paris: Payot.

Senis, Angela. 2016. Le phonème face à la théorie du langage de J. R. Firth [The phoneme and J. R. Firth's theory of language]. *Modèles Linguistiques* 74. https://journals.openedition.org/ml/2027. (28 March, 2021.)

Sinclair, John. 1991. *Corpus, concordance, collocation*. Oxford: Oxford University Press.

Stampe, David. 1969. The acquisition of phonetic representation. *Princeton Center for Language Study* 5. 443 454.

Stankiewicz, Edward (ed.). 1972. *A Baudouin de Courtenay anthology: The beginnings of structural linguistics*. Bloomington, IN: Indiana University Press. https://publish.iupress.indiana.edu/projects/a-baudoin-de-courtenay-anthology (13 June, 2022.)

Strauss, Steven L. 1982. *Lexicalist phonology of English and German*. Dordrecht: Foris.

Sweet, Henry. 1877. *Handbook of phonetics*. Oxford: Clarendon.

Taylor, John. 1990. Schemas, prototypes and models in search of the unity of the sign. In Savas L. Tsohatzidis (ed.), *Meanings and prototypes: Studies in linguistic categorization*, 521–534. London & New York, NY: Routledge.

Taylor, John. 2002. *Cognitive grammar*. Oxford: Oxford University Press.

Taylor, John. 2003. Polysemy's paradoxes. *Language Sciences* 25. 637–657.

Taylor, John. 2006. Where do phonemes come from? A view from the bottom. *International Journal of English Studies* 6. 19–54.

Taylor, John. 2017. Phonology and cognitive linguistics. *Journal of Cognitive Linguistics* 2. 1–24.

Trubetzkoy, Nikolai S. 1939. *Grundzüge der Phonologie* [Principles of phonology]. Göttingen: Vandenhoek & Ruprecht.

Twaddell, William Freeman. 1935. *On defining the phoneme.* Baltimore, MD: Waverly Press.

Vachek, Joseph. 1933. What is phonology? *English Studies* 15. 81–92.

Vachek, Joseph. 1964. *On some basic principles of 'classical' phonology.* Berlin: Akademie Verlag. https://www.degruyter.com/document/doi/10.1524/stuf.1964.17.16.409/html. (28 March, 2021.)

Vinogradov, Viktor. 1962. Jan Baudouin de Courtenay. *Slavia Orientalis* XI. 447–460.

Wells, John. 1982. *Accents of English*, vol. 2. Cambridge: Cambridge University Press.

CHAPTER 2

A Swedish merger

Production and perception
of the short vowels /œ/ and /ɵ/

Lena Wenner
Institute for Language and Folklore, Sweden

In Sweden, an ongoing sound change is resulting in the pronunciation of short /œ/ and short /ɵ/ becoming more similar. This chapter examines the relationship between the two sounds in the region of Uppland, situated in Central Sweden. It summarises the results of three tests conducted to investigate the informants' production and perception of this sound change as well as their attitudes towards it. By combining the results of the production test with the informants' categorisations in the perception test, the original study showed that those informants with a small phonetic distance between /œ/ and /ɵ/ in their own speech were better at categorising vowel stimuli correctly than the speakers who had a larger phonetic distance.

Keywords: sociophonetics, sound change, perception, vowel, phoneme merger, phonetics, dialectology, Swedish

1.   Introduction

When conversing with others, we adapt the way we speak, both consciously and unconsciously. Some changes are so small we do not notice them; others we are aware of. Such changes are often temporary, but some are permanent, in which case a new linguistic feature is transferred to future generations. In Sweden, one change that appears to have been under way for a considerable amount of time is that short *ö* [œ] and short *u* [ɵ] are approaching one another. As a result, some people pronounce words like *mörkna* [mœrkna] 'darken' and *murkna* [mɵrkna] 'rot' the same way.

The principal aim of this chapter is to summarise the main results of a research project carried out in 2010.[1] The study was conducted in the Swedish

---

1.   The full results of the study can be found in Wenner (2010), published in Swedish.

https://doi.org/10.1075/silv.31.02wen
© 2024 John Benjamins Publishing Company

region of Uppland (see Figure 1) to investigate the ongoing sound change in the local dialect concerning the sounds [œ] and [ɵ]. The purpose was to determine which group of people is leading this change, i.e. what the significance is of age, gender and social status in relation to early adoption of a new linguistic feature, with the additional question of whether the change is manifesting itself earlier in some words than in others.

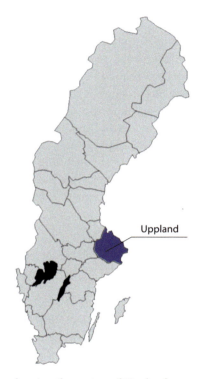

Figure 1. Map of Sweden, showing the region of Uppland

The research questions were the following:

- How is the pronunciation of /œ/ influenced by the phonetic environment? Do certain consonants have features that prompt the shift of /œ/ in a particular direction?
- Can differences be identified in the pronunciation of /œ/ that correspond to a person's gender, age or social status?
- How conscious are language users of a subtle vowel change? Do they notice the change in other speakers before adopting it themselves, or does a merger occur without speakers being aware of it?

To find answers to these questions, three tests were conducted: a production test to investigate how the participants pronounced the two phonemes, a perception test to investigate whether they perceived the difference between the phonemes, and an attitudinal test to investigate their opinions of the phoneme merger.

A total of 78 informants took part in the study. In order to determine whether social factors are significant in the sound change, the informants were subsequently organised into different groups to reflect their gender, age and education. The data were obtained from 38 men and 40 women, divided into three age groups. At the time of recording, the youngest group of speakers ranged from 12 to 20 years of age, the intermediate group from 30 to 60, and the oldest group from 70 to 85. The creation of groups that correspond roughly to generations meant this analysis was able to provide evidence of change in apparent time.

This chapter begins by describing the background of the ongoing vowel change concerning [œ] and [ɵ] in Sweden and by introducing theories on speech production and perception underlying the analysis. The subsequent three sections deal first with the production test, including key findings, then the perception test and finally the attitudinal test. Each section provides details of the relevant methodologies. The chapter ends with a comparison of the three tests and a summarising discussion.

2. Background

Phonetic developments that are universal are normally physiologically driven. For instance, Labov (1981: 299) has shown that lax vowels tend to fall. A traditional view of linguistic change is that unconscious changes move towards simplicity, i.e. less effort. If /œ/ and /ɵ/ were to merge, it would be a simplification in that it would no longer be necessary to distinguish two very similar sounds. The difference between /œ/ and /ɵ/ is also one of the last contrasts that children learn; this is because the sounds are so close phonetically that the difference is hard to identify (Ståhle 1976: 9). It is not difficult to imagine an eventual merger, since in the spoken language only about ten potential minimal pairs where confusion could arise. If the distinction were important, it would be retained. Evidence of the merger lies in the increasing difficulty people have in spelling words like *glögg* 'mulled wine' and *glugg* 'opening'.

Lindblom (1986: 33) assumes that the speaker wants to achieve a sufficient number of distinctive contrasts with minimal articulatory effort. Sounds located at the edge of the vowel space involve greater articulatory effort. Moreover, the consonant context affects how the vowel is produced. If quantity is observed as an autonomous feature, standard Swedish has nine vowels. According to the

UCLA Phonological Segment Inventory Database (UPSID), this is very close to the average for the world's languages. However, front-rounded vowels are highly unusual in other languages, occurring in just five percent of those in UPSID (Maddieson 1986: 251–253). Based on Lindblom's theory, this could indicate a universal rule that speakers avoid this type of vowel whenever possible in order to maintain a clearer contrast when the front-back distinction is accompanied by the unrounded–rounded distinction. Consequently, the reason for the change to /œ/ would be that it is moved toward the middle of the vowel system and thereby closer to the back vowels where rounding is more common. This would involve a simplification whereby the Swedish vowel system would become more similar to the typological average. Examples of similar cases of simplification are younger Swedish speakers pronouncing /ø:/ almost as /ɑ:/, e.g. *möta* 'meet' pronounced as *mata* 'feed', i.e. the front rounded vowel is pronounced like a back vowel; or the occasions when they pronounce /æ:/ as /ɑ:/, e.g. *mäta* 'measure' pronounced as *mata* 'feed', which involves a lesser degree of openness (Wenner 2019).

When a phoneme merger is in the process of becoming established, speakers are aware of the two phonemes that are approaching one another and know how to pronounce both. There is no conflict between the phonemes being auditorially indistinguishable yet acoustically distinct. Labov et al. (1991) have studied sound changes where the symmetry between production and perception has collapsed. They call this phenomenon "near-merger". Later, when there are no longer any speakers that keep the phonemes auditorially separate, the near-merger becomes a full merger. The question that remains unanswered is how the speaker learns to articulate every occurrence from one category in a certain way, but every occurrence from another category in a different way if they do not perceive any differences between the two categories (Labov 1994: 368). Veatch (2005) attempts to explain this by stating that children are so perceptive that they can detect and mimic a distinction that adults are not aware they are making. In a community, there may only be a small distinction that is barely audible, but when the children in the community grow up, they retain the distinction, and the phonemes may again move away from one another.

One of the best-known statements relating to mergers is Garde's Principle, which states that "mergers are irreversible by linguistic means" (Labov 1994: 311). Labov discusses cases where phonemic splits are possible and claims that sociolinguistic forces are most often responsible for the learnability of a distinction. Villena-Ponsoda and Vida-Castro (2004: 438) confirm this in their description of a merger that is unmerged in Andalusia. Their explanation is that overt prestige pressure on southern Spanish speakers leads to a convergence towards the standard distinction. They conclude that certain social and regional features of a language that are deeply rooted in the speech community and fully accepted by the speakers can change due to the influence of cvert prestige (ibid.: 442). Further research on this process of phonemic splitting of /s/ and /θ/ in Andalusian Spanish reinforces this idea (Molina-García 2019; Regan 2020).

Vowel changes are often dependent on a particular consonant context. Experimental studies have shown that there are features in the auditory system that perceptually compensate for coarticulation (Mann & Repp 1980). A sound is perceived as higher pitched when it follows a sound with lower formant frequencies and vice-versa, which results in the neutralisation of the assimilation effect. Pronunciation changes do not begin in the brain of the speaker or the listener but in the transfer between individuals, which includes the speaker's production system and the listener's decoding system. The most important reason for why variation in production does not necessarily lead to sound change is the listener's ability to normalise (Mann & Repp 1980; Lindblom et al. 1995).

Even if a specific linguistic change can be explained by internal factors, social forces should be considered when explaining how and why a change occurs. Sundgren (2009: 130) argues that the choice between two variants has a social function, with an individual's often unconscious choice of one variant having the effect of creating, changing or retaining their social identity.

3.   Production test

The informants were given 72 informal questions, each to be answered with a single word. The questions were presented verbally in the form of a simple sentence intended to elicit a certain word, e.g. "What is the opposite of *ljusna*?" 'lighten', to which the answer was supposed to be *mörkna* 'darken'. When the informant produced the correct word, they had to repeat it at least three times, so that there would be multiple options to choose from in the event that one of them was of insufficient quality.

For the analysis, Praat (Boersma & Weenink 2022) and Akustyk were used. Akustyk is an open-source add-on for Praat specifically designed for sociolinguists, offering automated tools for speech analysis, synthesis, plotting and data management. The three lowest formant frequencies (F_1, F_2 and F_3) were analysed in the broadband spectrogram, and an LPC analysis was performed. LPC (Linear Prediction Coding) analysis is a technique for estimating the vocal tract transfer function. To minimise incorrect data, different filters should be set depending on the gender of the person being analysed (Vallabha & Tuller 2002: 147). For the LPC analysis, the original speech signals were sampled down to 10 kHz for the voices of men and 11 kHz for those of women. The values in hertz were converted to values on the Bark frequency scale. The Bark scale is based on the results of psychoacoustic experiments and ranges from 1 to 24 Barks, which correspond to the first 24 critical bands of hearing and thereby correspond better to the human hearing system than frequencies in hertz (Smith 2011).

An interesting question in the discussion of the merging of /œ/ and /ə/ is where the phonemes meet, whether at the location of /œ/, the location of /ə/ or whether both phonemes approach one another and meet at a point between the two original phonemes. In this study, the third alternative seemed to be the most common.

3.1 Key results of the production test

The distance between two sounds can be calculated with a measurement that includes the three lowest formants. This gives the phonetic (i.e. Euclidean) distance between the sounds and makes it possible to calculate how the sounds relate to one another in three-dimensional space (see Eriksson & Wretling 1997: 1045). For every informant group, the mean value of the phonetic distance between /œ/ and /ə/ was calculated in order to obtain a measurement of how the phonemes relate to each other. The greater the distance, the more clearly the phonemes were distinguished.

Figures 2 and 3 present the results from the production test. These showed that, on average, women had a greater distance between the phonemes /œ/ and /ə/ than men. The average difference between the men's and women's phoneme distance was 0.37 Bark. There was also an age difference for both men and women, with the youngest age group (12–20) differentiating the least between the phonemes and the oldest age group (70–85) differentiating the most. Similarly, there was a weak pattern for the social status variable, where those with the highest social status distinguished the least between the phonemes, while those with the lowest social status distinguished the most.

Linear regression analysis was used in order to investigate whether the differences in pronunciation for the variables of gender, social status and age were statistically significant. Although the number of observations in this study was too small to fully interpret the results and the correlations observed were not always linear, the method did give an indication of the correlations.

The differences between men and women were significant ($p < .001$), with women presenting a greater phonetic distance between /œ/ and /ə/ than men. This could be interpreted as a reflection of adherence to the standard norm. Nordberg (2005) reaches the same conclusion in his study. Kuronen (2001: 96) shows that though the qualitative difference between /œ/ and /ə/ is very small, it is, again, the men who distinguish the least between the two phonemes.

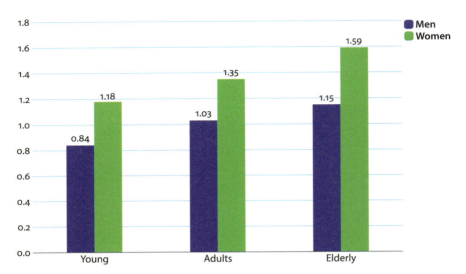

Figure 2. Comparison between the three age groups with regard to phonetic distance

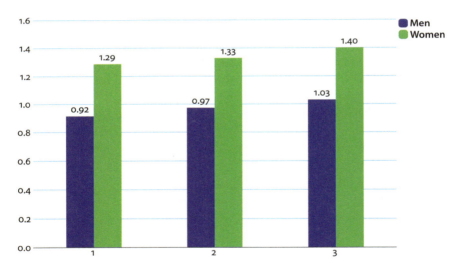

Figure 3. Comparison between the three status groups with regard to phonetic distance. 1 = highest social status, 3 = lowest social status

No clear social values could be linked to distinction or merging, but differences were identified between the three age groups. The phonetic distance generally reduced with every generation, such that the oldest made the greatest distinction between the phonemes and the youngest made the least. The difference between these two groups was significant ($p < .01$). This comparison between generations indicates an ongoing change in which the phonemes /œ/ and /ɵ/ are approaching one another.

3.2 Contextual effect

With regard to the purely phonetic analysis (in which the social variables were omitted), the main interest was in investigating correlations between particular consonant contexts and to what degree /œ/ and /ɵ/ are approaching one another. In order to ensure that the consonant context stayed as constant as possible, one stage of the analysis investigated only the 13 minimal and almost minimal word pairs in the material. The aim was to identify whether there is a hierarchy for which words have the greatest distance between /œ/ and /ɵ/ and in which words the vowels are closest to each other. This had the potential to indicate the cases in which phoneme mergers occur the earliest or most easily.

As shown in Table 1, the distance was smallest between the word pairs *förste/furste* 'first/prince', *mörkna/murkna* 'darken/rot', *rött/rutt* 'red/route', and *rösta/rusta* 'vote/equip'. The greatest distance was between *ögla* 'loop' and *uggla* 'owl'. A pattern can be observed, with the distance being smallest in the word pairs that have /r/ adjacent to the vowel. In the word pairs with the greatest distance, the vowel is initial in two of the words and follows an /h/ in the third. This was not unexpected, since in these positions the articulator is set for the pronunciation of the initial vowel. Stevens and House (1963:116) show that there is little difference in articulation between a vowel in the context /h-d/ and a vowel that is pronounced in isolation.

According to previous research (Ståhle 1976), a variably merged /œ/ occurs mainly in the position before /r/, which seemed to be the case in this study as well. However, there was no tendency, as suggested by Ståhle (1976:9), for word pairs from the same declension paradigm to be closer to one another. The word pairs *sjöng/sjung* 'sang/sing' and *högg/hugg* 'chopped/chop' both had distances above the mean value for the word pairs in the analysis, which could be facilitated by the fact that the semantic load of the distinction is high.

Labov (1994:542) asserts that regular distribution is most common during the beginning of a change and that lexical distribution comes later. When a vowel's place of articulation changes, Labov suggests that it is a question of regular sound change. This also seemed to be the case in this study. A pattern was observed in the influence of the consonant context, which implied that the consonant context is more important for the extent to which the minimal pairs differ than both words belonging to the same word class or the frequency of the words (for word frequencies, see Allwood 2000). The analysis of the 13 minimal pairs also showed that the phonetic distance between /œ/ and /ɵ/ was greater among the older informants and that the women had a greater phonetic distance than the men. These results were more evident in the test with the 13 minimal pairs than in the analysis of the entirety of the data obtained using the word list in the production test described

Table 1. Word pairs sorted by increasing phonetic distance between /œ/ and /ɵ/

Word pair	Distance (Bark)
förste/furste 'first/prince'	0.851
mörkna/murkna 'darken/rot'	1.069
rött/rutt 'red/route'	1.197
rösta/rusta 'vote/equip'	1.288
lögnare/lugnare 'liar/calmer'	1.293
döma/dumma 'judge/stupid'	1.541
sjöng/sjung 'sang/sing'	1.611
mössa/Musse 'cap/Mickey Mouse'	1.615
pölsa/pulsa 'hash/plod'	1.653
gömma/ljumma 'hide/warm'	1.780
högg/hugg 'chopped/chop'	1.943
öppen/uppe 'open/up'	1.991
ögla/uggla 'loop/owl'	2.122
Mean value	1.535

above. An explanation for this could be that the consonant context was constant for the word pairs, leading to clearer results.

4. Perception test

Various theories exist regarding how speakers perceive sound. By combining electropalatography and electromagnetic articulography, Simonsen et al. (2008) show that there may be considerable articulatory variation between speakers in producing the same sound. Traunmüller (1981:1465) states that phonemes must be discerned in order to be classified or distinguished and that if something is perceived as an /a/ then it is an /a/ regardless of how it is produced. He claims that only the features that the listener perceives can play a distinctive role in the communication process – articulatory features cannot. Traunmüller maintains that distinctive features should be described in perceptual terms. A description in acoustic terms is certainly possible but is complicated by the transformation in the auditory system. Against this background, a perception test provides interesting results because it reflects auditory perception.

A male informant was recorded saying the minimal pair *döma* /dœm:a/ 'to judge' and *dumma'* /dəm:a/ 'stupid'. Based on these two authentic forms, Praat was used to create two synthetic stimulus continua. In one continuum, the formant values were changed from the frequencies for /dœm:a/ to gradually approach the frequencies for /dəm:a/. In the other continuum, the formant values were changed from the frequencies for /dəm:a/ to gradually approach those for /dœm:a/. This process resulted in 22 different vowel qualities. Each stimulus appeared six times in the subsequent test, leading to a total of 132 forms that the test participants had to assess.

The hypothesis was that it is easier for the listener to distinguish between the vowels if they are heard in context. For this reason, the vowels were not played in isolation; forms that occur naturally in the language were used instead. This way the informants could use the entire word to support their assessment. Moreover, a listener tends to determine not which individual vowel they hear, but which word.

The stimuli were presented randomly to the informants, who were given the task of identifying each stimulus as either *döma* or *dumma*. They were asked to mark the word they heard and to not change their mind but reply intuitively. Even if they were uncertain of which word they had heard, they had to select one, so that data could be collected on difficult variants as well, since these would be of great interest for the study. Such difficult variants would aid in locating a phoneme boundary in the listener's perception. In order to be able to make statistical calculations, the informants' classifications of a stimulus as /ə/ were allocated zero points, and those classified as /œ/ were allocated one point.

One of the central questions was which informants had been most successful in the perception test. Based on each informant's perceptual deviation for a stimulus and the group's deviation for the same stimulus, a measurement was given in which those informants with a higher value than the group mean deviated more for this stimulus than the mean informant. Some listeners were very accurate in their identification of /œ/ and /ə/, categorising the same stimulus in the same way every time. Other listeners had much more variation. The listeners were divided into three groups based on their perception pattern. The majority had a gradual perception pattern, six had a categorical perception pattern, and four showed a great level of uncertainty in their identification of the two sounds. Despite these differences regarding how the informants identified stimuli in the perception test, there were no significant differences in the comparison between their perception and the extra-linguistic factors of gender, age and social status.

4.1   Discussion of the perception test

The results of the analysis in the previous section showed that many more informants interpreted /œ/ as /ɵ/ than /ɵ/ as /œ/. An explanation could be that they favoured one alternative when they were uncertain of what they were hearing. Several test subjects said that when uncertain, they interpreted the stimuli as *dumma* /dɵm:a/. The frequency of the word may well have been the reason. The word *dumma* is more common than *döma* in the everyday language and in consciousness, making it seem reasonable to interpret an ambiguous stimulus as *dumma*.

The over-representation of /ɵ/ in the responses from the perception test could also be blamed on a shortcoming in the test design. When producing synthetic sounds, it is unavoidable that the sound quality varies between stimuli. It proved easier to produce stimuli from the formant frequencies for /œ/ than for /ɵ/. This could be because it is easier to produce vowels that should sound like central vowels. Also, sounds in the proximity of schwa can vary in quality, and it is uncertain whether formant frequencies are even the most characteristic clues for auditory perception (cf. Ladefoged 1967; Johnson 2005). There are also studies showing asymmetries in perception when two sounds are acoustically similar (Plauché, Delogu & Ohala 1997). It may also be the case that words pronounced in isolation are particularly difficult to categorise. In normal speech, there is considerable variation in pronunciation, but the context helps the listener to interpret the sounds correctly – most often without the need for thought.

5.   Attitudinal test

A simple attitudinal test was conducted, which showed that all the informants were aware that /œ/ and /ɵ/ can merge and that none of them found this particularly attractive. The test consisted of 17 open questions on how one may react to a merger between /œ/ and /ɵ/ in private and public situations. In addition, the informants were asked to describe who they believed to be the prototypical speaker with a merger with respect to age, gender, social status and geographical residence. The analysis also examined whether the attitudes deviated from the informants' own pronunciation and whether age, gender and social status affected their opinions towards the merger. A difference in tolerance was observed between those who believed they merged the vowels themselves and those who believed they kept them apart. The latter believed to a greater extent that the merger was ugly. An additional difference observed was that those who believed they had a merger between /œ/ and /ɵ/ appeared to be more aware of their language use in general than those who believed they distinguished between the two.

The former group stated their opinion regarding their language use – more so than the latter – and reported that they had received comments in the past concerning their language, both factors that may have influenced the results.

One difficulty is that self-reporting reflects the norm rather than actual practice (Andersson & Thelander 1994:59). When people describe their own language, it often becomes evident that they believe they speak the way they want to or think they should. Therefore, a question arises: why do changes occur if they are considered unattractive?

Various theories (see, e.g. Auer et al. 2005) have been proposed regarding how linguistic change spreads, e.g. the desire to belong to or sound like a particular group of language users. Since all the informants in the study were aware that the merger between /œ/ and /ɵ/ exists, a link was expected between positive attitudes to the merger and a merger in the individual's own speech. However, no such link was found when this hypothesis was tested. An explanation could be that subconscious attitudes guide linguistic change more than conscious attitudes (Kristiansen 2015). This, though, is a debated distinction that has been criticised by e.g. Preston (2004:64), who argues that "attitude study, within a linguistic setting, should proceed along both lines of enquiry: what are the linguistic facts of identification and reaction, and what are the underlying constructs which promote and support them?". As stated above, the merger between /œ/ and /ɵ/ may be physiologically driven, resulting from a simplification process concerning articulation and perception that is occuring naturally.

A further question that can be discussed is whether it is a change in attitude towards a linguistic change that leads to a change in production, or whether the change in production takes place first, in turn leading to an attitudinal change. Kristiansen and Jørgensen (2005:295) maintain that good agreement between language use and hidden attitudes supports the hypothesis that attitude changes prior to language use. The attitudinal test conducted for this study showed that young people do not hold particularly strong opinions on the pronunciation of a variably merged /œ/, which could indicate that the attitudes toward the merger are in the process of changing. It also revealed that the younger group of speakers have a smaller distance between /œ/ and /ɵ/ in their production. From this can be deduced that strong feelings for or against a sound change are not necessary for innovations to be integrated into a language. According to the attitudinal test, it may suffice that people believe both forms are equally good options.

6. Comparison between production and perception

When it was established that there were differences in how the informants perceived stimuli, the desire arose to investigate whether there was a correlation between the informants' perception and their pronunciation. A subgroup of 19 informants therefore became the focus of study, with the purpose of investigating any correlation between the informants' production and their perception. This was achieved by subtracting the perceptual deviation from the phonetic distance for each informant. The hypothesis was that people with a large phonetic distance between /œ/ and /ɵ/ are better at categorising stimuli.

The nine informants with the smallest phonetic distance (less than 1.14) were placed in one group and the remaining ten in another. The mean value for the distance in the first group was 0.77, while for the latter it was 1.48. A t-test established that the difference in pronunciation between the two groups was significant ($p < .001$).

Only one informant with a large phonetic distance performed better in the perception test than the average informant. Similarly, only two informants from the group with a small phonetic distance fared worse than the average informant. The fact that 16 of the 19 informants ended up in the same perception group as the other informants in their production group indeed indicates a correlation between production and perception, but not with the expected result. It appears that people with a small phonetic distance in their own language find it easier to categorise stimuli than the people who more clearly distinguish between /œ/ and /ɵ/ in their own speech. A correlation analysis conducted between the informants' perceptual deviation and phonetic distance confirmed that there was a certain positive correlation ($r = 0.236$) that might be significant for a larger population.

The explanation could be that people who only have small differences between the phonemes in their speech are aware that small qualitative differences can produce a meaningful contrast, while people who more clearly distinguish the phonemes also expect greater differences between the phonemes of other speakers. It must also be noted that one of the informants who clearly distinguished the phonemes in his own speech reported in the attitudinal test that he often misunderstands people with a variably merged /œ/ and /ɵ/.

A subject that has been repeatedly discussed is whether an ongoing change occurs first in production or in perception. In a perception test performed on users of the Stockholm dialect of Swedish, Janson (1986) shows that the differences in the categorisation of a continuum of sounds into the /ɑː/ and /oː/ phonemes are very small between the different groups of informants, despite pronunciation varying greatly between generations. Janson (1983:31) similarly concludes that a sound change first affects production, with the argument that the old perception pattern must remain in place even if one's own usage changes. Labov (1994:355), on the other hand, suggests that studies of ongoing linguistic change have shown that changes in perception precede changes in production: the speaker pronounces two vowels differently but does not perceive the difference between them. However, Hansen (2006), investigating the confusion of the vowels /œ̃/ and /ɛ̃/ in French, concludes that whether the change process is first noticed in production or in perception depends on which stage the change is at. A recently started change is first visible in production. When the change approaches its final stage, speakers no longer need to perceive the distinction, so the change then often takes place in their perception before they change their pronunciation.

6.1 Results of the combined analysis

The results of the combined analysis of the informants' production and perception showed that there was a correlation, with those who distinguished the least between the phonemes /œ/ and /ɵ/ being the ones who better discerned the differences in the perception test. This could be because people with a small phonetic distance feel more certain that small nuances can indicate a difference in meaning, while people who more clearly distinguish the phonemes expect greater differences between them in others. Based on this explanation, it seems reasonable to assume that sound change begins in production. Once the phonemes are located closer to each other in the vowel space, perception is affected, as listeners are forced to distinguish between phonemes with fewer qualitative differences. Molina-García (2019) arrived at a similar conclusion, since the speakers in his study who displayed a very small phonetic distance between the merged sounds were perceived correctly by the listeners.

Speakers may be aware of change occurring in the speech community even if they do not always hear the difference and are unaware that they have already adopted it themselves. In line with this, certain informants in the present study noticed when others had a variably merged /œ/, while being unaware that they themselves had a merger, or at least such a small distance between phonemes that others had trouble discerning their /œ/ and /ɵ/ sounds. This result is also supported by Kerswill's perception test, in which informants listened to recordings of their own vowels and were not always able to classify them correctly (Kerswill 1980).

7. Summarising discussion

The results of the study show that the phonetic distance between /œ/ and /ɵ/ decreases for each age group as the oldest speakers have the largest difference between the phonemes and the youngest speakers have the smallest distance. Significant differences in the phonetic distance between /œ/ and /ɵ/ were also found between men and women. Previous research argues that women's speech adheres more closely to the standard than men's speech (Trudgill 1986: 161; Wolfram 1969: 76; Hudson 1996: 195; Nordberg 1971). This concurs with the results of this study, in which the women had a greater phonetic distance between the phonemes /œ/ and /ɵ/ than the men. An explanation for this could be that women are encouraged to follow societal norms, also with regard to language. At the same time, other studies show that girls and women are the most innovative in introducing and using new non-standard forms (e.g. Eckert 1989; Labov 2001). There are also studies that show bigger differences *within* gender categories than between them (e.g. Bucholtz 1999; Eckert 2000; Eriksson 2001; Matsumoto & Britain 2003; Røyneland 2007). Regarding the question of which linguistic features belong to the norm, the deciding factor is the social status of the language users. It could therefore make sense to investigate whether gender and social status covary, but since social status is a continuous variable, it is difficult to draw a fair dividing line between groups. In this study, social status was based on the informants' educational level. There were no statistically significant differences between the groups, but a trend was perceived where those with a lower social status kept the phonemes apart the most, while those with the highest social status differentiated the least. Nordberg (2005: 130), who investigated the small Swedish town of Eskilstuna, has also shown that high-status social groups tend to merge the sounds, with the opposite applying to low-status social groups.

Labov (1994: 78) argues that a change from below can be introduced by any social class, but that there are no results determining that the highest social classes lead such developments. This does not necessarily contradict the results in the present study. Firstly, the difference between social classes is not as pronounced in Sweden as it is in many other countries. Secondly, the merger may indeed initially have been started by people with a lower social status. In poetry and drama, it has been this group that has been attributed with the merger (Ståhle 1976: 8 f.). In recent times, with people commuting from Uppland to their jobs and careers in Stockholm, a merger in Stockholm speech could be perceived more favourably by the commuters than by Stockholmers.

If in various locations the phonemes are indeed moving apart, the relationship between short /œ/ and short /ɵ/ could be viewed as a near-merger. This means that the speakers produce distinctions that neither they themselves nor other listeners can use to distinguish different sounds from one another. The comparison of the informants' own productions and their responses in the perception test showed that informants with a small phonetic distance in their own speech more easily distingished /œ/ and /ɵ/ in the perception test than those people who more clearly kept /œ/ and /ɵ/ apart in their own speech. One possible explanation may be that people with a small distance between the phonemes in their own speech have a greater understanding of the fact that small differences in quality may also signal a difference in meaning, while people who more clearly keep the phonemes apart also expect there to be larger differences between the phonemes produced by other speakers. According to Labov (1994:359), there is great individual variation within a society, with some speakers having a total merger, others a near-merger and still others making a distinction.

One reason why a full merger is unlikely to occur in this case is that many language users are aware of the confusion between /œ/ and /ɵ/. The attitudinal test revealed that many people saw this trend as undesirable. This alone may be enough to spark a counter-reaction, with those who still have not merged the phonemes aiming to make an even greater distinction between them than before.

A main cause of dialect levelling is increased mobility, which leads to people coming into contact with new people and thus new pronunciation patterns. As is well-known, people adjust their speech both consciously and unconsciously to fit into a new environment. Studies have found that new arrivals in a community do not necessarily adopt the local language; rather they shift toward the national standard (Thelander 1985). Since the variably merged /œ/ is not part of the standard language, increased mobility could lead to a retreat of the merged pronunciation.

An explanation of dialect levelling that provides the opposite result is that an approximation of /œ/ and /ɵ/ assisted by the phoneme system becomes unbalanced when old pronunciation habits meet new patterns. In such a situation, speakers can find it difficult to maintain all distinctions that exist. It becomes easier to have a single realisation of /œ/ and /ɵ/ than two different realisations located close together. The assumption that a merger between two phonemes will happen more readily in such cases is not far-fetched, especially since maintaining the contrast between /œ/ and /ɵ/ is not necessary.

The results of this research showed that merging was not as common as expected. Gordon (2004:264) writes that in-depth studies of ongoing sound changes do not always point clearly in a particular direction. Based on the attitudinal test and considering popular awareness of the variably merged /œ/, a greater number of these sounds could have been expected in the production test. The merger is probably so marked that it is perceived as more common than is actually the case. Moreover, linguistic change does not occur as quickly as researchers often believe. Nordberg (2001) points out that the development of /ɑ:/ to /o:/ took centuries to complete. It remains to be seen whether /œ/ and /ɵ/ will merge into one phoneme in Swedish or whether the differences that exist today will remain or even increase again in future.

Acknowledgements

I am very grateful to the editors and the two anonymous reviewers for their insightful comments.

References

Allwood, Jens. 2000. *Talspråksfrekvenser. Frekvenser för ord och kollokationer i svenskt tal- och skriftspråk* [Language frequencies. Frequencies for words and collocations in spoken and written Swedish] (Swedish Gothenburg papers in theoretical linguistics 21). Göteborg: Göteborg University.

Andersson, Roger & Mats Thelander. 1994. Internal migration, biography formation and linguistic change. In Bengt Nordberg (ed.), *The sociolinguistics of urbanization. The case of the Nordic countries* (Soziolinguistik und Sprachkontakt 7), 51–86. Berlin & New York: De Gruyter.

Auer, Peter, Frans Hinskens & Paul Kerswill (eds.). 2005. *Dialect change. Convergence and divergence in European languages.* New York, NY: Cambridge University Press.

Boersma, Paul & David Weenink. 2022. *Praat: Doing phonetics by computer.* https://www.fon.hum.uva.nl/praat/. (16 May, 2022.)

Bucholtz, Mary. 1999. "Why be normal?": Language and identity practices in a community of nerd girls. *Language in Society* 28(2). 203–223.

Eckert, Penelope. 1989. *Jocks & burnouts. Social categories and identity in the high school.* New York, NY & London: Teachers College Press.

Eckert, Penelope. 2000. *Linguistic variation as social practice. The linguistic construction of identity in Belten High* (Language in Society 27). Malden, MA & Oxford: Blackwell.

Eriksson, Anders & Pär Wretling. 1997. How flexible is the human voice. A case study of mimicry. In George Kokkinakis, Nikos Fakotakis & Evangelos Dermatas (eds.), *5th European Conference on Speech Communication and Technology (EUROSPEECH'97),* 1043–1046. Grenoble: European Speech Communication Association.

Eriksson, Lisa. 2001. Absolutister, anpassare och andra – något om dialektens betydelse för ungdomars självbild [Absolutists, adapters and others – on the significance of dialect for young people's self-image]. In *Språk, kön och kultur: Rapport från fjärde konferensen om språk och kön, Göteborg den 6.–7. oktober* 2000, 101–107.

Gordon, Matthew. 2004. Investigating chain shifts and mergers. In Jack K. Chambers, Peter Trudgill & Natalie Schilling-Estes (eds.), *The handbook of language variation and change* (Blackwell Handbooks in Linguistics 2), 244–266. Malden, MA: Blackwell.

Hansen, Anita Berit. 2006. *Le rôle de la perception dans le changement phonétique – l'exemple des voyelles nasals du français parisien* [The role of perception in phonetic change – the example of nasal vowels in Parisian French]. Unpublished manuscript from a colloquium in Louvain-la-Neuve 2006.

Hudson, Richard. 1996. *Sociolinguistics* (Cambridge Textbooks in Linguistics), 2nd edn. Cambridge: Cambridge University Press.

Janson, Tore. 1983. Sound change in perception and production. *Language* 59. 18–34.

Janson, Tore. 1986. Sound change in perception. An experiment. In John Ohala & Jeri Jaeger (Eds.), *Experimental phonology*, 253–260. Orlando, FL: Academic Press.

Johnson, Keith. 2005. Speaker Normalization in Speech Perception. In David B. Pisoni & Robert E. Remez (eds.), *The Handbook of Speech Perception*, 363–389. Oxford: Blackwell.

Kerswill, Paul. 1980. *On the nature of contrast in phonology. Evidence from a phoneme merger in South-West Norwegian.* Unpublished MPhil dissertation. Cambridge: University of Cambridge.

Kristiansen, Tore. 2015. The primary relevance of subconsciously offered attitudes. Focusing the language ideological aspect of sociolinguistic change. In Alexei Prikhodkine & Dennis R. Preston (eds.), *Responses to language varieties: Variability, processes and outcomes*, 85–116. Amsterdam: John Benjamins.

Kristiansen, Tore & Jens N. Jørgensen. 2005. Subjective factors in dialect convergence and divergence. In Peter Auer, Frans Hinskens & Paul Kerswill (eds.), *Dialect change. Convergence and divergence in European languages*, 287–302. New York, NY: Cambridge University Press.

Kuronen, Mikko. 2001. Acoustic character of vowel pronunciation in Sweden-Swedish and Finland-Swedish. *Working Papers in Linguistics* 49. 94–97. Lund: Lund University.

Labov, William. 1981. Resolving the Neogrammarian controversy. *Language* 57. 267–308.

Labov, William. 1994. *Principles of linguistic change. Vol. 1: Internal factors* (Language in Society 20). Oxford: Blackwell.

Labov, William. 2001. *Principles of linguistic change. Vol. 2: Social factors* (Language in Society 29). Oxford: Blackwell.

Labov, William, Mark Karan & Corey Miller. 1991. Near-mergers and the suspension of phonemic contrast. *Language Variation and Change* 3. 33–74.

Ladefoged, Peter. 1967. *Three areas of experimental phonetics* (Language and Language Learning 15). London: Oxford University Press.

Lindblom, Björn. 1986. Phonetic universals in vowel systems. In John Ohala & Jeri Jaeger (eds.), *Experimental phonology*, 13–44. Orlando, FL: Academic Press.

Lindblom, Björn, Susan Guion, Susan Hura, Seung-Jae Moon & Raquel Willerman. 1995. Is sound change adaptive? *Rivista di Linguistica / Italian Journal of Linguistics* 7. 5–37.

Maddieson, Ian. 1986. *Patterns of sounds* (Cambridge Studies in Speech Science and Communication). Cambridge: Cambridge University Press.

Mann, Virginia & Bruno Repp. 1980. Influence of vocalic context on perception of the [Σ]–[s] distinction. *Perception and Psychophysics* 28. 213–228.

Matsumoto, Kazuko & David Britain. 2003. Investigating the sociolinguistic gender paradox in a multilingual community: A case study from the Republic of Palau. *The International Journal of Bilingualism* 7(2). 127–152.

Molina-García, Álvaro. 2019. Percepción y distancia acústica: La variación paramétrica individual en la escisión fonemática de /θ/ en el español andaluz. Datos de la ciudad de Málaga [Perception and acoustic distance: The individual parametric variation in phonemic split of /θ/ in Andalusian Spanish. Data of the city of Malaga]. *Estudios de Lingüística Universidad de Alicante* 33. 111–140.

Nordberg, Bengt. 1971. En undersökning av språket i Eskilstuna [A study of the language in Eskilstuna]. *Språkvård* 1971(3). 7–15.

Nordberg, Bengt. 2001. Samma gamla tal [The same old speech]. *Språkvård* 2001(2). 31–41.

Nordberg, Bengt. 2005. /ö/, /u/ och liknande vokaler [/ö/, /u/ and similar vowels]. In Björn Melander et al.. (eds.), *Språk i tid. Studier tillägnade Mats Thelander på 60-årsdagen* (Skrifter utgivna av Institutionen för Nordiska Språk vid Uppsala Universitet 67), 123–135. Uppsala: Uppsala University.

Plauché, Madelaine, Cristina Delogu & John J.Ohala. 1997. Asymmetries in consonant confusion. In George Kokkinakis, Nikos Fakotakis & Evangelos Dermatas (eds.), *5th European Conference on Speech Communication and Technology (EUROSPEECH'97)*, 2187-2190. Grenoble: European Speech Communication Association.

Preston, Dennis. 2004. Language with an attitude. In Jack K. Chambers, Peter Trudgill & Natalie Schilling-Estes (eds.), *The handbook of language variation and change*, 39–66. Malden, MA: Blackwell.

Regan, Brendan. 2020. The split of a fricative merger due to dialect contact and societal changes. A sociophonetic study on Andalusian Spanish read-speech. *Language Variation and Change* 32(2). 159–190.

Røyneland, Unn. 2007. Språklege innovatørar og tradisjonalistar. Om kjønnsparadokset i sosiolingvistikken [Linguistic innovators and traditionalists. On the gender paradox in sociolinguistics]. In Gunnstein Akselberg & Johan Myking (eds.), *Å sjå samfunnet gjennom språket* (Heidersskrift til Helge Sandøy på 60-årsdagen), 179–189. Oslo: Novus.

Simonsen, Hanne G., Inger Moen & Steve Cowen. 2008. Norwegian retroflex stops in a cross linguistic perspective. *Journal of Phonetics* 36. 385–405.

Smith, Julius O. 2011. *Spectral audio signal processing*. http://ccrma.stanford.edu/~jos/sasp/. (20 March, 2022.)

Ståhle, Carl Ivar. 1976. "Mötet uppnas på sundag" ["The meeting opens on Sunday"]. In Bertil Molde (ed.), *Studier i dagens svenska* (Skrifter utgivna av Nämnden för Svensk Språkvård 44), 1–15. Stockholm: Läromedelsförlagen.

Stevens, Kenneth & Arthur House. 1963. Perturbation of vowel articulations. *Journal of Speech and Hearing Disorders* 6. 111-128.

Sundgren, Eva. 2009. The varying influence of social and linguistic factors on language stability and change. The case of Eskilstuna. *Language Variation and Change* 21. 97–133.

Thelander, Mats. 1985. Från blåknut till brakknut. Om provinsiella drag i flyttares språk. [From *blåknut* to *brakknut*. On regional features in the language of migrants]. *Nysvenska Studier* 63. 5–126.

Traunmüller, Hartmut. 1981. Perceptual dimension of openness in vowels. *Journal of the Acoustical Society of America* 69. 1465–1475.

Trudgill, Peter. 1986. *Dialects in contact* (Language in Society 10). Oxford & New York, NY: Basil Blackwell.

UPSID (UCLA Phonological Segment Inventory Database). http://www.linguistics.ucla.edu/faciliti/sales/software.htm#upsid. (17 September, 2021.)

Vallabha, Guatam & Betty Tuller. 2002. Systematic errors in the formant analysis of steady-state vowels. *Speech Communication* 38. 141–160.

Veatch, Thomas. 2005. *Near merger*. http://www.tomveatch.com/Veatch1991/node130.html. (17 September, 2021.)

Villena-Ponsoda, Juan Andrés & Matilde Vida-Castro. 2004. The effect of social prestige on reversing phonological changes. Universal constraints on speech variation in southern Spanish. In Britt-Louise Gunnarsson et al.. (eds.), *Language Variation in Europe: Papers from the Second International Conference on Language Variation in Europe, ICLaVE 2*, 432 444. Uppsala: Uppsala University.

Wenner, Lena. 2010. *När lögnare blir lugnare. En sociofonetisk studie av sammanfallet mellan kort ö och kort u i uppländskan* [When *lögnare* becomes *lugnare*. A sociophonetic study of the merger between short *ö* and short *u* in Uppland Swedish] (Skrifter utgivna av Institutionen för Nordiska Språk vid Uppsala Universitet 80). Uppsala: Uppsala University.

Wenner, Lena. 2019. Vokaler i förändring [Ongoing vowel change]. In Jenny Nilsson, Susanne Nylund Skog & Fredrik Skott (eds.), *Sånt vi bara gör*, 241 242. Stockholm.

Wolfram, Walter. 1969. *A sociolinguistic description of Detroit negro speech* (Urban Language Series 5). Washington, DC: Center for Applied Linguistics.

CHAPTER 3

Social patterns in s-palatalisation in Moroccan and Turkish ethnolectal Dutch
One half of a sociolinguistic study

Frans Hinskens[1,2] & Etske Ooijevaar[1]
[1] Meertens Instituut, Netherlands | [2] Radboud Universiteit Nijmegen, Netherlands

This is a study of variable s-palatalisation in Turkish and Moroccan ethnolectal Dutch, with special attention to its social distribution. Following a discussion of the phenomenon of ethnolectal variation, this chapter introduces the Roots of Ethnolects project as well as the present sub-study. It then explores palatalisation both in general and specifically in the realisation of /s/, before presenting the details of this study on s-palatalisation in the Roots of Ethnolects data, including methodology, the speakers studied, material and data, coding, measurement and analysis. Lastly, it discusses the findings from the point of view of the research questions guiding the Roots of Ethnolects project as well as issues for further research.

Keywords: ethnolect, Centre of Gravity, first and second language acquisition, language contact, language variation, palatalisation, social meaning

1. Introduction

Demographic diversity in present-day Europe appears to be on the rise as a result of mobility and migration of all types and at all geographical levels. When occurring on a national level, it tends to be referred to as mobility, while cross-border mobility is usually referred to as migration. This differentiation is not coincidental but derives from a historical fact: in western Europe migration is rooted either in processes of decolonisation or in labour migration. One of the cultural consequences of this increase in demographic diversity is multilingualism. This comes on top of traditional endogenous variation (mostly dialect variation), which initially often also entailed social variation, though only in urban areas. With the

https://doi.org/10.1075/silv.31.03hin
© 2024 John Benjamins Publishing Company

Chapter 3. Social patterns in s-palatalisation in Moroccan and Turkish ethnolectal Dutch

erosion of traditional dialects and the emergence of dialect/standard language continua, the emerging vertical variation has also begun to correlate with social and demographic variables such as educational level, occupation and income. Increasingly rich verbal repertoires are emerging, constituted by old and young dialect variation alongside and increasingly as a result of multilingualism. At the crossroads of endogenous variation and multilingualism ethnolects develop. Ethnolects are varieties of a language (usually the dominant language) that originated in a specific ethnic or cultural group.

This contribution focuses on the variable s-palatalisation in Turkish and Moroccan Dutch, with special attention to its social distribution. It first discusses the phenomenon of ethnolectal variation (Section 2), after which it introduces the Roots of Ethnolects project as well as this sub-study (section 3). It then looks at palatalisation both in general (4.1 and 4.2) and specifically in the realisation of /s/ (4.3), before presenting the details of the methodology of this study on s-palatalisation in the Roots of Ethnolects data (Section 5), covering the speakers studied (5.1), material and data (5.2), coding and measurement (5.3) and analyses (5.4). Sections 6 and 7 are devoted to the findings and the discussion of these as well as to issues for further research.

2. Ethnolectal variation

Ethnolectal variation is often rooted in substrate effects of the original language of an ethnic minority group, in L2 acquisition phenomena and in the native dialects. Much is still unclear about ethnolects, such as how stable they can become or whether they spread.[1]

Useful overviews of important 'early' work and more recent studies, regarding the international perspective as well as past and present ethnolects of Dutch, can be found in Muysken (2013) and Hinskens (2019).

In general, there are two distinct approaches to the study of ethnolects: the language-centred and the ethnographic approach. Whereas the ethnographic approach conceives language systems as infinite resources from which speakers may freely choose to shape their identity, the language-centred approach tries to disentangle the laws, generalisations and restrictions concerning these resources. The language-centred approach is typically characterised by:

---

1. Parts of the present section as well as the below sections on the Roots of Ethnolects project, the speakers, and the material and data are based on parts of Hinskens (2019) and Hinskens et al. (forthcoming 2022).

- the use of terminology such as 'ethnolect', 'multi-ethnolect' and 'multicultural variety';
- 'objective' definitions of ethnicity (language, race, descent);
- quantitative methodology (often in the Labovian tradition);
- focus on form, structure and the distribution of variation; and
- a macro-social perspective.

The ethnographic approach, on the other hand, is typically characterised by:

- the use of terminology such as 'style' and '(pan-)ethnic style';[2]
- 'subjective' definitions of ethnicity (social construction, perception);[3]
- attention to both reactive and initiative uses of linguistic and paralinguistic features;
- interpretive methodology;
- focus on social meaning ('indexicality') and its fluidity; and
- a micro-social perspective.

3. The roots of ethnolects project

The research project "The roots of ethnolects: an experimental comparative study" pays systematic attention to language contact, universal traits of second language acquisition and to endogenous dialects as sources of variation.[4] The project focuses on synchronic variation in the speech of bilingual and monolingual native speakers of Dutch, including members of the 'white' majority who have mainly Dutch-born forebears and members of two specific ethnic minority groups. The Roots of Ethnolects project examines the emergence, position and social spread of two young ethnolects of Dutch in the cities of Amsterdam and Nijmegen (see Figure 1).

These two ethnolectal varieties are spoken by second and third generation migrants of Turkish and Moroccan descent. While there has been labour migration from Mediterranean countries such as Spain, Portugal and Italy since the 1950s, in the 1970s, the bilateral labour recruitment agreements that had just been

---

2. On concepts and terminology, see Kern 2011: 4–10.

3. See Fought (2013).

4. Conceived and supervised by the late Pieter Muysken (Nijmegen) and Frans Hinskens (Amsterdam). The project was financed 2005–2015 by the Netherlands Organisation for Scientific Research (NWO), Meertens Instituut and Radboud Universiteit Nijmegen. Other researchers involved were Hanke van Buren (Nijmegen), Roeland van Hout (Nijmegen), Esther van Krieken (Nijmegen), Wouter Kusters (Amsterdam), Linda van Meel (Nijmegen and Amsterdam) and Arien van Wijngaarden (Amsterdam).

Chapter 3. Social patterns in s-palatalisation in Moroccan and Turkish ethnolectal Dutch

Figure 1. Sampling points for the Roots of ethnolects project

signed with Turkey (1964) and Morocco (1969) presented important impulses for migration. Table 1 contains relevant demographic facts (from 2005, the year the project and the fieldwork started) about the two cities represented in the project.

Table 1. Three relevant demographic facts about the Dutch cities of Amsterdam and Nijmegen

City	Total no. of inhabitants	Moroccan descent (%)	Turkish descent (%)
Amsterdam	742,783	8.7	5.1
Nijmegen	158,215	2.0	3.2

The proportions (Amsterdam: Moroccan > Turkish, Nijmegen: Moroccan < Turkish) are consistent with those of the Migration Map of the Meertens Institute.[5] According to this source, of the inhabitants of Amsterdam who were between 30

---

5. https://www.meertens.knaw.nl/migmap/. (3 November, 2021.)

and 50 years of age in 2007, 5.17% were of Moroccan and 3.60% of Turkish descent. Of the inhabitants of Nijmegen who were between 30 and 50 years of age in 2007, 1.49% had Moroccan ancestry and 2.61% had Turkish ancestry.

The approach of the project is language-centred rather than ethnographic. One set of research questions concerns the linguistic make-up of ethnolects: to what extent are they rooted in substrates, in phenomena that are typical of second language acquisition, and in endogenous non-standard varieties? Another set of questions concerns the place of the ethnolect in the verbal repertoires of its speakers, such as whether the variable features are subject to style-shifting. Yet other questions concern the spread of ethnolectal features to other ethnic groups.

The data for the Roots of Ethnolects project were collected in such a way that they fitted a factorial design, with equal numbers of young male speakers[6] from Amsterdam and Nijmegen. They are of three backgrounds, Moroccan, Turkish and 'white' Dutch, and two age groups – with age group serving as an apparent time or cross-sectional operationalisation of acquisition, one of the hypothesised roots of ethnolectal variation. The speakers with Moroccan and Turkish backgrounds grew up bilingually in the Netherlands with at least one parent who was born in Morocco or Turkey, respectively; hence they are also native speakers of some variety of modern Dutch. Among the 'white' Dutch speakers, a distinction is made between those with strong and those with weak or no network ties with boys from other ethnic groups. Each of the resulting sixteen subgroups (4 backgrounds × 2 age groups × 2 cities) is represented by six speakers.

Except in the case of the subgroup of 'white' Dutch boys who have few if any friends from other ethnic groups, four recordings were made of every single speaker, with three of these concerning conversations: one with a speaker whose main background is Moroccan, one with a speaker with a Turkish background and one with a 'white' Dutch boy with friends from other ethnic groups. The conversations were typically held in school canteens; most conversations lasted about one hour. The speaker and the interlocutor were often friends, and the fieldworker was usually absent for a part of the recording session. The additional recording of these speakers comprises an individual elicitation session. Both the individual elicitation sessions and the conversations were recorded on a Marantz Professional CD recorder CDR300. The quality of the recordings allowed for full acoustic analysis and did not cause any problems.

The findings mainly concern four different variable phenomena: three are phonetic-phonological in nature, one morpho-syntactic. The variables involve the realisation of /z/ (palato-alveolar or dental, voiced or voiceless), the diphthong

---

6. It was decided to study just one gender so as to keep the design manageable and for budget reasons. Boys were chosen since, in these communities, males are less oriented to standard norms (see, e.g. Brouwer 1989 and Van Hout 1989 for the Dutch language area).

Chapter 3. Social patterns in s-palatalisation in Moroccan and Turkish ethnolectal Dutch

/ɛi/ (diphthongal or monophthongal, with a mid or low prominent first element), the contrast /ɑ-a/ (where both length and place of articulation were found to vary) and grammatical gender marking in determiners and adnominal flexion.

As to the origin of these features: substrate effects are only discernible for the dental variant of /z/, and L2 effects only for the variation in grammatical gender marking both in determiners and adnominal flexion.[7] Effects of the surrounding endogenous dialects dominate, being visible in the devoicing of /z/, the monophthongisation and variation in the height of /ɛi/ as well as in the place of articulation of the low vowels /a/ and /ɑ/.

Stylistic variation due to accommodation to the interlocutor was found in the use of the dental variant of /z/, of /a/ before obstruents in Moroccan Dutch, and in the fact that fewer standard grammatical gender determiners were used in interactions with interlocutors with a Moroccan Dutch and Turkish Dutch background. These effects are all instances of audience design; however, this does not hold for the style effect in the variable use of monophthongal variants of /ɛi/.

Spread to other groups has been established for the dental variant of /z/, which originated in Moroccan Dutch (a variety that has a certain covert prestige, indexing roughness and toughness) but has clearly been adopted by the Turkish Dutch. Spread to other groups has also been established for the endogenous local dialect variants of /ɛi/, which are being abandoned by teenagers from monolingual Dutch families in favour of the new, supra-regional non-standard [ai]. The older dialect variants [ɛ:] and [a:] are being rescued by speakers of Moroccan and Turkish Dutch; these dialect features are thus being recycled as ethnolect features.[8]

Of the variable phenomena that emerged from the initial inspections and inventories of non-standard phenomena in the Roots of Ethnolects recordings, pronominal adverbs or R-pronouns (such as *ermee*, lit. 'therewith' or 'with it', and new variants such as *met die* and R-less *mee*, lit. 'with that' and 'with') and the palatalisation of onset /s/ before a consonant and in particular before a velar voiceless or voiced fricative (/x/ and /ɣ/, respectively) have not yet been investigated. The latter phenomenon will be the focus of this study.

3.1 The present study

In the Amsterdam area and especially in the urban vernacular, /s/ is variably realised grave and slightly palatal (Hinskens 2004); the process is not subject to internal conditioning, but socially it is largely confined to the lower strata and

---

7. I.e. L2 effects in the Dutch of Turkish and Moroccan migrants, which were passed on in the in-group varieties of Dutch.

8. For more information on data, methods and findings from the study of the three phonetic variables, see Van Meel (2016), among others.

the more casual style levels. In Limburg dialects /s/ is palatalised in onset clusters (Goossens 1969:51–52, 127). Otherwise, s-palatalisation is rare and at best sub-phonemic in the Dutch language area and this applies a fortiori in contexts where /s/ precedes a velar fricative. In the Roots of Ethnolects recordings, on the other hand, s-palatalisation is far from rare. It occurs, for example, in:

(1) a. *schaken* 'play chess'   (N12M01)
     b. *onbeschoft* 'rude'   (A12D02)
     c. *is goed* 'is good/fine'   (A12T02)
     d. *anders geweest* '[have/has] been different'   (A20D04)
     e. *klasgenoot* 'classmate'   (N12M03)

The codes between brackets identify individual speakers. A and N stand for Amsterdam and Nijmegen, respectively, 12 and 20 for the age groups 10–12 and 18–20 years, and M, T and D for Moroccan Dutch, Turkish Dutch and white Dutch (specifically those with strong network ties with boys from other ethnic groups). The examples in (1) show that s-palatalisation occurs in both cities and among speakers of both age groups and from all three backgrounds – albeit variably, whereby the variation is not a question of yes or no, but rather of more or less. In the study of which this contribution is the first fruit, the aim is to uncover the distribution of s-palatalisation, including both the social and socio-stylistic as well as the linguistic distribution.

In general, a /sɣ/ or /sx/ sequence in Dutch can occur in three grammatical contexts:

- word internally: within a word, as in e.g. *school* 'school', *schrijven* '[to] write', *misschien* 'maybe', see also (1a, b);
- word boundary: the cluster is broken up by a word boundary, as in e.g. *is goed* 'is good/fine', *als chemisch* 'like chemical', *dus geen* 'so/hence no', see also (1c, d);
- compound word: the cluster is broken up by the boundary between the constituent parts of a compound word, as in e.g. *wasgoed* 'laundry', *reisgeld* 'travel money', *huisgenoten* 'housemates', see also (1e).

The examples given above in (1) show that /s/ before a velar fricative can be palatalised in any of these environments, changing the standard variant [s], a 'hisser', into a sound approaching the 'husher' [ʃ]. The aim of the analyses in the following pages is to determine to what extent the embedding of the cluster plays a role in s-palatalisation. However, the intention is also to gain an understanding of possible effects of the segmental environment; from the examples given, palatalisation can occur at least after schwa, /ɪ/, /r/ and /ɑ/ and before a velar fricative followed by /a/, /ɔ/, /u/ and schwa – but this too must be investigated systematically.

The analyses are limited to the investigation of and findings for social and socio-stylistic effects. The last section in this chapter outlines the research currently being conducted on internal conditioning.

4. S-palatalisation

Studies have been conducted on phonological and phonetic as well as variationist aspects of palatalisation. Palatalisation is subphonemic in some languages, allophonic in others and in yet others (as in the consonant inventories of many Slavic languages[9]) palatalisation has led to a systematic widening of segment inventories. Variationist research deals almost without exception with variable, subphonemic palatalisation of the sibilant /s/ and is mainly socio-phonetic and either quantitative or interpretive ('understanding' in Dilthey's (1883) sense) in nature.

4.1 Palatalisation

First, a brief word on palatalisation in general. Bhat (1978) studies phonetic palatalisation, observing among other things that palatalisation "generally gets strengthened and even newly introduced into a stretch of speech as the rapidity of speech increases" (ibid.: 65).

Bateman (2011) focused on phonemic palatalisation, both secondary (where a consonant acquires a secondary palatal articulation) and full palatalisation, resulting in "a change in place (toward palatal) and often manner of articulation" (ibid.: 589). The latter type is often accompanied by affrication.

Bateman investigated a wide range of languages,

> aiming to provide a basic typology of palatalization targets (consonants that undergo palatalization), palatalization triggers (sounds that trigger palatalization), and of possible palatalization patterns one might expect to find, or to not find, in the world's languages. (ibid.: 588)

Thus, the author tried to unearth generalisations concerning larger (natural or other) classes of sounds and individual sounds that are subject to or trigger palatalisation.[10] Bateman found "implicational relationships among palatalisation

---

9. See Padgett (2003) and Rubach (2011) among many others. For another concise overview see https://en.wikipedia.org/wiki/Slavic_palatalization and links mentioned there (last accessed by the principal author on 13 October, 2021)

10. González (2014) is a study of palatalisation as an areal feature in members of six language families spoken in the Chaco linguistic area (western Paraguay, eastern Bolivia and northern

targets and triggers", allowing predictions regarding patterns of palatalisation in "the world's languages, with the most significant prediction being that we should find no language where labials show exclusive palatalisation (full or secondary)" (ibid.: 600).

The variable s-palatalisation studied here concerns full and not secondary palatalisation and seems to be triggered by a following velar fricative. Bateman's research shows that only front and/or high vowels trigger palatalisation. In her study of palatalisation gestures in the production of /t/ and /d/ in Belgian Standard French, Corneau (1999) demonstrates that subphonemic "palatalisation is due to the coarticulation of the stop with a following high front vowel or a palatal approximant" (Corneau 1999: 61). This may mean that the velar fricative in Turkish and Moroccan Dutch contains a palatal specification. However, it is also conceivable that the palatalisation is essentially a co-articulation effect consisting of the tongue body retracting during the articulation of the sibilant in anticipation of the realisation of the velar.

4.2 Variable palatalisation of coronals other than /s/

The sibilant /s/ is not the only coronal that undergoes (variable) palatalisation, although cross-linguistically it does seem to occur most often in this sense. The coronal plosives and the nasal sometimes undergo variable palatalisation as well, also in unrelated languages.

Carvalho (2004) studied the sociolinguistic distribution of palatalisation of /di/ and /ti/ in Uruguayan Portuguese in data collected in a bilingual town on the Uruguayan–Brazilian border. The author argues that the process is related to increasing urbanisation and thus the orientation towards Brazilian Portuguese, where palatalisation is abundant (in this regard, see Monteiro, Section 4.3 below). Qualitative data suggest that exposure to Brazilian television plays an indirect role in the process.

Sokhey (2015) focuses on palatalisation of the nasal /n/ in Cairene Arabic. After an acoustic description, the occurrence of the palatalised nasal is related to the use of /t, d/ in three speech contexts. The hypothesis is explored that palatalised /n/ may be "used strategically in conversations by its speakers to assume certain 'expressive postures'" (Sokhey 2015: V).

Argentina). Along the lines of the dissertation underlying Bateman (2011), González maps triggers, targets, results, direction (progressive or regressive) as well as the phonological status (lexical versus post-lexical) of the palatalisation process for the languages studied.

4.3 Variable palatalisation of /s/

Prior to looking specifically at the palatalisation of /s/, a variable process targeting /s/ should be mentioned that is related to but different from palatalisation, namely fronting. Articulatorily fronting is the opposite of palatalisation, which is sometimes analysed as retraction (of the tongue tip, to be specific).

Variable s-fronting has been studied in a wide range of languages and language varieties, including the English of Johannesburg (Bekker 2007; Bekker & Levon 2017), San Francisco (Calder 2019), southern California (Podesva & Hofwegen 2016), south-east England (Holmes-Elliot & Levon 2017) and Glasgow (Stuart-Smith 2007, 2020) as well as Copenhagen Danish (Pharao et al. 2014; Pharao & Maegaard 2017) and early L1 Mandarin (Li 2017).

In almost all these communities, fronting seems to index female gender and/ or queerness (referring to gays or drag queens; Calder 2019), also perceptually (Pharao et al. 2014), sometimes in conjunction with higher social-economic class (Bekker 2007) and with urbanity (Bekker 2007; Podesva & Hofwegen 2016; Bekker & Levon 2017). In Glasgow, depending on the type of phonetic analysis, a "reduction of gender differentiation" or a "change in gendered differentiation" appears to be taking place (Stuart-Smith 2020).[11]

S-palatalisation is mostly achieved through retraction, in a sense the counterpart of s-fronting. Monteiro (2009) is a study of syllable-final s-palatalisation in Portuguese from Macapá in the Brazilian state of Pará. Variable s-palatalisation is a common and recurrent phenomenon in varieties of Brazilian Portuguese, and it has been the object of study in varieties spoken in cities in at least seven different states. In her analysis of s-palatalisation in Macapá, Monteiro focuses on both social and structural factors.

Rutter (2014) is another study of variation in the realisation of /s/ in L1 acquisition – of American English in this case. Rutter studied variable s-retraction in /str/ onset clusters in the speech of eight children aged 4;1–8;1 and their primary caregivers. The author found that 5;1-year-old children "were starting to exhibit the usage patterns of their mothers". The distributional patterns suggest that the acquisition of the new variant proceeds by lexical diffusion rather than by rule.

Marzo et al. (2018) study s-palatalisation in Citétaal, an urban vernacular Dutch that is spreading in the easternmost region of the northern, Dutch-speaking part of Belgium. The authors found macro-social correlates such as gender, migrant/native born, and age group. They also found certain parameters of the interactional context to affect the process, including 'emotional/neutral' as well as

---

11. A compact survey of the literature, with emphasis on the aspect of social meaning, can be found in Eckert (2019: 761, 764).

priming, word class and the phonetic context.[12] Advanced statistical analyses brought to light patterns seemingly consistent with the hypothesis that the (unspecified) social meaning of the variable "results from a combination of social and interactional categories at play in variant selection and that this combination adopts a prototype structure, characterised by salient and less salient categories" (Marzo et al. 2018: 127).

Mourigh (2017) argues that in the Hollandic village of Gouda sibilant palatalisation has been conventionalised as a Moroccan-Dutch youth speech feature. The palatal variant is "used for the purposes of stance-taking. Speakers use it as a marker for casual, tough and impudent stance in certain contexts" (Mourigh 2017: 445), especially in informal settings.

As the brief literature survey in this section has shown, s-palatalisation occurs in varieties of different languages in different parts of the world. Variable s-palatalisation, like s-fronting, can be socially meaningful. However, insofar as the variation has a social meaning (and this assumes: insofar as one is aware of it), this meaning is not necessarily identical for all varieties. Whether s-palatalisation has a social meaning in Moroccan and Turkish ethnolectal Dutch is one of the questions that may be addressed on the basis of the patterns of its social distribution and spread that emerge from the analysis of the Roots of Ethnolects data.

5. S-palatalisation in the roots of Ethnolects data: Method and approach

5.1 Speakers

The present study is based on data from 34 speakers (a proper subset of the speaker sample for the Roots of Ethnolects project), divided into groups determined by the speakers' ethnic and linguistic backgrounds (Moroccan Dutch, Turkish Dutch and white Dutch), age (10–12 years versus 18–20 years) and city of residence (Amsterdam versus Nijmegen). Table 2 illustrates the speaker design for this study and the number of speakers in each group.

Table 2. The speaker design for the present study

Ethnic background	Moroccan Dutch		Turkish Dutch		White Dutch	
Age group	10–12	18–20	10–12	18–20	10–12	18–20
Amsterdam	3	4	3	4	2	3
Nijmegen	3	2	2	3	3	2

---

12. For this study, it is interesting that in Marzo et al.'s data a following velar fricative triggers significantly more palatalisation than other consonants.

5.2 Material and data

This study on s-palatalisation is based on analyses of Roots of Ethnolects recordings of conversational speech. During an earlier phase of the project, ten to fifteen minutes of each conversation had already been orthographically transcribed and annotated in ELAN (Brugman & Russel 2004). The first three minutes of each conversation were not transcribed. All transcriptions were checked by a second transcriber.

The aim for the present study was to gather at least 15 realisations of /s/ before /x/ or /ɣ/ per speaker per conversation. After they had been checked, the transcribed parts of the recordings were examined and, wherever necessary, more /s/-realisations were collected from the same recording. To avoid bias from high frequency words, every word was selected at most three times per speaker per conversation. This resulted in an initial collection of over 1400 instances of /sx/ or /sɣ/.

5.3 Coding and measurement

With the help of ELAN, each occurrence per speaker per conversation was registered with the exact time of occurrence in the conversation. Next, each realisation of /sx/ or /sɣ/ was annotated and coded for the grammatical position of the cluster, i.e. word internal, split by a word boundary or by the boundary between the constituent parts of a compound (see Section 3.1 above). Additionally, information on the phonological nature of the segment preceding /s/ and that following /x/ or /ɣ/ was coded, i.e. a consonant, a front vowel, a back vowel or schwa. Some words with an initial /s/ followed by a velar fricative were preceded by a pause, which was included as such in the coding.

Using the transcriptions and annotations, each sequence of /s/ preceding /x/ or /ɣ/ was measured for duration using Praat (Boersma & Weenink 2010); only /s/ realisations longer than 40 ms were selected for further acoustic measurement. A total of 1304 observations remained. Considering the total of 34 speakers, this amounts to an average of 38.35 observations per speaker. Each single /s/ realisation was carefully localised in the speech signal and then manually segmented. The boundaries of each /s/ were determined on the basis of a visual estimation of its spectral properties.

Cross-linguistically, there is a linear relationship between the degree of palatalisation and the spectral Centre of Gravity of /s/. The Centre of Gravity (CoG) is "a measure for how high the frequencies in a spectrum are on average" (Praat Manual).[13] It is the frequency that "divides the spectrum into two halves

---

13. https://www.fon.hum.uva.nl/praat/manual/Manual.html (last accessed by the principal author on 10 October, 2021).

such that the amount of energy in the top half (higher frequencies) is equal to that in the bottom half (lower frequencies)".[14] As for /s/: the more retracted the tongue tip during the realisation of /s/, the lower the CoG. Thus, [s] has higher CoG values than [ʃ]. Gordon et al. (2002) carried out acoustic measurements of /s/ and /ʃ/ in six different languages and found that /ʃ/ has lower spectral peak values and lower CoG values than /s/ in each of these languages. The same has been established for the Dutch equivalents of both fricatives by Rietveld and Heuven (2013: 156–159; see also Ditewig et al. 2021: 153–154). Moreover, Reidy (2016) found that in English the spectral properties of word initial /s/ and /ʃ/ show different dynamics. From 'onset' to 'midpoint', /s/ shows a sharper increase in maximum frequency values than /ʃ/. In the present study, the palatalisation of /s/ was therefore measured dynamically (using Praat) on the basis of two specific CoG measurements, the first at 25% and the second at 55% of the duration, both with a 10 ms window length. For occurrences not longer than 40 ms, this means that there is a 2 ms time difference between the end of the first and the beginning of the second measurement window. A smaller time difference would not improve the quality of the measurements and, thus, the palatalisation measure. All measurements were normalised per speaker via z-scores. Based on the mean and standard deviation of CoG1 and CoG2 per speaker, z-values for CoG1 and CoG2 were calculated; then, per occurrence, diff_zCoG2_zCoG1 was calculated as zCoG2 – zCoG1. The difference between the z-scores of CoG2 and CoG1, labelled diffZCoG2-ZCoG1, is the dependent variable. Since [ʃ] has lower CoG values than [s], this means: the lower the value, the more palatalisation.

5.4 Data analyses

Mixed Models regression analysis (LMER) was conducted with diffZCoG2-ZCoG1 for the effects of the independent variables City, Age Group, Speaker Background (white Dutch, Moroccan Dutch or Turkish Dutch) and Addressee Background (white Dutch, Moroccan Dutch or Turkish Dutch), for both main effects and a range of interaction effects. Speakers and words were included as random effects. Based on the Akaike information criterion (AIC), the best model was chosen. Finally, using this model of social conditioning, groups were determined that exhibit their own patterns of s-palatalisation.

The results of this first step in the analyses – the measurement of the impact of the four social factors – are presented sequentially in Section 6 below.

---

14. https://www.phonetik.uni-muenchen.de/~hoole/kurse/akustik_ba/fricative_uebung_kurz_anleitung.pdf. (last accessed by the principal author on 11 October, 2021)

Chapter 3. Social patterns in s-palatalisation in Moroccan and Turkish ethnolectal Dutch   **69**

Two series of analyses were carried out. In the first, the starting point was the model without any independent variables. An independent variable was added in each subsequent step, first for the main effects, then an interaction effect was added to the model (one at a time) with all four independent variables. This involved only the six first-degree interaction effects (City × Age, City × Background Speaker, City × Background Addressee, Age × Background Speaker, Age × Background Addressee, Background Speaker × Background Addressee). In the second series of analyses, after the null model, a model was examined four times with one main effect each, then six models with two main effects, four models with three main effects and, finally, the model with four main effects. The model that emerged from this as superior (also via comparison with ANOVAs) was then expanded six times with one interaction effect at a time. The last step was to compare the winning model with that of the first series.

6.   Findings

For the difference measure (diff_zCoG2_zCoG1), a significant main effect was found in the initial, relatively simple approach, namely that Turkish Dutch young men palatalise more than their white Dutch peers. An interaction effect was also revealed, consisting of the Nijmegen Turkish Dutch speakers palatalising less than the Nijmegen white Dutch and Amsterdam Turkish Dutch speakers.

From the series of complex and more comprehensive analyses, a model emerges that is superior to this (with a considerably smaller AIC); see Table 3. The model formula is:

(2)   lmer(diff_zCoG2-zCoG1 ~ plaats + leeftijd + plaats:agspreker + (1|spreker) + (1|word), data = spalRoE)[15]

This winning model shows significant main effects for City (Nijmegen more palatalisation than Amsterdam; $p = .00558$) and Age Group (18–20-year-olds less palatalisation than 10–12-year-olds; $p = .05000$); see Figure 1. Note: the lower the index value, the more palatalisation.

Furthermore, there is an interaction effect meaning that (a) the Amsterdam Turks palatalise more than the Amsterdam Whites and the Nijmegen Turks ($p = .01941$), and (b) the Nijmegen Turks palatalise less than the Nijmegen Whites and the Amsterdam Turks ($p = .01657$).

---

15. *Plaats* means 'city', *leeftijd* 'age/age group' and *agspreker* is short for *achtergrond spreker*, meaning 'background speaker'.

Table 3. Random and fixed effects structure of the linear mixed-effects model. Total number of observations = 1303

Random effects	Variance	Std. Dev.			
Word (intercept)	0.017806	0.1334			
Speaker (intercept)	0.003528	0.0594			
Residual	0.285413	0.5342			
Fixed effects	Estimate	Std. Error	df	t-value	Pr (> /t/)
Intercept	0.29770	0.09932	27.86075	2.997	0.00567**
City (Nijmegen)	−0.21752	0.07148	24.12070	−3.043	0.00558**
Age	0.01024	0.00499	26.73859	2.053	0.05000*
Interactions					
CityAmsterdam * SpeakerBgMD	−0.08350	0.06798	26.46117	−1.228	0.23014
CityNijmegen * SpeakerBgMD	−0.03475	0.06709	19.16992	−0.518	0.61040
CityAmsterdam * SpeakerBgTD	−0.16717	0.06700	25.49026	−2.495	0.01941*
CityNijmegen * SpeakerBgTD	0.17702	0.06744	19.21877	2.625	0.01657*

Signif. codes: '***' < 0.001 '**' < 0.01 '*' < 0.05 '.' < 0.1

A striking similarity between the two series of analyses is that the background of the interlocutor never plays a role. Thus, insofar as style variation is a matter of audience design (*sensu* Bell 1984), s-palatalisation is not subject to style variation.

There are two notable differences between the series of analyses. First, the main effects do not overlap, but the interaction effects do, and second, the complex approach shows an additional pattern in this respect. The fact that the complex approach yields different results is not surprising, since in this approach all logically possible models are tested and compared with each other, whereas in the simple approach only a subset of the conceivable models is measured and compared. The simple approach therefore contains a proper subset of the complex approach, which is superior, as the 'winner' here is the winner of the models from both series of analyses.

The main effect for the factor group City is that Nijmegen speakers palatalise their /s/ more than Amsterdam speakers. The finding that s-palatalisation in Nijmegen appears to be significantly stronger may be related to the fact that, in the southern varieties (not only dialects), velar fricatives are traditionally articulated palato-velar. If this is indeed the cause of the stronger s-palatalisation in Nijmegen, it is in line with the consideration mentioned above (see Section 4.1 above) that s-palatalisation before a velar fricative may be a co-articulation effect. The fact that s-palatalisation is significantly weaker in Amsterdam, in combination with the

Chapter 3. Social patterns in s-palatalisation in Moroccan and Turkish ethnolectal Dutch 71

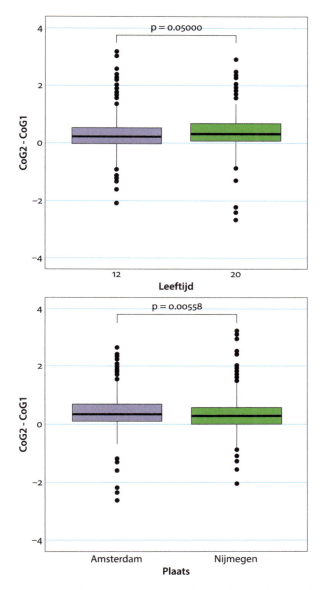

Figure 2. The effects of age (*leeftijd*, top) and city (*plaats*, bottom) on s-palatalisation

general fact that the Dutch capital, Amsterdam, has traditionally been the cultural centre of the country, could mean that s-palatalisation is not part of the contemporary norm – not even of what Grondelaers et al. (2019) call the new 'cool' norm for spoken Standard Dutch. From the main effect for Age, one might assume that linguistic socialisation is accompanied by the unlearning of s-palatalisation.

Together, the two patterns constituting the interaction effect in the winning model roughly give the following picture:

(3) AT > { AD, ND } > NT

When the main effect for City for the D speakers is included, the picture changes to:

(3') AT > ND > AD > NT

Three facts are interesting. First, here too, the speakers of Moroccan Dutch do not play a role. It can only be established that they do not appear to differ significantly from the white Dutch speakers in any analysis (and the white Dutch form the reference group for the effect of Background Speaker). Ergo:

(3") AT > { ND, NM } > { AD, AM } > NT

Second, the speakers of Turkish Dutch appear to distort the pattern that emerges from the main effect for City (i.e. Nijmegen > Amsterdam). Third, the factor group Age Group does not distort the effect of the factor group City, nor does it show a statistically significant interaction effect with the Background of the Speakers.

7. Discussion and issues for further research

As far as the data and the results of these first analyses allow, preliminary answers can be derived for the three sets of research questions guiding the Roots of Ethnolects project, described in Section 3 above. One set of questions concerns the origin of ethnolectal features (whether they are rooted in substrates, in phenomena that are typical of second language acquisition or in endogenous non-standard varieties), another concerns the place of the ethnolect in the verbal repertoires of its speakers (including style-shifting) and the final set concerns the spread of ethnolectal features to other ethnic groups.

Regarding the emergence of this variable ethnolectal phenomenon: Turkish has a contrast between coronal /s/ and palatal /ʃ/, while (Moroccan) Arabic does not, having instead a contrast between /s/ and pharyngealised emphatic /sˤ/.[16] In Arabic, however, there is a non-sibilant palato-alveolar /ʃ/ (Maddieson 1984:310, and 1984:178 for sources mentioned for both languages; Harrell 1962; Caubet 1993:11; Comrie 1997), although some varieties of Berber do have a phoneme /ʃ/

---

16. In Arabic, there are also voiced counterparts of both short and long counterparts of each pair, although the latter may be allophones; see Hinskens (2011).

(Kossmann & Stroomer 1997: 464, 467).[17] The fact that the speakers of Turkish Dutch have different patterns in the s-palatalisation for velar fricatives than the speakers of Moroccan Dutch may have something to do with the fact that Turkish, unlike Moroccan Arabic, has a phoneme /ʃ/; closer inspection of the literature should reveal whether /ʃ/ also occurs in clusters in Standard Turkish and/or in specific Turkish dialects. As there is no significant difference between the Moroccan Dutch and the white Dutch speakers, it can be concluded that there is an effect from the surrounding dialects in the case of the Moroccan Dutch speakers. Witness the interaction effect between City and Speaker Background, which amounts to the finding that the Turkish Dutch distort the geographical pattern (that s-palatalisation is significantly weaker in Amsterdam), thus escaping this influence – probably in favour of the substratum effect, at least in the case of the Amsterdam Turks. In general s-palatalisation is not typical of the acquisition of Dutch as a second language.

As far as the position of s-palatalisation in the verbal repertoires of the speakers is concerned, s-palatalisation distinguishes Turkish Dutch in particular – in Amsterdam due to its relatively frequent use, in Nijmegen, on the other hand, due to its remarkably low use by Turkish Dutch speakers. S-palatalisation is not subject to style-shifting, as there is no main effect for Addressee Background nor any interaction between Speaker Background (in this case Turkish Dutch) and Addressee Background.

Finally, with regard to the social spread of this feature, relatively high values can only be found for the Amsterdam Turks in this sample. The further spread does not yet seem to have commenced, and it is unclear whether it will. A follow-up study could shed light on this.

Other questions for further research concern the semiotic aspect, more specifically the question to what extent s-palatalisation indexes a social-emblematic meaning. The fact that in this data, at least from the perspective of language style as audience design (Bell 1984), no style-shifting occurs seems to imply that s-palatalisation in these groups has no profiled indexical value. However, complementary data are needed for a conclusive answer to this question.

In the second phase of this study, the internal conditioning of s-palatalisation will be determined for each of the groups AT, ND + NM, AD + AM and NT using the same statistical procedures applied in the assessment of the effects of the social factors. Thus, for the internal effects, the following will be compared:

---

17. In the Tables 1 and 2 of his overview, Kossmann (2012) presents the consonant inventories of Ahaggar Tuareg and Kabyle, two varieties of Berber. In the first, the palatal realisations are not phonemic, while in the second they are so.

- the Nijmegen speakers with those from Amsterdam; and
- the speakers aged 10–12 years with those aged 18–20 years.

Furthermore, a triangular comparison will be made between:

- the Amsterdam Turkish Dutch, the Nijmegen Turkish Dutch and all other speakers (i.e. the Amsterdam and Nijmegen white and Moroccan Dutch).

As discussed above, the Moroccan Dutch and the white Dutch are being grouped together, since they do not appear to differ significantly from each other in terms of s-palatalisation in any analysis. Note that Ditewig et al. (2021) reach the same conclusion in the analysis of other data.

The impact of three language-internal independent variables will be investigated: the segment preceding /s/, the segment following /x/ or /ɣ/ and the prosodic position. Previous analyses (which will not be discussed here) have demonstrated that there is neither a main nor an interaction effect of grammatical position, or rather the grammatical boundary that separates /s/ and /x/ or /ɣ/, but that the position of the /s/ may well vary with the prosodic boundary and that prosodic structure is indirectly linked to grammatical structure (Nespor & Vogel 1986).

The independent variables "segment preceding /s/" and "segment following /x/ or /ɣ/" both have the values consonant, pre-vocal, post-vocal and schwa; some words containing /s/ followed by a velar fricative were preceded by a pause. Regarding vowels, the distinction front–back seems to be of great importance, because front vowels often trigger palatalisation, as also shown by Bateman (2011), discussed in Section 4.1 above. The value of the variable prosodic position must first be specified per occurrence on the basis of the score for 'grammatical position' and the annotations and transcriptions of the speech material. Grammatical position is recoded into prosodic position as follows:

- word internal → either segment boundary or foot boundary;
- compound word → prosodic word boundary; and
- word boundary → either prosodic word boundary or phonological phrase boundary.

This new independent variable will be ordinal in nature, with the hierarchy:

(4) segment boundary < clitic boundary < prosodic word boundary < phonological phrase boundary

Insofar as the following velar fricative plays an active role as a trigger, it is to be expected that a deeper prosodic boundary will lead to a lower probability of s-palatalisation.

It is not surprising that there is neither a main nor an interaction effect of grammatical position on s-palatalisation, since s-palatalisation is a phonetic process and phonetic processes are blind to grammatical structure. However, as soon as s-palatalisation starts to phonologise, prosodic position is likely to have an effect, in addition to the segmental environment. This independent variable will be tested both on its own and in conjunction with the two segmental factors.

The ultimate aim is to discover whether the groups distinguished based on the findings of the above analyses for the impact of the social factors show any differences in the internal conditioning of s-palatalisation. This may well be the case, given that the speakers of Turkish Dutch radically distort the distribution related to the factor group City.

Juan Villena has conducted thorough socio-phonetic research on the sibilants of Andalusian varieties of Spanish, including 'Seseo' and related phenomena (Villena-Ponsoda 2001) and the aspiration and reduction of word-final /s/. Insofar as he has addressed processes of palatalisation, he did so in his study of the raising and fronting of /a/ resulting from the aspiration of /s/ > [h] in eastern Andalusian (Villena-Ponsoda 1987: 93–94). We can only hope that our study has something of the elegant precision with which Juan brings together phonetic, linguistic and social mechanisms.

Acknowledgements

Thanks are due to the editors, Khalid Mourigh, and the anonymous reviewers for their invaluable feedback and helpful suggestions. Many thanks also to the 34 speakers studied in this contribution. We are grateful to the then BA students Talitha Eikenhout, Xamorah Henar, Aouatif Jiah, Chantal Reijm and Deveny van Tiel for identifying, coding and labelling relevant observations (as part of a course on Language Variation and Language Contact taught by the first author in 2016–2017) and hence taking the first essential step in transforming the audio material into data. Additional thanks to Xamorah Henar for carrying out the CoG measurements. We are also grateful to the Centre for Language Studies (Radboud Universiteit) for a Small Research Grant that allowed Ms Henar's efforts to be funded. Etske Ooijevaar prepared and supervised the CoG measurements and developed the first version of the script for the Mixed Models regression analysis in R. She also designed the graph in Figure 1.

References

Bateman, Nicoleta. 2011. On the typology of palatalization. *Language and Linguistics Compass* 5(8). 588–602. https://www.researchgate.net/publication/220531585_On_the_Typology _of_Palatalization. (15 May, 2022.)

Bekker, Ian. 2007. Fronted /s/ in General White South African English. *Language Matters* 38. 46–74.

doi Bekker, Ian & Erez Levon. 2017. The embedded indexical value of /s/-fronting in Afrikaans and South African English. *Linguistics* 55. 1109–1139.

doi Bell, Alan. 1984. Language style as audience design. *Language in Society* 13(2). 145–204.

Bhat, D. N. Shankara. 1978. A General study of palatalization. In Joseph Greenberg, Charles Ferguson & Edith Moravcsik (eds.), *Universals of human languages*, vol. 2, 47–92. Stanford, CA: Stanford University Press.

Boersma, Paul & David Weenink. 2010. *Praat: Doing phonetics by computer.* https://www.fon.hum.uva.nl/praat/. (16 May, 2022.)

Brouwer, Dédé. 1989. *Gender variation in Dutch. A sociolinguistic study of Amsterdam speech.* Nijmegen: Radboud University Nijmegen dissertation.

Brugman, Hennie & Albert Russel. 2004. Annotating multi-media/multi-modal resources with ELAN. In Maria Teresa Lino et al.. (eds.), *Proceedings of the Fourth International Conference on Language Resources and Evaluation (LREC'04)*. https://aclanthology.org/L04-1285/. (16 May, 2022.)

doi Calder, Jeremy. 2019. The fierceness of fronted /s/: Linguistic rhematization through visual transformation. *Language in Society* 48. 31–64.

doi Carvalho, Ana Maria. 2004. I speak like the guys on TV: Palatalization and the urbanization of Uruguayan Portuguese. *Language Variation and Change* 16. 127–151.

Caubet, Dominique. 1993. *L'Arabe Marocain: Tome 1: Phonologie et morphosyntaxe* [Moroccan Arabic: Book 1: Phonology and morphosyntax]. Paris & Louvain: Peeters.

Comrie, Bernard. 1997. Turkish phonology. In Alan S. Kaye & Peter T. Daniel (eds.), *Phonologies of Asia and Africa*, vol. 2, 883–898. Winona Lake, IN: Eisenbrauns.

Corneau, Caroline. 1999. An EPG Study of Palatalization in French. In John Ohala (Ed.), *Proceedings of the XIVth International Congress of Phonetic Sciences, San Francisco 1–7 August 1999 (ICPhS 99)*, vol. 1, 61–64.

Dilthey, Wilhelm. 1883. *Einleitung in die Geisteswissenschaften. Versuch einer Grundlegung für das Studium der Gesellschaft und der Geschichte* [Introduction to the human sciences. An attempt to lay a foundation for the study of society and history], vol. 1. Leipzig: Duncker & Humblot.

doi Ditewig, Sanne, Laura Smorenburg, Hugo Quené & Willemijn Heeren. 2021. An acoustic-phonetic study of retraction of /s/ in Moroccan Dutch and endogenous Dutch. *Nederlandse Taalkunde* 26(3). 147–170.

doi Eckert, Penelope. 2019. The limits of meaning: Social indexicality, variation, and the cline of interiority. *Language* 95(4). 761–776.

doi Fought, Carmen. 2013. Ethnicity. In Jack Chambers & Natalie Schilling (eds.), *The handbook of language variation and change*, 2nd edn., 388–406. Malden, MA: Wiley-Blackwell.

González, Hebe Alicia. 2014. Procesos fonológicos como rasgos areales: El caso de la palatalización en las lenguas chaqueñas [Phonological processes as areal features: The case of palatalization in the Chaco languages]. *Liames* 14(1). 11–39.

Goossens, Jan. 1969. *Strukturelle Sprachgeographie. Eine Einführung in Methodik und Ergebnisse* [Structural linguistic geography. An introduction to methodology and results]. Heildelberg: Winter.

doi Gordon, Matthew, Paul Barthmaier & Kathy Sands. 2002. A cross-linguistic acoustic study of voiceless fricatives. *Journal of the International Phonetic Association* 32. 141–174.

Chapter 3. Social patterns in s-palatalisation in Moroccan and Turkish ethnolectal Dutch 77

doi Grondelaers, Stefan, Roeland van Hout & Paul van Gent. 2019. Re-evaluating the prestige of regional accents in Netherlandic Standard Dutch: The role of accent strength and speaker gender. *Journal of Language and Social Psychology* 38(2).

Harrel, Richard. 1962. *A short reference grammar of Moroccan Arabic*. Washington, DC: Georgetown University Press.

Hinskens, Frans. 2004. *Nieuwe regenboogkleuren. Jonge typen niet-standaardtaal en hun taalkundig belang* [New rainbow colours. New types of non-standard language and their linguistic relevance]. Inaugural address, Vrije Universiteit Amsterdam. Amsterdam: VU University Press. https://pure.knaw.nl/ws/portalfiles/portal/460748/rede.pdf.

doi Hinskens, Frans. 2011. Emerging Moroccan and Turkish varieties of Dutch: Ethnolects or ethnic styles? In Friederike Kern & Margret Selting (eds.), *Ethnic styles of speaking in European metropolitan areas*, 103–131. Amsterdam & Philadelphia, PA: John Benjamins.

Hinskens, Frans. 2019. Ethnolects: Where language contact, language acquisition and dialect variation meet. *7th International Conference on Modern Greek Dialects and Linguistic Theory (MGDLT7)*. 1–27.

Hinskens, Frans, Khalid Mourigh & Pieter Muysken. Forthcoming 2024. Urban contact dialects in the Netherlands. In Paul Kerswill & Heike Wiese (eds.), *Urban contact dialects and language change: Insights from the Global North and South*. London: Routledge.

doi Holmes-Elliot, Sophie & Erez Levon. 2017. The substance of style: Gender, social class and interactional stance in /s/-fronting in southeast England. *Linguistics* 55. 1045–1072.

Hout, Roeland van. 1989. *De structuur van taalvariatie: Een sociolinguïstisch onderzoek naar het stadsdialect van Nijmegen* [The structure of language variation. A sociolinguistic study on the urban dialect of Nijmegen]. Nijmegen: Radboud Universiteit Nijmegen dissertation.

Kossmann, Maarten. 2012. Berber. In Zygmunt Frajzyngier & Erin Shay (eds.), *The Afroasiatic languages*, 18 101. Cambridge etc.: Cambridge University Press.

Kossmann, Maarten & Harry Stroomer. 1997. Berber phonology. In Alan S. Kaye (ed.), *Phonologies of Asia and Africa (including the Caucasus)*, vol. 1, 461–475. Winona Lake, IN: Eisenbrauns.

doi Li, Fangfang. 2017. The development of gender-specific patterns in the production of voiceless sibilant fricatives in Mandarin Chinese. *Linguistics* 55. 1021–1044.

doi Maddieson, Ian. 1984. *Patterns of sounds*. Cambridge: Cambridge University Press.

doi Marzo, Stefania, Eline Zenner & Dorien Van de Mieroop. 2018. When sociolinguistics and prototype analysis meet: The social meaning of sibilant palatalization in a Flemish Urban Vernacular. In Eline Zenner, Ad Backus & Esme Winter-Froemel (eds.), *Cognitive contact linguistics placing usage, meaning and mind at the core of contact-induced variation and change*, 127–156. Berlin, Munich & Boston, MA: Mouton de Gruyter.

Meel, Linda van. 2016. The roots of ethnolects. A sociophonological study in Amsterdam and Nijmegen. Nijmegen: Radboud Universiteit Nijmegen dissertation. Digital version: http://www.lotpublications.nl/the-roots-of-ethnolects. (16 May, 2022.)

Monteiro, Renata Conceição Neves. 2009. A produção palato-alveolar de /S/ nas vozes do Amapá [The palato-alveolar production of /S/ in the voices of Amapá]. João Pessoa: Universidade Federal da Paraíba MA thesis.

doi Mourigh, Khalid. 2017. Stance-taking through sibilant palatalisation in Gouda Moroccan Dutch. *Nederlandse Taalkunde* 22(3). 421–446.

Muysken, Pieter. 2013. Ethnolects of Dutch. In Frans Hinskens & Johan Taeldeman (eds.), *Language and space: Dutch*, 739–761. Berlin & Boston, MA: De Gruyter Mouton.

Nespor, Marina & Irene Vogel. 1986. *Prosodic phonology*. Dordrecht: Foris.

Padgett, Jaye. 2003. The Emergence of Contrastive Palatalization in Russian. In: D. Eric Holt (ed.), *Optimality Theory and Language Change*. Dordrecht: Springer, 307 335.

Pharao, Nicolai & Marie Maegaard. 2017. On the influence of coronal sibilants and stops on the perception of social meanings in Copenhagen Danish. *Linguistics* 55. 1141–1167.

Pharao, Nicolai, Marie Maegaard, Janus Spindler-Møller & Tore Kristiansen. 2014. Indexical meanings of [s+] among Copenhagen youth: Social perception of a phonetic variant in different linguistic contexts. *Language in Society* 43. 1–31.

Podesva, Robert & Janneke van Hofwegen. 2016. /s/exuality in smalltown California: Gender normativity and the acoustic realization of /s/. In Erez Levon & Ronald Beline Mendes (eds.), *Language, sexuality, and power: Studies in intersectional sociolinguistics*, 168–188. Oxford: Oxford University Press.

Reidy, Patrick F. 2016. Spectral dynamics of sibilant fricatives are contrastive and language specific. *The Journal of the Acoustical Society of America* 140. 2518–2529.

Rietveld, Toni & Vincent van Heuven. 2013. *Algemene fonetiek* [General phonetics]. Bussum: Coutinho.

Rubach, Jerzy. 2011. Slavic Palatalization. In Marc van Oostendorp, Colin J. Ewen, Elizabeth Hume & Keren Rice (eds), *The Blackwell Companion to Phonology, Volume V. Phonology across Languages*. Oxford/Boston: Blackwell-Wiley, 2908 2935.

Rutter, Ben. 2014. The acquisition of newly emerging sociophonetic variation: /str-/ in American English. *Journal of Child Language* 41. 1166–1178.

Sokhey, Navdeep Kaur. 2015. The women (and men) who speak Funnyi: Negotiating social meanings through palatalization of the Cairene nasal. Austin: University of Texas at Austin MA thesis.

Stuart-Smith, Jane. 2007. Empirical evidence for gendered speech production: /s/ in Glaswegian. In Jennifer Cole & José Ignacio Hualde (Eds.), *Laboratory phonology* 9, 65–86. New York, NY: Mouton de Gruyter.

Stuart-Smith, Jane. 2020. Changing perspectives on /s/ and gender over time in Glasgow. *Linguistics Vanguard* 6(s1).

Villena-Ponsoda, Juan Andrés. 1987. Forma, sustancia y redundancia contextual en el vocalismo andaluz [Contextual form, substance and redundancy in Andalusian vowels]. In Juan Andrés Villena-Ponsoda, *Forma, sustancia y redundancia contextual: El caso del vocalismo del español andaluz*, 87–94. Malaga: Universidad de Málaga.

Villena-Ponsoda, Juan Andrés. 2001. *La continuidad del cambio lingüístico* [The continuity of linguistic change]. Granada: Universidad de Granada.

CHAPTER 4

Coronalisation in the German multi-ethnolect
Evidence for regional differentiation?

Peter Auer & Daniel Duran
Albert-Ludwigs-Universität Freiburg, Germany | Leibniz-Zentrum
Allgemeine Sprachwissenschaft, Germany

We investigate coronalisation, i.e. the fronting of the palatal fricative /ç/, in the multi-ethnolect spoken by young people in the city of Stuttgart. In contrast to a previous study on the Berlin multi-ethnolect, which claims a merger of /ç/ with /ʃ/, we only find a weak and unstable tendency among our speakers to reduce the difference between the two dorsal fricatives /ç/ and /ʃ/, as compared to a group of similar speakers living in a relatively monoethnic neighbourhood. Depending on the phonetic measurements used, this tendency mostly remains below the threshold of significance. We discuss two interpretations of these findings, one linked to the ambient German dialects, the other postulating the beginning of regional differentiation between the German multi-ethnolects.

Keywords: (German) multi-ethnolects, coronalisation, dorsal assimilation in German, regional differentiation in multi-ethnolects

1. Introduction

The coronalisation of the palatal fricative /ç/, i.e. its fronting toward the coronal variant /ɕ/ or even merging with post-alveolar /ʃ/, is one of the phonological features most stereotypically associated with the German multi-ethnolect.[1] The feature is used pervasively in representations of young speakers of migrant background (Auer 2013). Phonetic studies on multi-ethnolectal German in Berlin (Jannedy & Weirich 2017) have shown that coronalisation is also a phonetic reality and that speakers of migrant (mainly Turkish) background indeed (tend

---

1. We are aware of the problems associated with this term but use it for lack of a satisfactory alternative.

https://doi.org/10.1075/silv.31.04aue
© 2024 John Benjamins Publishing Company

to) merge the two dorsal fricatives. In this chapter, we present phonetic evidence that this feature of the Berlin multi-ethnolect is not used in the same way across Germany. Based on an acoustic study of speakers in Stuttgart (in the southwest of Germany), we show that a (quasi-)merger cannot be found there, which raises the question of a possible regional differentiation of the multi-ethnolect.

2. Phonological and social-dialectological background

German is well known for being one of the rare languages of the world the sound structure of which includes a palatal fricative. The sound is not phonemic but takes part in a text-book example of allophonic (complementary) distribution known as dorsal assimilation: [ç] only occurs after front vowels (such as in [ɪç] *ich* 'me' or [bɛçɐ] *Becher* 'cup'). After back vowels, the velar fricative [x] is required (cf. [nɔx] *noch* 'still', [kuːxn] *Kuchen* 'cake'). As the front variant of the dorsal fricative also occurs morpheme-initially (as in [çemiː] *Chemie* 'chemistry' or [vɛltçən] *Wäld+chen* 'wood+DIM') and after sonorants in standard German (cf. [zɔlç] *solch* 'such', [mançə] *manche* 'some'), it is often assumed that the underlying form is /ç/, although this analysis is disputed (cf. Robinson 2001 for phonological details). Historically, /x/ is the older form, having developed a fronted variant after front vowels through assimilation.

The palatal fricative [ç] (or /ç/ if it is regarded as a phonological unit) is phonetically unstable in the non-standard varieties of continental West Germanic. In a large area between Low and Upper German, stretching from Aachen in the west to Leipzig in the east, it tends to merge with the post-alveolar std.G. fricative /ʃ/ with the phonetic value [ɕ] (see Dogil 1993 on Saarland dialects). Conrad (2021) presents a phonetic study on coronalisation in Luxembourgish.

As Herrgen (1986) shows, coronalisation is an innovation of the nineteenth century; it emerged in urban centres and has still not spread to all the dialects of the countryside in between. Coronalisation is therefore typical of the vernaculars of large industrial cities in Germany, such as Mannheim, Frankfurt, Cologne or Leipzig. Note that Berlin is not part of this coronalisation zone. In Berlin, /ç/ > /ʃ/ is observed only in certain words (most notably in the high frequency word [nyʃt] *nicht(s)* 'not/nothing') and in the context after vocalised /R/, as in [kʁɐʃə] *Kirche* 'church'.

Coronalisation does not affect the front/back allophony of the dorsal fricatives, of course; however, instead of [ç] and [x], it groups together [ɕ] ~ [ʃ] and [x] as allophones. Hall (2014) describes coronalisation as a markedness reduction, in which the features [dorsal] in /ç/ and [labial] in /ʃ/ are deleted and only the common feature [coronal] is preserved.

Chapter 4. Coronalisation in the German multi-ethnolect

This analysis of coronalisation as simplification is supported by the fact that the replacement of [ç] by [ʃ] or [ɕ] also occurs in L2 learners of German whose L1 does not have the palatal fricative, such as English or Polish (the phonology of which includes /ɕ/). The same applies to the brought-along languages of almost all immigrants. However, whether coronalisation was also a feature of so-called "guestworkers' German" (the pidgin-like fossilised learner variety of first-generation work migrants in the 1960s and 1970s) is largely unknown, since no systematic sound studies were conducted. Phonetic transcripts of the German of Spanish and Italian workers recorded at the time in Heidelberg suggest that it was not the rule (cf. Heidelberger Forschungsprojekt "Pidgindeutsch" 1975: 135–146), despite Heidelberg being part of the dialectal coronalisation zone.[2] Today, the Italians and Spanish no longer represent the majority among multi-ethnolect speakers. For L1 speakers of the most important immigrant language in Germany, i.e. Turkish, no data from first-generation *Gastarbeiter* are available. It therefore remains open to speculation whether present-day multi-ethnolectal speakers, whose (grand)parents came to Germany as "guestworkers", were exposed to and acquainted with coronalisation in their families.

3. Previous work on multi-ethnolectal coronalisation

The German multi-ethnolect is part of the repertoire of many (young) speakers whose families came to Germany as migrant workers or refugees and who were born and raised in Germany. For these speakers, German is a native language in addition to one or more other family languages. It is not a learner variety (see, with particular reference to grammar, Wiese 2009; Freywald et al. 2011; Auer 2013; and Siegel 2020, among others). The multi-ethnolect initially developed in this group of speakers (presumably first among Turks); however, some of its features have spread to young Germans who do not share this sociolinguistic background and have a "monolingual" German biography.

The earliest available recordings of this multi-ethnolectal young speakers' variety of German were collected in an ethnographic study on a group of (mainly) Turkish/German bilingual adolescents in a Frankfurt youth gang (Tertilt 1998). Their language clearly shows frequent coronalisation. It is not easy to decide, though, whether this is an innovation of the emerging multi-ethnolect or rather copied from the Frankfurt urban vernacular, which is part of the dialectal coronalisation zone mentioned above. The same applies to Keim's study conducted in

---

2. Of the six speakers for whom detailed phonetic transcriptions are available, only two use /ʃ/ instead of /ç/, one varies between the two, and three consistently use the palatal fricative.

Mannheim at the turn of the century among adolescent girls and young adults, also with a Turkish family background (Keim 2002, 2007). On the other hand, a study undertaken in Hamburg (located outside the dialectal coronalisation zone) in the late 1990s (Dirim & Auer 2004), although having a different focus, found no evidence of coronalisation in multi-ethnolectal German in the city at the time. Similarly, in a study of 15 participants in Münster (Westphalia, also outside the coronalisation zone), Bücker (2007) observed frequent coronalisation in only two of her participants, while 12 speakers did not use the feature at all.

The decisive evidence for coronalisation as a feature of the German multi-ethnolect independent from dialectal coronalisation comes from Berlin, where numerous (socio)phonetic and perceptual studies have been undertaken on the topic. Jannedy and Weirich (2014), Jannedy et al. (2015), and Jannedy and Weirich (2017) performed acoustic analyses on the dorsal fricatives in three minimal pairs (such as *fischte*, std.G. [fɪʃtə] 'fished, 3SG' vs. *Fichte*, std.G. [fɪçtə] 'spruce') read by three groups of speakers, one from Kiel and two from Berlin. The Berlin groups consisted of 86 university students (not further characterised) and 32 speakers from the neighbourhood of Kreuzberg, where many people with migration background live and which is often associated with multi-ethnolectal German (called "hood German" by these authors). Spectral data in the bandwidth from 500 to 12,000 Hz were analysed using a variety of measurement techniques (Centre of Gravity, standard deviation, skewness, kurtosis, discrete cosine transformation (DCT)). In the results produced by the DCT the authors found significantly smaller differences between the two dorsal fricatives in the Berlin-Kreuzberg group, both in comparison to the other Berlin group and the Kiel group. There was also a significant difference between the three minimal pairs, i.e. a lexical effect. Jannedy and Weirich (2017) performed a perception test with a subset of the data, in which speakers from northern Germany had to identify the words they heard. The word *Fichte* as produced by speakers from Berlin-Kreuzberg was categorised correctly significantly less often than the productions by the other Berlin and the Kiel speakers. The authors assume that the merger of /ʃ/ and /ç/ in the stimuli made it more difficult for these listeners to keep *Fichte* 'spruce' and *fischte* 'fished' apart.

Weirich et al. (2020) show that coronalisation of the dorsal fricative evokes social stereotypes about people with migration background (i.e. people from Kreuzberg, in their study), at least in older listeners who themselves do not have such a background. These respondents matched coronalised stimuli with negative concept categories more often when the stimuli were primed as "hood German" than when they were primed as "German of French learners". Jannedy and Weirich (2014) primed stimuli with information about the neighbourhood of the speaker, using resynthesised fricatives on a continuum from [ʃ] to [ç] in a forced-

Chapter 4. Coronalisation in the German multi-ethnolect

choice identification task. Older, but not younger speakers heard significantly more [ʃ] when the stimulus was primed as coming from a Kreuzberg speaker. This age difference suggests that coronalisation is on the verge of losing its social meaning; the merger is already on the way to becoming the unmarked Berlin vernacular for younger people.

While Jannedy and Weirich's data are experimental, Wiese and Freywald (2019) investigated the occurrence of coronalised fricatives in the first-person singular pronoun *ich* in a corpus of spontaneous speech from young Berlin-Kreuzberg speakers, based on auditory analysis. The group was compared to a control group of young speakers from a less multi-ethnic neighbourhood. The coronalised form occurred more than 25 times as often in the Kreuzberg group than in the control group, and it accounted for more than a third of the fricatives in words with Std.G. [ç] in the Kreuzberg group.

In sum, there is strong evidence that coronalisation is indeed a prominent feature of the German multi-ethnolect as spoken in Berlin, and that multi-ethnolectal coronalisation is not restricted to the dialectal coronalisation zone. There is, however, much less (and no acoustic) research on coronalisation among multi-ethnolectal speakers outside Berlin and outside the coronalisation zone. This research on the city of Stuttgart intends to fill this gap.

While the study presented in the following sections uses the acoustic methods employed by Jannedy and Weirich in order to ensure comparability, i.e. it is based on data collected in rather formal settings, the first author also performed a preliminary auditory study on the basis of a corpus of spontaneous speech gathered in informal settings (see Auer 2013 and 2017 for details), restricted to ten male speakers and to the pronoun *ich*. They were recorded between 2009 and 2012 at youth centres and schools, and had lived in Germany from early childhood. Almost all speakers were attending either *Hauptschule* or *Werkrealschule* (the lowest hierarchical level in the German school system); a few had started vocational training. They all lived in high-immigration neighbourhoods and were 14–18 years old at the time. All were fluent speakers of German but showed distinct grammatical features of the multi-ethnolect (cf. Siegel 2020; Auer & Siegel 2021). Coronalisation was found to a limited degree only, with an average realisation of std.G. /ç/ as /ʃ/ of 5.9%, and as [ɕ] of 11.3%. (This is about half the coronalisation rate reported by Wiese and Freywald.) However, since coronalisation is a gradient phenomenon and auditory transcription is not unproblematic, an acoustic study is necessary.

4. Data

The city of Stuttgart and the metropolitan area surrounding it is among the German regions with the highest rates of foreigners (residents without German citizenship) and persons with a migration background (residents with German, often dual citizenship, but at least one parent who immigrated). In 2018, when the data were collected, the percentage of these two groups together accounted for 44.5% of the city's 611,665 inhabitants (25.4% and 19.2%, respectively),[3] which was about twice as much as in Germany as a whole at the time.[4] This percentage had risen by roughly 7% from 37.2% in the year 2000. As early as 2011, 44% of all children and adolescents under the age of 18 were being raised in migrant families (cf. Haußmann 2012).[5] The largest groups until 2015 were of Turkish or ex-Yugoslavian/Albanian background; since then, Syrian and other refugees have also become important groups, with sub-Saharan African immigration following most recently.

The speech data for the core group in this study were collected in 2018 from 32 students attending school in high-immigration, multi-ethnic neighbourhoods of the city. As a control group, 12 students at a *Realschule* with a similar social background to the core group, but from one of the relatively monoethnic and monolingual suburbs of the larger Stuttgart area, were recruited. Informed consent to participate in the study was obtained from the subjects as well as the school principals prior to data collection. The speakers of the core group were selected on the basis of a short screening test, in which peers from another school were asked whether the voices played to them came from a speaker brought up in a multilingual family. As those with the highest scores on this test were selected, the core group potentially overestimates the prevalence of coronalisation (provided it is indeed a relevant marker of the multi-ethnolect).

Speech data were recorded during school time in quiet rooms under varying acoustic conditions. In each session, pairs of friends from the core or control group, respectively, were recorded during (a) a reading task, (b) a Diapix task with two custom-made sets of pictures, and (b) an unstructured interview. For this analysis, (b) and (c) were combined and will be referred to as "spontaneous

---

3. Source: Statistisches Amt, Landeshauptstadt Stuttgart. https://statistik.stuttgart.de/statistiken/tabellen/7392/jb7392.php. (1 June, 2022.)

4. In 2017, the respective percentages were 11.5% and 12% (official statistics by the Statistisches Bundesamt), totaling 19.3 million people.

5. The statistics do not include mixed families, i.e. those in which one parent has no migration background.

Chapter 4. Coronalisation in the German multi-ethnolect

speech" from here on. The reading task included three minimal pairs in various non-adjacent, unrelated sentences.

All recordings (46 hours in total) were transcribed orthographically using ELAN (Brugman & Russel 2004) by linguistically trained native speakers of German (often by the researchers themselves). A first segmentation on word and phone level was then automatically created through forced alignment, using the MAUS system via its online interface WebMAUS Basic and its "German (DE)" language model[6] (Kisler et al. 2017). The target fricative segments /ʃ/, /ç/ and /x/[7] in word-final and word-medial position were identified, manually corrected and labelled phonemically according to the expected standard German realisation. The realisation of word-final /g/ after /ɪ/ varies in standard German between stop realisation /k/ and fricative realisation /ç/. The sound was categorised accordingly. Occasional occurrences of Swabian dialectal palatalisation of /s/ before stops were labelled /ʃ/. Table 1 provides a summary of the data set.

Table 1. Overview of the number of speakers and tokens by speaker group, gender (F = female, M = male) and speaking style (read speech vs. spontaneous speech)

Group		Speakers	/ʃ/		/ç/		/x/	
			read	spont.	read	spont.	read	spont.
core	F	14	232	282	481	656	296	499
	M	18	322	538	576	798	347	516
control	F	8	137	200	264	343	171	232
	M	4	62	140	116	183	73	135

5. Methods

Fricatives are acoustically characterised by continuous noise, with different energy distributions in the spectrum for different types. Various acoustic measures have been proposed to distinguish different fricative categories (and other obstruents) in automated phonetic-linguistic analysis and speech technology applications (cf. Shadle & Mair 1996). Phonetic analysis is most often conducted on VCV tokens

---

6. https://clarin.phonetik.uni-muenchen.de/BASWebServices/interface/WebMAUSBasic. (1 June, 2022.)

7. Note that we use slashes rather than square brackets in our notation of the allophone /ç/ in order to refer to the canonical form. /x/ was included in order to check the validity of our measurements.

or even on sustained fricatives produced in isolation (e.g. by Hoole et al. 1993; Maniwa et al. 2009).

It has been shown repeatedly that spectral properties provide reliable acoustic information to characterise and distinguish between different places of articulation (cf. Flipsen et al. 1999; Jongman et al. 2000), although some older studies (such as Forrest et al. 1988) had cast doubt on this method (see Shadle & Mair 1996). The following acoustic properties of fricatives have been used for the analysis of coronalisation in previous studies: (a) Centre of Gravity (COG, sometimes also referred to as the centroid or spectral mean), (b) standard deviation (SD), (c) skewness, and (d) kurtosis.

The spectral Centre of Gravity is a measure of the average frequency of a spectrum, where most of the energy is concentrated. This measure is probably the most often employed spectral moment in phonetic analysis. Hoole et al. (1993) and Zharkova (2016) found a higher COG for [s] than for [ʃ], while Gordon et al. (2002) found a higher COG for /ʃ/ than for /x/, and a higher COG for /ç/ than for more posterior fricatives in some of the languages analysed.

Standard deviation is a measure of the extent to which the energy in a spectrum deviates from the Centre of Gravity. Skewness is a measure of the asymmetry of the frequency distribution of a spectrum around the mean, with a skewness of zero corresponding to a symmetrical spectrum. Kurtosis is a measure of the spectrum's peakedness. Taken together, these spectral moments allow for an objective characterisation of the shape of a spectrum.

We computed all spectral moments using a custom-made Praat script. First, a 40 ms Hamming window was set around the midpoint of each target segment. A pre-emphasis filter of $F = 100$ Hz was then applied to that window, and a spectrum was computed using the Fourier transform. Finally, a bandpass filter was applied to the spectrum from 500 to 12,000 Hz with a smoothing of 100 Hz, before the spectral moments were extracted with the central moment power set to $p = 2.0$. We also applied a non-linear transformation to the recorded speech signal from Hertz to Bark (as did, e.g. Hoole et al. 1993 and Jannedy & Weirich 2017). Forrest et al. (1988), for example, found that sibilants are better discriminated on the Bark scale than on the linear scale.

In addition to the frequently applied spectral moments, we used an additional, low-dimensional representation of the overall shape of the segment spectra: discrete cosine transformation (DCT) coefficient modelling (cf. Zahorian & Jagharghi 1993; Watson & Harrington 1999; Harrington 2010). This transformation decomposes the overall shape of the spectrum into a set of coefficients that correspond to the amplitudes of half-cycle cosine waves (similar in principle to a discrete Fourier transform). The first coefficients represent with increasing resolution the global shape properties of the spectrum, such as its mean, slope, curvature, etc. Examples of the two representations are shown in Figure 1.

Chapter 4. Coronalisation in the German multi-ethnolect 87

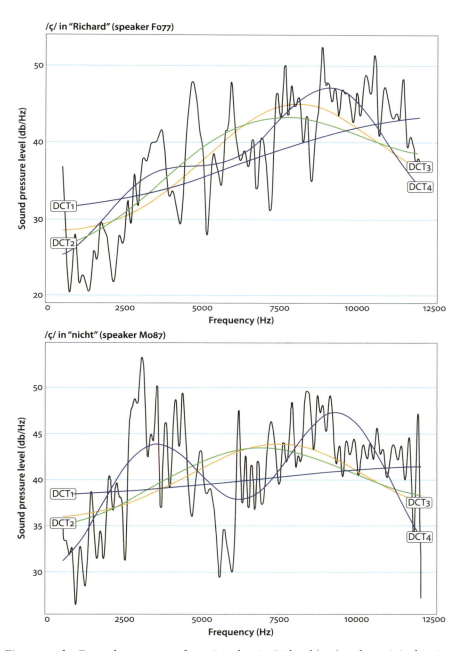

Figures 1a, b. Exemplary spectra of one /ç/ token in *Richard* (top) and one /ç/ token in *nicht* (bottom) (black line) as read by two control group speakers. The smoothed trajectories of the DCT are shown by the coloured lines, representing coefficients 1–4.

Our application of DCT coefficient modelling is similar to the method employed by Jannedy et al. (2015) and Jannedy and Weirich (2017). We computed the DCT coefficients in R, using the DCT-function provided by the emuR package (Winkelmann et al. 2021). Statistical significance and p-values for pairwise comparisons were calculated by using the ggpubr R package (Kassambara 2020).

6. Results

We first present the averaged spectra of /ç/ and /ʃ/ by gender and group (core vs. control) for read and spontaneous speech for visual comparison (Figure 2). The values for /x/ are included in order to demonstrate the validity of the methods and procedures. /x/ is always very clearly distinct from the two other sounds.

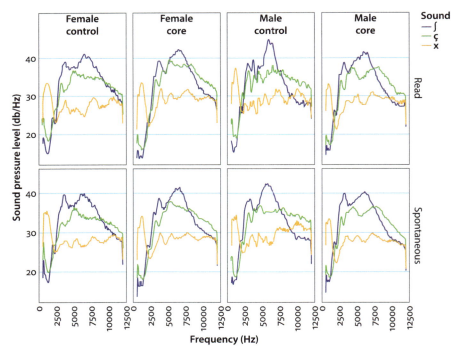

Figure 2. Averaged spectra of /ç/, /ʃ/ and /x/ by speaker gender and group for read and spontaneous speech.

Across all groups and conditions, /ʃ/ shows more energy than /ç/ in the spectral range between approx. 2500 and 7500 Hz, whereas /ç/ shows more energy than /ʃ/ above approx. 8000 Hz. The spectral energy of /ʃ/ has two peaks in the area of approx. 3000 Hz and 6000 Hz, while the peaks for /ç/ are in the range of approx. 5000 Hz; occasionally, there is an additional peak around 7500 Hz, but the energy curve tends towards a continuous decline after the 5000 Hz peak. Particularly, the energy distribution for /ʃ/ is remarkably similar in the core and in the control group. The energy distributions for /ç/ are always distinct from those for /ʃ/ but show more variation. Most notably, the male core group speakers show a second peak for this sound across conditions in the higher energy range, which is absent in the male control group speakers. However, there is no evidence for a merger between the two sounds in the core group as compared to the control group.

In order to test for potential differences between groups and conditions, we compared the Euclidean distances between the spectral moments.

The four spectral moments (Figure 3) and five DCT coefficients (Figure 4) can be interpreted as dimensions of a vector within an abstract n-dimensional feature space. The Euclidean distance (ED) between two points within such a spectral feature space is interpreted as a measure of the dissimilarity between the two corresponding data points (e.g., the average spectra of two different speech sounds). We performed the following statistical tests based on both the Hertz and the Bark values.

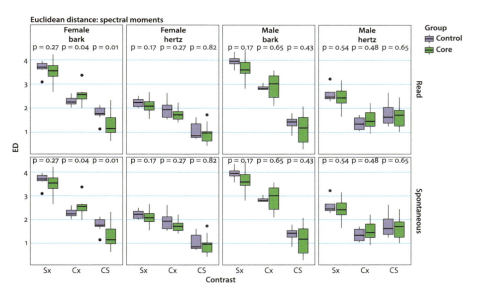

Figure 3. Euclidean distances between the z-scaled spectral moments Centre of Gravity, standard deviation, skewness and kurtosis, in the Hertz and Bark-scaled data. "CS" is the distance between /ç/ and /ʃ/, "Cx" is the distance between /ç/ and /x/, and "Sx" is the distance between /ʃ/ and /x/. Significance levels are shown above each pair of comparison.

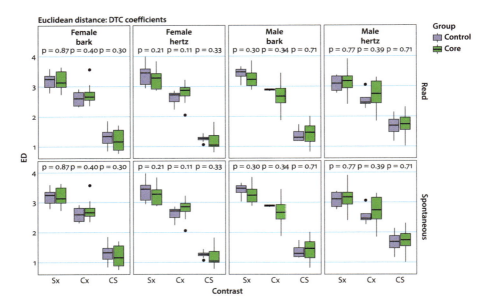

Figure 4. Euclidean distances between the z-scaled DCT coefficients 0–4. "CS" is the distance between /ç/ and /ʃ/, "Cx" is the distance between /ç/ and /x/, and "Sx" is the distance between /ʃ/ and /x/. Significance levels are shown above each pair of comparison.

Since the values of the spectral moments COG, SD, skewness and kurtosis have different orders of magnitude, we computed z-scores for these values. This guarantees that all four spectral moments contribute equally to the comparison. We also computed z-scores for the DCT coefficients. Since the zeroth DCT coefficient encodes the mean of the signal, it is an order of magnitude larger than the higher-order coefficients. If we had computed the distances on the non-normalised coefficient vector, they would have been dominated by the zeroth DCT coefficient.

ED was computed separately for each speaker and speaking style for the contrasts /ç/ ~ /ʃ/, /ç/ ~ /x/ and /ʃ/ ~ /x/, based on the distances between the average realisations of the fricative types in connected speech within one speaking style. As expected, the distances between /ʃ/ and /x/ are always larger than between /ç/ and /ʃ/, and /x/ and /ç/, respectively.

In general, the Euclidean distances (EDs) in the Bark-scaled data show larger differences between the three contrast types than the corresponding consonant contrasts in the Hertz scaled data. In Hertz, none of the contrasts between the core and the control group reaches significance.

In the Bark-scaled data, the female core group speakers have significantly smaller EDs between /ç/ and /ʃ/ than the female control group speakers. Correspondingly, they have significantly larger EDs between /ç/ and /x/. This may be indicative of a coronalisation of /ç/, i.e. a shift of /ç/ towards /ʃ/, within the feature space over spectral moments. The male speakers show the same trend, with a larger median ED between /ç/ and /x/ and a smaller median ED between /ç/ and /ʃ/ in the core group as compared to the control group. However, there is much more variability in the male speakers' productions, and thus, these differences are not significant.

Figure 4 shows the Euclidean distances between the z-scaled DCT coefficients 0–4. Once more, the distances between /ç/ and /ʃ/ are smaller than the distances between the other two contrasts for all speaker groups, both on the Hertz and the Bark scale. The female core group speakers produce more similar /ç/ and /ʃ/ sounds (i.e. smaller distances) than the control group on both scales. The high p-values, however, show that these differences are not significant. In contrast to Figure 3, the values for the male speakers do not differ between the core and control group (their EDs between /ç/ and /ʃ/ are sometimes even smaller in the control than in the core group).

In order to analyse possible interactions between the predictors "group", "gender" and "style", we performed an analysis of variance (ANOVA) for the Euclidean distances over the five DCT coefficients for the /ç/ ~/ʃ/ contrast. For the Hertz-scaled data, the results (see Table 2) show a significant effect of gender. Post-hoc pairwise t-tests with Bonferroni correction show significant differences between female control group speakers and male core group speakers as well as between male and female core group speakers. For the the Bark-scaled data, the results show no significant effect of any of the three factors (including their interactions). We applied the ANOVA function from the car library in R to compute "type 3" analysis of variance tables, i.e. testing each factor in the model after all others (Fox & Weisberg 2019). Post-hoc pairwise t-tests with Bonferroni correction show the same pattern as for the data in Hertz.

Table 2. Type 3 ANOVA for Euclidean distances in the data in Hertz according to speaker group, gender and speaking style (interactions not shown, as none of them is significant).

	Sum Sq	Df	F	Pr(>F)	
(Intercept)	12.6991	1	123.5529	<0.001	***
group	0.0389	1	0.3785	0.54015	
gender	0.4594	1	4.4697	0.03762	*
style	0.0000	1	0.0000	1.00000	

In sum, there is only very limited evidence of coronalisation, or, more precisely, of a tendency to make the realisation of /ʃ/ and /ç/ converge. Only in one type of measurement (using spectral moments, in Bark) and only in one gender group (female) is the distance between the two sounds /ç/ and /ʃ/ significantly smaller in the core group of speakers than in the control group.

It should be noted at this point that Jannedy and Weirich (2017) failed to obtain significant differences when using Euclidean distances over spectral moments, and only did when using DCT coefficients. These measurements produced the more valid results in their case, and they were supported by the perceptual tests. In our study, the DCT coefficients did not produce significant results.

The Berlin study was based on minimal pairs in a reading experiment, whereas the results reported here compare measurements across all tokens. In order to exclude the possibility that this methodological difference was responsible for the diverging results, we also calculated differences over minimal pairs. Our reading list included the following minimal pairs:

> *fischte* 'fished' vs. *Fichte* 'spruce'
> *Kirche* 'church' vs. *Kirsche* 'cherry'
> *Wicht* 'gnome' vs. *wischt* 'wipes'

It also included the quasi-minimal pairs *Löcher* 'holes' vs *(Feuer-)Löscher* '(fire) extinguisher' and *Teich* 'pond' vs. *Tisch* 'table'.

Figure 5 shows the results for the data on minimal pairs in Hertz and Bark based on the z-scores derived from the DCT coefficients, i.e. in an attempt to replicate the findings of Jannedy and Weirich.

The pairwise comparisons in Figure 5 show no significant differences between the core and the control group (see the p-value annotations in the figure). It should be noted that these pairwise comparisons are based on a small subset of the data: there are only 85 tokens for *Fichte* vs. *fischte*, 104 for *Kirche* vs. *Kirsche*, 263 for *Löcher* vs. *(Feuer-)Löscher*, 142 for *Teich* vs. *Tisch* and 99 for *Wicht* vs. *wischt*. For female speakers, the overall median distance for all pairs is smaller for the core group than for the control group on the Hertz scale. On the Bark scale, there is no consistent pattern for female speakers. Similarly, no pattern can be observed for the male speakers, neither in the Bark-scaled nor in the Hertz scaled data. Only *Löcher* vs. *(Feuer-)Löscher* (both in Bark and Hertz) and *Wicht* vs. *wischt* (only in Hertz) show a smaller difference between the /ʃ/ and /ç/ sounds in the core male group speakers.

Figure 6 shows the results for the data in Hertz and Bark based on the z-scores derived from the spectral moments. Again, there is no significant difference for any pairwise comparison, and, in contrast to the measurements based on the DCT coefficients, there is also no consistent trend regarding a possible difference between female and male speakers.

Chapter 4. Coronalisation in the German multi-ethnolect   93

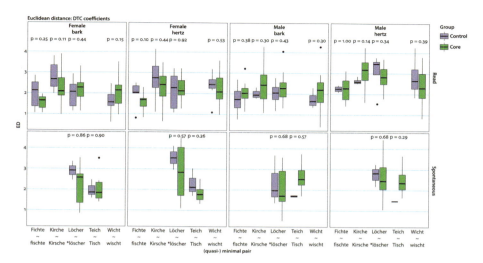

Figure 5. Boxplots of the distribution of Euclidean distances between z-scaled DCT coefficients for (quasi-)minimal pairs with a /ç/ ~ /ʃ/ contrast. Significance levels are shown above each pair of comparison.

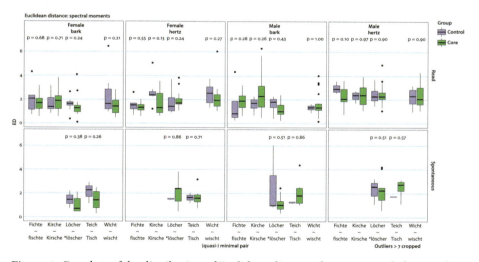

Figure 6. Boxplots of the distribution of Euclidean distances between z-scaled spectral moments between the minimal pairs with a /ç/ ~ /ʃ/ contrast. Outliers with values > 7 are not shown. Significance levels are shown above each pair of comparison.

7. Discussion

In summary of the findings, we can conclude that this study shows at best a weak tendency among speakers living in a multi-ethnic neighbourhood of Stuttgart to reduce the difference between the two dorsal fricatives /ç/ and /ʃ/ when compared to a group of speakers of similar age and educational background living in a relatively monoethnic neighbourhood. Depending on the phonetic measurements used, this tendency mostly remains below the threshold of significance. Only measurements using spectral moments (COG, SD, skewness and kurtosis) show a significant difference, and only in the female speakers. Measurements using DCT coefficients do not produce statistically significant results. The analysis of minimal pairs confirms a slight tendency towards coronalisation of /ç/ in certain lexical items, especially in female speakers, when using spectral moments, but it also shows a high degree of variability in the data, with no clear and no statistically significant difference observed between the speaker groups.

It should be remembered here that the data were collected among speakers who were judged by their peers to 'sound like coming from a multilingual family'. This pre-selection over-estimates the prevalence of coronalisation among speakers with a migratory background. On the other hand, data collection in a formal, school-related context may have induced the speakers to use less (multi-)ethnolectal phonetics, which might have led to an underestimation of this feature's prevalence in everyday talk.

Our results diverge from the findings of Jannedy and Weirich (2017) for Berlin, despite similar methods having been used. Jannedy and Weirich claim a (quasi-) merger between the two sounds, regardless of gender. At the same time, the results of this study confirm the auditory analysis presented in Auer (2013), based on informal data from Stuttgart speakers from a similar background as the core group in the present study. In both cases, some coronalisation was found, but the effect is small. Most speakers use the coronalised fricative only occasionally and/or with a weak amount of fronting. It must be concluded that even though the subjects of this study were perceived as multi-ethnolect speakers (as indicated by the peer-ratings in the screening test), this perception was not grounded in their phonetic realisations of /ç/.

There are at least two possible interpretations for the results. One is that multi-ethnolectal coronalisation is restricted to the dialectal coronalisation zone of the German language space, to which the city of Stuttgart does not belong. Coronalisation as a feature of the multi-ethnolect would then only have emerged where it also existed in the ambient spoken language of the autochthonous population, from which it was copied or by which it was strengthened. This inter-

Chapter 4. Coronalisation in the German multi-ethnolect   95

pretation is supported to a certain extent by the fact that multi-ethnolectal coronalisation is reported to occur frequently in the cities of Mannheim and Frankfurt (part of the coronalisation zone), but much less in places such as Hamburg or Münster, where it is not part of the autochthonous local language use.

However, since dialectal features are otherwise rare or absent in German multi-ethnolects (Auer 2020), such an interpretation in terms of contact is rather unlikely. It is unclear why speakers with an immigration background should accommodate the local speech only with regard to this particular feature. In addition, since multi-ethnolectal coronalisation is strong in some places outside the dialectal coronalisation zone such as Berlin, it would have to be assumed that it has spread beyond the dialectal coronalisation zone.

Jannedy and Weirich (2017:395) suggest that the dialectal coronalisation zone is expanding independently of the multi-ethnolect. They observe that the merger of the dorsal fricatives also occurs in "some older east German speakers" (2017:395). According to this interpretation, two very different social groups would have contributed independently to the merger of the dorsal fricatives in Berlin: older East Berlin speakers without, and younger speakers with a migration background. There is, however, no independent evidence for such a spread of the dialectal coronalisation zone beyond the Central German dialects to places such as Berlin.

A second, and more likely interpretation of the results is that the German multi-ethnolects have begun to diversify geographically, i.e. that they themselves are undergoing 'dialectalisation'. Such a regional differentiation in the multi-ethnolect would seem to be grounded in a different attitudinal embedding of the feature in, for example, Berlin and Stuttgart.

The coronalisation of /ç/, leading, in the extreme case, to a merger with /ʃ/, is one of the most stereotypical features of multi-ethnolectal speech in Germany. It is strongly associated with the stereotype of immigrant street culture. In Stuttgart, there is evidence that young people are well aware of this stereotype and avoid the feature precisely because of the way in which it indexes a certain social 'persona' (Auer 2017). When asked about their language during the interviews, the young people in this study insisted on a difference between what they often called "street language" and what they called "language of respect", the latter being appropriate when speaking with adults, and particularly so in the school context. The data for the acoustic analysis performed within the framework of this study were collected in a formal situation in the school context. Under the regime of the prevalent stereotypical interpretation of coronalisation as an index to street culture, non-integration, lack of social aspiration, and educational failure, it stands to reason that identification with this stereotype is avoided in such a situation.

In Berlin, on the contrary, coronalisation seems to have lost this sociolinguistic meaning and is said to have become part of a socially unmarked youth vernacular (Jannedy et al. 2019). This de-ethnicisation may be responsible for the lacking situational sensitivity of the feature: even though data collection required a formal context in Berlin as well, there was no reason for the speakers to avoid it even in this situation. Being the unmarked way of speaking in the city and thus no longer part of "street language", it could be used even in a school context, which, in Stuttgart, required a "language of respect". Hence, diverging patterns of evaluation may be responsible for the different usage patterns observed in Berlin and Stuttgart.

In one of the analyses performed for this study, the female core group speakers were found to outperform the female speakers in the control group with regard to coronalisation, while there was no such difference observed in the male speakers. Jannedy and colleagues found no gender differences in Berlin. Although gender differences as such are compatible with the view that coronalisation is a sociolinguistic "marker" or "stereotype" in Stuttgart (but not in Berlin), this gender pattern is unusual. It is normally assumed that female speakers show a stronger orientation towards the prestigious variant (the non-coronalised standard pronunciation, in our case). Thus, the expectation would be for the male, and not the female, core group speakers to use more or even strongly coronalised fricatives. More importantly, the pattern observed for gender also contradicts the pattern found in the same data set for other multi-ethnolectal features. In Duran and Auer (forthcoming), we show that the vowel space of the same group of speakers (core group) is reduced when compared with that of the control group. This centralisation of the vowel space is significantly stronger in the male than in the female speakers. Male speakers also show more obstruent voicing (Duran & Auer, submitted, b) and use more grammatical features of the multi-ethnolect. These features make the multi-ethnolectal way of speaking diverge from autochthonous Stuttgart speech. The same gender pattern would therefore be expected in the case of coronalisation. It seems, then, that there are indeed gender differences in our data, but that in the case of coronalisation, they do not converge with those found in other features. However, since the finding that only female speakers use this feature significantly more often than the female speakers in the control group was not robust and only surfaced in one type of measurement, its social relevance should not be overrated.

References

Auer, Peter. 2013. Ethnische Marker im Deutschen zwischen Varietät und Stil [Ethnic markers in German between variety and style]. In Arnulf Deppermann (ed.), *Das Deutsch der Migranten (Jahrbuch des Instituts für Deutsche Sprache 2012)*, 9–40. Berlin & Boston, MA: De Gruyter.

Auer, Peter. 2017. *Doing difference* aus der Perspektive der Soziolinguistik – an einem Beispiel aus der Lebenswelt von 'Jugendlichen mit Migrationshintergrund' [Doing difference from the perspective of sociolinguistics – an example from the lifeworld of 'adolescents with a migration background']. In Stefan Hirschauer (ed.), *Un/doing Difference. Praktiken der Humandifferenzierung*, 287–306. Weilerswirst: Velbrück Wissenschaft.

Auer, Peter. 2020. Dialect (non-)acquisition and use by young people of migrant background in Germany. *Journal of Multilingual and Multicultural Development*.

Auer, Peter & Vanessa Siegel. 2021. Grammatical gender in the German multiethnolect. *Journal of Germanic Linguistics* 33(1). 5–29.

Brugman, Hennie & Albert Russel. 2004. Annotating multi-media/multi-modal resources with ELAN. In Maria Teresa Lino et al.. (eds.), *Proceedings of the Fourth International Conference on Language Resources and Evaluation (LREC'04)*. Lisbon: European Language Resources Association (ELRA).

Bücker, Tanja. 2007. Ethnolektale Varietäten des Deutschen im Sprachgebrauch Jugendlicher [Ethnolectal varieties of German in the language use of adolescents]. *Studentische Arbeitspapiere Sprache und Interaktion (SASI)* 9. Münster: Centrum Sprache und Interaktion. http://audiolabor.uni-muenster.de/SASI/?page_id=64. (13 May, 2022.)

Conrad, François. 2021. Regional differences in the evolution of the merger of /ʃ/ and /ç/ in Luxembourgish. *Journal of the International Phonetic Association*. 1–18.

Dirim, İnci & Peter Auer. 2004. *Türkisch sprechen nicht nur die Türken: Über die Unschärfebeziehung zwischen Sprache und Ethnie in Deutschland* [Not only the Turks speak Turkish: On the fuzzy relationship between language and ethnicity in Germany]. Berlin & New York, NY: De Gruyter.

Dogil, Grzegorz. 1993. Phonologische Nachbarschaft trotz akustischer Ferne. Untersuchungen zur /ç/ – /x/-Neutralisierung im Saarland [Phonological neighbours despite acoustic distance. Studies on the neutralisation of /ç/ – /x/ in Saarland]. In Maria Bonner & Max Mangold (eds.), *Nachbarschaften: Thematische und systematische-Festschrift für Max Mangold zum 70. Geburtstag*, 57–66. Saarbrücken: Saarbrücker Druckerei und Verlag.

Duran, Daniel & Peter Auer. (submitted, a). The vowel space of multiethnolectal (Stuttgart) German.

Duran, Daniel & Peter Auer. (Submitted, b.) *Plosive voicing in multi-ethnolectal Stuttgart German.*

Flipsen, Peter, Lawrence Shriberg, Gary Weismer, Heather Karlsson & Jane Mc Sweeny. 1999. Acoustic characteristics of /s/ in adolescents. *Journal of Speech, Language, and Hearing Research* 42(3). 663–677. (18 May, 2022)

Forrest, Karen, Gary Weismer, Paul Milenkovic & Ronald N. Dougall. 1988. Statistical analysis of word-initial voiceless obstruents: Preliminary data. *The Journal of the Acoustical Society of America* 84(1). 115–123. (18 May, 2022)

Fox, John & Sanford Weisberg. 2019. *An {R} companion to applied regression*, 3rd edn. Thousand Oaks, CA: Sage. https://socialsciences.mcmaster.ca/jfox/Books/Companion/ (13 May, 2022.)

Freywald, Ulrike, Katharina Mayr, Tiner Özelik & Heike Wiese. 2011. Kiezdeutsch as a multiethnolect. In Friederike Kern & Margret Selting (eds.), *Ethnic styles of speaking in European metropolitan areas*, 45–73. Amsterdam & Philadelphia, PA: John Benjamins.

Gordon, Matthew, Paul Barthmaier & Kathy Sands. 2002. A cross-linguistic acoustic study of voiceless fricatives. *Journal of the International Phonetic Association* 32(2). 141–174. (18 May, 2022)

Hall, Tracy Alan. 2014. Alveolopalatalization in Central German as markedness reduction. *Transactions of the Philological Society* 112(2). 143–166.

Harrington, Jonathan. 2010. *Phonetic analysis of speech corpora*. Malden, MA: Wiley-Blackwell.

Haußmann, Michael. 2012. 44 Prozent der Stuttgarter Kinder und Jugendlichen leben in reinen Migrantenhaushalten. *Statistik und Informationsmanagement Monatshefte* 2012(3). 97–98.

Heidelberger Forschungsprojekt ,Pidgindeutsch'. 1975. *Sprache und Kommunikation ausländischer Arbeiter* [Language and communication of foreign workers]. Kronberg: Scriptor.

Herrgen, Joachim. 1986. *Koronalisierung und Hyperkorrektion: Das palatale Allophon des /ch/-Phonems und seine Variation im Westmitteldeutschen* [Coronalisation and hypercorrection: The palatal allophone of the /ch/ phoneme and its variation in West Central German]. Stuttgart: Franz Steiner Verlag. (18 May, 2022)

Hoole, Philip, Noel Nguyen-Trong & William Hardcastle. 1993. A comparative investigation of coarticulation in fricatives: Electropalatographic, electromagnetic, and acoustic data. *Language and Speech* 36(2–3). 235–260. (18 May, 2022)

Jannedy, Stefanie & Melanie Weirich. 2014. Sound change in an urban setting: Category instability of the palatal fricative in Berlin. *Laboratory Phonology* 5(1). (18 May, 2022)

Jannedy, Stefanie & Melanie Weirich. 2017. Spectral moments vs discrete cosine transformation coefficients: Evaluation of acoustic measures distinguishing two merging German fricatives. *The Journal of the Acoustical Society of America* 142(1). 395–405. (18 May, 2022)

Jannedy, Stefanie, Melanie Weirich & Louisa Helmke. 2015. Acoustic analyses of differences in [ç] and [ʃ] productions in Hood German. In The Scottish Consortium for ICPhS 2015 (ed.), *Proceedings of the 18th International Congress of Phonetic Sciences (ICPhS 2015)*. Glasgow: University of Glasgow. https://www.internationalphoneticassociation.org/icphs-proceedings/ICPhS2015/Papers/ICPHS0328.pdf. (13 May, 2022.)

Jannedy, Stefanie, Norma Mendoza-Denton & Melanie Weirich. 2019. Social capital and the production and perception of fine phonetic detail in Berlin. In Theresa Heyd, Ferdinand von Mengden & Britta Schneider (Eds.), *The sociolinguistic economy of Berlin*, 125–144. Boston, MA & Berlin: De Gruyter. (18 May, 2022)

Jongman, Allard, Ratree Wayland & Serena Wong. 2000. Acoustic characteristics of English fricatives. *The Journal of the Acoustical Society of America* 108(3). 1252 . (18 May, 2022.)

Kassambara, Alboukadel. 2020. *ggpubr: "ggplot2" based publication ready plots*. https://CRAN.R-project.org/package=ggpubr. (13 May, 2022.)

Keim, Inken. 2002. Sozial-kulturelle Selbstdefinition und sozialer Stil: Junge Deutsch-Türkinnen im Gespräch [Sociocultural self-definition and social style: Young, female German-Turks in conversation]. In Inken Keim & Wilfried Schütte (eds.), *Soziale Welten und kommunikative Stile. Festschrift für Werner Kallmeyer zum 60. Geburtstag*, 233–259. Tübingen: Narr.

Keim, Inken. 2007. *Die ,türkischen Powergirls'. Lebenswelt und kommunikativer Stil einer Migrantinnengruppe in Mannheim* [The 'Turkish power girls'. Lifeworld and communicative style of an immigrant group in Mannheim]. Tübingen: Narr.

Kisler, Thomas, Uwe Reichel & Florian Schiel. 2017. Multilingual processing of speech via web services. *Computer Speech & Language* 45. 326–347. (18 May, 2022)

Maniwa, Kazumi, Allard Jongman & Travis Wade. 2009. Acoustic characteristics of clearly spoken English fricatives. *The Journal of the Acoustical Society of America* 125(6). 3962–3973. (18 May, 2022)

Robinson, Orrin W. 2001. *Whose German? The ach/ich alternation and related phenomena in standard and colloquial.* Amsterdam & Philadelphia, PA: John Benjamins.

Shadle, Christina H. & Sheila J. Mair. 1996. Quantifying spectral characteristics of fricatives. *Fourth International Conference on Spoken Language Processing (ICSLP '96).* 1521–1524. (18 May, 2022)

Siegel, Vanessa. 2020. *Multiethnolektale Syntax. Artikel, Präpositionen und Pronomen in der Jugendsprache* [Multiethnolectal syntax. Articles, prepositions and pronouns in adolescent language]. Heidelberg: Winter.

Tertilt, Hermann. 1998. *Turkish Power Boys. Ethnographie einer Jugendbande* [Turkish power boys. Ethnography of a youth gang]. Frankfurt: Suhrkamp.

Watson, Catherine I. & Jonathan Harrington. 1999. Acoustic evidence for dynamic formant trajectories in Australian English vowels. *The Journal of the Acoustical Society of America* 106(1). 458–468. (18 May, 2022)

Weirich, Melanie, Stefanie Jannedy & Gediminas Schüppenhauer. 2020. The social meaning of contextualized sibilant alternations in Berlin German. *Frontiers in Psychology* 11. 566174. (18 May, 2022)

Wiese, Heike. 2009. *Kiezdeutsch* [Hood German]. Munich: Beck.

Wiese, Heike & Ulrike Freywald. 2019. Regionalsprachliche Merkmale in jugendsprachlichen Praktiken im multilingualen urbanen Raum [Regional characteristics of adolescent speech in multilingual urban space]. In Joachim Herrgen & Jürgen Erich Schmidt (eds.), *Sprache und Raum. Ein internationales Handbuch der Sprachvariation. Band 4: Deutsch (HSK 30.4)*, 995–1012. Berlin & Boston, MA: De Gruyter Mouton.

Winkelmann, Raphael, Klaus Jaensch, Steve Cassidy & Jonathan Harrington. 2021. *EmuR: Main package of the EMU Speech Database Management System.*

Zahorian, Stephen A. & Amir J. Jagharghi. 1993. Spectral-shape features versus formants as acoustic correlates for vowels. *The Journal of the Acoustical Society of America* 94(4). 1966–1982. (18 May, 2022)

Zharkova, Natalia. 2016. Ultrasound and acoustic analysis of sibilant fricatives in preadolescents and adults. *The Journal of the Acoustical Society of America* 139(5). 2342–2351. (18 May, 2022)

CHAPTER 5

Sociophonetic variation in a context of dialect contact
Standardisation and semi-standardisation in Canarian Spanish

Manuel Almeida & Juan M. Hernández-Campoy
Universidad de La Laguna, Tenerife, Spain
Universidad de Murcia, Spain

The social contexts of language and dialect contact are an exceptional scenario in which to analyse some of the most innovative outcomes of language change. In these dynamic contexts, mixed language varieties often develop, constructed from elements and structures of the languages or dialects that participate in the contact. In the specific case of dialect contact, one of the most creative hybrid outcomes is interdialectalisms, forms that can coexist in a speech community with vernacular and standard variants. The study of the structural and social relationships between these alternatives may contribute towards a better understanding of the mechanisms underlying changes in progress.

Keywords: dialect contact, change in progress, interdialectalisms, standardisation, media

1. Introduction

The study of the significant relationship between language and society, by correlating linguistic constituents with extralinguistic factors, has allowed sociolinguistics to decipher language variation in terms of orderly heterogeneity as for its mechanisms and social motivations, and, consequently, to account for variability in language. It is certainly obvious that linguistic change must be regarded from both the social and linguistic perspective, as it is, after all, a sociolinguistic phenomenon. Studies carried out since the 1960s have demonstrated that sound change takes place within a speech community and that sociodemographic factors (such as social class, age, gender and social networks) as well as geographical

https://doi.org/10.1075/silv.31.05alm
© 2024 John Benjamins Publishing Company

Chapter 5. Sociophonetic variation in a context of dialect contact 101

factors and certain linguistic environments are paramount in the diffusion of innovations (Chambers & Trudgill 2004 [1980]: 153–159). However, the way in which a linguistic change presents before it starts and how it *does* start is a mystery: "language change is one of the most mystifying and fascinating phenomena that dialectologists and linguistic scientists encounter" (Trudgill 1990: 7).

In language contact situations, the rate of interaction (high/low contact) crucially determines the "natural" or "abnatural" processes leading to language change (see Trudgill 1978, 1989; Bailey 1982). In high-contact situations, simplification is the usual process (change from synthetic to analytic structure, reduction in redundancy, and increase in regularity), whereas complication (shift from analytic to synthetic structure, general increase in redundancy and irregularity) is the usual result in cases of low contact. As also applies to languages, in high dialect-contact situations changes are more likely to occur faster and tend towards simplification, whereas in low dialect contact changes usually occur more slowly and entail complication. Other social factors, such as the status of the groups that speak the different languages or varieties, the institutional support they receive, the attitudes of individuals, the type of contact, etc., can also lead to the formation of more or less regular patterns of linguistic variation in the communities where these changes occur. The concurrence of these factors could also explain the greater or lesser speed of changes. For instance, it is unlikely that the standardisation process of the Canarian dialect is linked to face-to-face contact between Canarian speakers and Standard Spanish speakers, since the latter group consists of only very few individuals on the islands. It is mainly through the mass media that the Canarian population is in contact with the national standard.

In situations of dialect contact, one of the most usual changes is the emergence of intermediate varieties, which manifest themselves in different ways (see Cerruti & Tsiplakou 2020). One of the most innovative outcomes of such intermediate varieties is interdialectalisms, meaning forms and structures created from elements that exist in both dialects. These hybrid alternatives have been documented at all levels of language: phonetic, morphosyntactic and lexical (Trudgill 1986: 58–63; Chambers & Trudgill 2004 [1980]: 106–118; Siegel 2012 [2010]: 56–60). According to Trudgill (1986: 62), "the label 'interdialect' is intended to refer to situations where contact between two dialects leads to the development of forms that actually originally occurred in neither dialect". At the lexical level, an example of an interdialectal form is the current use in British English of the compromise term "take out", which is used in the geographically intermediate areas of northern England (as transition zones) and separates the use of "carry out" in Scotland and Northern Ireland from "take away" used in central and southern areas, all referring to hot food bought for consumption off premises (Trudgill 1986: 63). A second example is the use of the term *Erdbirne* 'earth pear' in central areas of Germany, separating the use of *Grundbirne* 'ground pear' in the north from that of *Erdapfel* 'earth apple' found in the south to refer to a potato (Trudgill 1986: 63). At the phonetic level, the pronunciation of word-final postvocalic /s/ in *judías verdes* 'green beans' in Spanish evolves geographically from the categorical absence of /s/ in the south (Andalusia, Extremadura and Murcia: *judía*[ø] *verde*[ø]) to the categorical presence of /s/ in the north (*judía*[s] *verde*[s]), after passing through a transition zone (La Mancha), where there is an intermediate realisation (*judía*[ø] *verde*[s]) (see Figure 1).

Figure 1. Interdialectal forms in the United Kingdom (for "take away" and "carry out"), Germany (for *Grundbirne* and *Erdapfel*) and Spain (for plural pronunciation of *judías verdes*)

These three examples of interdialectalisms have been documented in transitional zones between two dialects. However, this does not mean that all hybrid forms exclusively arise in such geographic areas.

There are different interpretations regarding the origin of interdialectalisms. For Chambers and Trudgill (2004 [1980]: 110–111), these innovative variants can work as a neutrality strategy: by avoiding the use of the pre-existing forms associated with two dialects, the hybrid forms allow speakers to avoid identifying themselves with a particular dialect or, on the contrary, to identify themselves with both dialects at the same time. For Trudgill (1986: 58–63), interdialectalisms are the result of the imperfect learning of a second dialect. In this sense, they would result from a similar process to the one that underlies the formation of interlanguage during the learning of a second language (Selinker 1972). Almeida (2019) proposes that not all hybrid forms that arise in a dialect are due to the same causes. Some can indeed be explained as a consequence of the imperfect learning of a second dialect, as suggested by Trudgill (1986), but others have likely been developed in order to allow speakers to express a dual cultural identity, that is, to show feelings of identification with the cultures associated with each of the dialects that served as a model for the new form (the neutrality hypothesis, as mentioned above). It can also occur that interdialectal forms that originally arose as the result of the imperfect learning of a second dialect are socially used by speakers to express a hybrid cultural image.

2. Objectives

The present study aims to describe the linguistic and social variation observed in two phonological variables in the Spanish spoken in the Canary Islands (Spain): (c) and (h). According to a previous study carried out by Almeida (2019), these variables have three variants: a local vernacular realisation, a standard Castilian realisation, and an interdialectal variant as an intermediate alternative or compromise pronunciation (Table 1). Interdialectal forms could be viewed as cases of incomplete standardisation, or, simply, of semi-standardisation.

Table 1. Vernacular, standard and interdialectal variants of variables (c) and (h) in Canarian Spanish

		Standard	Vernacular	Interdialectal
Variable (c)[a]	*pecho* 'chest'	['petʃo]	['peco]	['pec̑o]
	chino 'Chinese'	['tʃino]	['cino]	['c̑ino]
Variable (h)	*bajo* 'under'	['baxo]	['baho]	['bahˣo]
	jabón 'soap'	[xa'βon]	[ha'βon]	[hˣa'βon]

a. In line with traditional variationist analysis, the two variables under study are represented in parentheses. Symbols used for standard and vernacular variants correspond to the IPA transcription system.

Following Trudgill (1974: 80), the selection of these linguistic variables was initially justified by (a) "the amount of apparent social significance in the pronunciation of the segment or segments involved", and (b) "the amount of phonetic differentiation involved". These justifications were based firstly, on the native knowledge of the speech area of one of the authors:

> wherever possible, field-workers should be native of the area, or people familiar with the local dialect. This is not always possible, of course, and even when it is there are some dangers – preconceptions are less likely to be wrong, but if they are wrong they are more likely to be adhered to (Trudgill 1983: 41);

and secondly, on the results obtained in previous studies (see Almeida & Díaz-Alayón 1989; Almeida 1992, 2019, 2020).

Table 2 shows the main articulatory and acoustic characteristics of the variants (based on Almeida 2019). Regarding the origins of the Canarian interdialectal variants, Almeida (2019) has proposed that the hybrid forms of (c) arose as a consequence of the imperfect learning of the corresponding form from the standard variety. The differences between the vernacular and standard variants of (c) are greater than those between the vernacular and standard variants of (h).

Among these differences there is one that appears particularly difficult to bridge: the duration of the plosive and fricative phases. In the vernacular variant of (c), the fricative phase is either absent or very short with respect to the occlusive. For Alvar and Quilis (1966), this represents the most important difference between the Canarian and the standard variants. From this follows that it is relatively difficult for a Canarian speaker to articulate the standard realisation [ʧ] correctly (see Table 3). On the other hand, the interdialectal forms of (h) seem to have arisen in order to express identification with both local (regional) and national cultural values (Almeida 2019). Despite it being relatively easy for a Canarian speaker to articulate the corresponding standard forms (as can be seen in Table 3), they often opt for the hybrid variant instead; that is, although the speaker's intention to project a dual cultural identity may be carried out by alternating the use of the vernacular and the standard variants (see for instance Villena-Ponsoda & Vida-Castro 2020 for Andalusia), it is likely that the interdialectal variants represent a more attenuated way of expressing their dual identity (Almeida 2019, 2020).

Table 2. Phonetic characteristics of the vernacular, standard and interdialectal variants of (c) and (h)

		Standard	Vernacular	Interdialectal
Variable (c)	Mode of articulation	Affricate	Stop	Affricate
	Place of articulation	Prepalatal	Mid-, postpalatal	Mid-, postpalatal
	Voicing	[− voiced]	[+/− voiced]	[+/− voiced]
	Duration of the occlusive phase	25–30% longer than the fricative phase	200–500% longer than the fricative phase	Approximately the same duration as the fricative phase
Variable (h)	Mode of articulation	Fricative	Fricative	Fricative
	Place of articulation	Velar	Glottal	Glottal-velar
	Voicing	[− voiced]	[+/− voiced]	[− voiced]

These variants represent two examples of change in progress. Among the different stages that a study of this type should take into account (see Weinreich et al. 1968), this chapter will focus on two that are closely related: transition and embedding. The first involves describing the different stages of change both linguistically and socially, while the second requires a description of how the forms subject to change are redistributed both in the linguistic and the social structure of the community. For this, a series of linguistic and social constraints apparently governing the two types of change will be examined (see Methodology). Before proceeding with a more specific analysis, it should be clarified that the inter-dialectal variants of (c) can be heard both in the formal and informal speech of Canarian speakers as well as in individuals from all social groups. By contrast, the hybrid and standard variants of (h) are only rarely heard in informal contexts and working-class individuals. It can therefore be argued that while the change affecting (c) is to some extent rooted in the community (at least as far as hybrid variants are concerned), (h) is in the early stages of a change in progress. The analysis may also help to gain an understanding of whether interdialectal forms, given their hybrid linguistic nature, are subject to the same linguistic and social constraints as the other two variants (the vernacular and the standard) or whether they have their own patterns of variation.

3. Methodology

3.1 The sample

The use of archived mass media sources, such as radio recordings, has proved an excellent source for sampling audio materials to measure and analyse linguistic change (see, for example, Van de Velde et al. 1996; Hernández-Campoy & Jiménez-Cano 2003; or Zhang 2012) as well as inter- and intra-speaker variation (Bell 1982; Coupland 1996; Cutillas-Espinosa & Hernández-Campoy 2006, 2007; Cutillas-Espinosa et al. 2010; Hernández-Campoy & Cutillas-Espinosa 2010, 2012; Soukup 2011; Hall-Lew et al. 2012; and Sclafani 2018, among others).

An interesting aspect regarding the two variables under study is their different frequency of use depending on the context of the situation, as mentioned above. In informal speech styles, it is not uncommon to hear interdialectal variants of (c), whereas interdialectal (or even standard) variants of (h) are heard only rarely. However, in formal styles, the innovative variants of (h) are more usual. This means that, for a sociolinguistic analysis of these variables, formal contexts, such as conferences, debates on radio and television, parliamentary speeches, etc., had to be used, despite the limitations this entails (for example, difficulties identifying the age and social class of some informants). A speech sample comprising around twenty hours of radio recordings obtained between 2006 and 2010 was used. Different radio programmes were recorded for the purpose: magazines (discussions, interviews, reports), news, entertainment, culture, sports, etc. Radio stations were selected based on coverage throughout the Canary Islands, with the most common being chosen, such as Radio Club Tenerife – Cadena SER, COPE, Radio Las

Palmas and Radio Nacional de España. Fragments corresponding to read speech were not taken into account.

To avoid as far as possible any distortion of the sociolinguistic analysis, the maximum number of cases per variable per speaker was 50.

3.2 Independent variables

This study analyses two types of independent variables: linguistic and social. The linguistic variables are stress (stressed vs. unstressed syllable), word-syllable position (word-initial vs. medial), and word frequency (low and moderate vs. high). The social variables are gender (women and men) and degree of public contact (high, medium and low).

3.2.1 *Linguistic variables*

3.2.1.a *Stress*

The variants of the two variables were observed in stressed position, as in *echar* 'to throw' (standard Sp. /eˈʧaɾ/) or *gente* 'people' (standard Sp. /ˈxente/), and in unstressed position, as in *ocho* 'eight' (standard Sp. /ˈoʧo/) or *caja* 'box' (standard Sp. /ˈkaxa/). In this regard, the starting hypothesis postulates that the innovative variants (standard and interdialectal) must be found more frequently in stressed position than in unstressed contexts. Given that speakers have to perfectly identify the contexts in which the new variants are produced, it must be assumed that they will use these forms in those contexts that are more cognitively relevant, that is, those marked by the [+ stress] feature. A stressed position within a word has been demonstrated to be more relevant than an unstressed position, both phonetically and cognitively. The greater prosodic prominence of stressed syllables explains the infrequency of articulatory weakening and deletion processes in this position (Yaeger-Dror 1993; Laver 1994: 511–517). For instance, in Santa Cruz de Tenerife, intervocalic /d/ deletion occurs more frequently in unstressed syllables, whereas the presence of this consonant is more stable in stressed syllables (Almeida 2011). Likewise, the weakening and deletion of vowels in Canarian Spanish, as in most Spanish dialects, mostly affect those in unstressed position (Almeida & Díaz-Alayón 1989: 30–32). The greater phonetic stability of stressed syllables is the factor that makes speakers pay more attention to these than to unstressed syllables (Wang et al. 2005) and allows them to identify a phoneme in this position more immediately during speech processing (Pitt & Samuel 1990).

3.2.1.b *Word-syllable position*

Two contexts were taken into account for syllable position within a lexical item: word-initial, as in *chino* 'Chinese' (standard Sp. /'tʃino/) or *genio* 'genius' (standard Sp. /'xenio/), and word-medial, as in *pecho* 'chest' (standard Sp. /'petʃo/) or *ceja* 'eyebrow' (standard Sp. /'θexa/). The hypothesis is that the vernacular variant must occur more frequently in word-medial position, while hybrid and standard variants must be more frequent word-initially. Various studies have shown that, cognitively, the initial position of the word is more salient than the internal. According to certain theories on speech processing, individuals recognise words in a sequential way, that is, according to the temporal order in which sounds appear in utterance sequences. For this reason, speakers tend to pay more attention to sounds located at the beginning of the word than to those found in internal position, which allows them to identify the word more accurately during lexical access (Marslen-Wilson & Welsh 1978; Vitevich 2002). According to Stemberger and Treiman (1986:163), "words are accessed as the acoustic information arrives, so that listeners begin to access words before the entire word has been heard; the beginning of the word is more important because it is used in the initial decisions". In other words, the beginning of a word is highly informative, since with the first sounds of a word, all those words that begin with the same sounds are activated. The number of possible options decreases as the remaining sounds are uttered sequentially in the production process, meaning a word can be perfectly recognised even before a speaker has provided all the acoustic information. In fact, experiments have shown that children aged between 18 and 21 months are able to associate a single image, from a selection of several, with a familiar word that is pronounced even before its utterance has been completed (Fernald et al. 2001). The fact that this skill is acquired at such an early age can be understood as a symptom of its importance during language processing.

3.2.1.c *Word frequency*

The influence of the greater or lesser frequency of words in the alternation between traditional and innovative variants was also analysed. The dictionary of frequencies elaborated by Almela et al. (2005) was taken as a reference in the analysis of the relationship between phonetic variation and word frequency. This dictionary is based on a corpus of twenty million words of Spanish oral and written texts from Spain and Latin America and includes the 10,000 most frequent words. Five degrees of word frequency are distinguished: low (up to three occurrences per million), moderate (4–10 occurrences per million), notable (11–25 occurrences per million), high (26–75 occurrences per million), and very high (more than 75 occurrences per million). For this analysis, the first three were grouped as one degree and the last two as another; in this way, only two groups were considered: high versus moderate/low frequency. Words such as *coche* 'car' and *mejor* 'better' belonged to the first group, while words such as *anoche* 'last night' and *página* 'page' were conceived as having a low–moderate frequency of use. The most frequent words tend to be stored in a more accessible place in memory to facilitate lexical selection during language processing. As they are more frequent, they are more predictable; thus, their selection is more automatic or immediate than in the case of less usual words, which would explain why processes of phonetic reduction (such as weakening and elision) affect frequent words more often than infrequent words (Bybee 2003 [2001], 2007). Consequently, it can be hypothesised that those words requiring greater articulatory effort will occur less frequently than those requiring less effort. Indeed, Zipf (1965 [1935]: 20–29) observed that longer words are less frequent in languages such as Latin, Peiping Chinese and English, and that aspirated stops are less frequent than unaspirated stops in Peiping and Cantonese Chinese as well as in Danish and Burmese (Zipf 1965 [1935]: 68–72).

3.2.2   *Social variables*

3.2.2.a   *Gender*
The changes studied here can be considered changes from above, since they imply the replacement of a vernacular with a hybrid or standard variant. This type of change is usually led by women (Labov 1982 [1966]: 385, 2001; for Spanish, see Almeida 1992; Moya-Corral & García-Wiedemann 1995: 91; Villena-Ponsoda 2000; Díaz-Peralta 2001: 124). Different theories have tried to explain why women use prestigious or standard forms of speech more frequently than men: due to an awareness that the symbolic strength of prestigious linguistic forms may compensate for the lack of power and status they have in our societies (Trudgill 1978 [1975]; Eckert 1989); that this is a manifestation of the importance they attach to their public image, given the social pressure they are under (Lakoff 1975); etc. On the other hand, the verification that women are indeed the ones who lead the changes entailing the abandonment of vernacular or traditional forms and their replacement with others coming from the outside community (normally from the standard variety, as in the changes in progress under research here) may also be interpreted as a kind of rebellion of women against the position of subordination they occupy in their community (Fasold 1990: 99).

3.2.2.b   *Degree of public contact*
Three groups of individuals were considered in this study: (a) people working in radio broadcasting, either as presenters in the studio or as interviewers/reporters outside the studio, (b) written press journalists and people from the world of politics and culture, and (c) ordinary people, mostly radio audience that call the radio

for various reasons (to share their experience of situations that have occurred in their neighbourhood or family, ask about lost objects, or request information on public events), but also others interviewed in the street or even inside the studio. The last is a fairly heterogeneous group, since it includes individuals from different professions and social classes, who are also not as used to speaking in public as the informants in the other groups.

The starting hypothesis assumes that the innovative forms (interdialectal and standard) should be more frequent among radio professionals and less so among ordinary people. To a large extent, this hypothesis is supported by the concept of "linguistic market" (Sankoff & Laberge 1978), which proposes that certain occupations seem to be more receptive to the use of the standard variety (or a variety closer to the standard) regardless of the social class of individuals. Within this framework, "the social and symbolic power of languages or language use does not derive from language as such, but from the settings (the particular contexts or markets) in which communication takes place" (Gogolin 2001). The speaker's occupation, for example, strongly determines the way they speak, despite their social and/or educational background: "people in certain occupations tend to use more standard varieties of language than other people at the same level of status, income, or education" (Guy 2011: 166). In this theory, linguistic competence refers to the linguistic capacity to handle diversity and "generate an infinite number of discourses as the social capacity to use this competency adequately in specific situations" (Gogolin 2001: 613). Those who work in radio broadcasting tend to seek acceptance from their listeners; in fact, audience ratings largely determine the type of format many programmes have. For this reason, in the case of Canarian radio stations, the expectation is that regional features should be prioritised to a certain extent over those coming from standard Spanish. Bell (2001) observed that four radio broadcasters from Wellington (New Zealand) who worked for two radio stations (national and local) used the innovative, non-standard voiced flap [ɾ] more frequently in the station that had an audience of low social status, whereas the more conservative variant, a voiceless or voiced stop ([d]/[t]), was more frequent when broadcasting through the national station, addressed to a high-status audience. In other words, the announcers adapted their speech style to that of the audience. Bell himself does admit that individuals may occasionally also design their speech based not on the real audience, but on an ideal, prototypical audience (what he calls "style as initiative") (see also Hernández-Campoy 2016). In this regard, Cutillas-Espinosa and Hernández-Campoy (2006) observed that the presenter of a radio programme in Murcia used the standard forms of (s), (r), and (l), and maintained consonant groups much more often (92%) than his audience (13.4%).

In the case of the Canarian sample, it is assumed that individuals who work in the world of radio broadcasting are more likely to want to demonstrate a sense of proximity to their listeners, but also to project an image that has certain intellectual authority, is cosmopolitan (or at least not too tied to the local world), sophisticated, etc. This attitude will lead them to make more use of hybrid and standard forms than individuals working in other professions that do not require such contact with the public. In addition, during the Franco regime, the imposition of the standard variety, or at least a variety very close to it, was the norm in Canarian radio broadcasting (as in other Spanish regions), especially in urban stations and in the most widely broadcast programmes (Yanes 2013). Those who wanted to work as announcers thus had to be mindful of their diction, since the announcer's test was extremely strict during this time. The regional accent was permitted once again when democracy arrived during the 1970s, although even today some announcers still feel that the standard should prevail over the Canarian variety in broadcasting.

4. Results

The general results (Table 3 and Figure 2) show that vernacular variants are used in the majority of cases, with percentages exceeding 75%. Standard variants are the least frequent, especially those of (c) (0.4% vs. 9.4% for standard variants of (h)), and hybrid variants have modest percentages ranging between 12% and 15%. The emergence of interdialectal forms, the fact that some of these variants are only valid to a certain extent in formal speech, and, finally, the evidence that vernacular forms are still the most frequent phonetic alternative, suggest that dialect standardisation is a slow process in the Canarian community. The results also corroborate the hypothesis regarding the different origins of the interdialectal forms for both variables.

Table 3. Absolute and relative frequencies of the variants of (c) and (h)

	Vernacular		Interdialectal		Standard		T
	N	%	N	%	N	%	
(c)	833	87.0	120	12.5	4[a]	0.4	957
(h)	1000	75.5	199	15.0	125	9.4	1,324

a. Due to the small number of standard variants of (c) (4 cases), the decision was taken to exclude these in the statistical analysis regarding the crossing of variables.

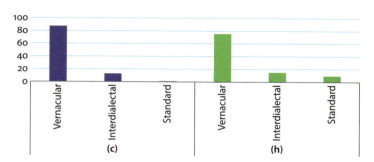

Figure 2. Frequencies for the variants of (c) and (h) in percentages

With respect to the analysis of dependent factors, a chi-square test was used in order to verify the significance of each variable. The analysis of internal factors (Tables 4 and 5 and Figure 3) revealed that differences are not significant ($p > .05$) in either of the two variables: the two variants of variable (c) and those of variable (h) show approximately the same percentages in all the contexts studied as independent variables (stressed and unstressed syllables, word-initial and word-medial position, and low/moderate and high frequency words). In the case of (c), the percentages for the vernacular variant range between 86% and 89%, while those for the innovative variant range between 11% and 14%. Regarding variable (h), the vernacular variant reaches 75–77%, while the hybrid reaches 13–16%, and the standard 8–10.5%. The fact that the two variables are not statistically significant may suggest that there are other factors present in the discourse that are neutralising the effect of the phonotactic constraints discussed above. The role of stress, for example, may be irrelevant due to discursive factors (such as focus). This may have modified the values that prosodic features such as duration or pitch tend to obtain within the frame of the word when analysed in isolation or when inserted into very short sentences. The results therefore suggest that further research is needed.

The analysis of social factors revealed that the differences obtained between groups are significant in most cases (Tables 6 and 7 and Figure 4). Regarding gender, women make more use of innovative forms (both interdialectisms and standard forms) than men. In the case of the hybrid variants of (c), women use them 15.2% and men 10.5% ($\chi^2(1) = 4.599$, $p = .033$). The hybrid variants of (h) are used 18.1% by women and only 12.6% by men, while the standard variant [x] obtains 11.8% and 7.5%, respectively ($\chi^2(2) = 17,220$, $p < .001$). The starting hypothesis is therefore validated in both variables: women use standard and hybrid variants more frequently than men. However, the differences between women and men are not particularly relevant, since they are around 5–6 percentage points only.

Regarding the degree of public contact, the results reveal a more complex situation. The variants of (c) do not exhibit differences in any of the three groups: there is an 87–88% use of vernacular forms, whereas interdialectal forms are used

Manuel Almeida & Juan M. Hernández-Campoy

Table 4. Results of the alternation in the variable (c). Internal factors

	Vernacular		Hybrid		χ^2 value (df)	Significance
	N	%	N	%		
Stress						
Stressed	219	88.7	28	11.3		
Unstressed	614	87.0	92	13.0	.478 (1)	.489
Word position						
Initial	75	86.2	12	13.8		
Internal	758	87.5	108	12.5	.126 (1)	.723
Word frequency						
Low/medium	260	87.5	37	12.5		
High	573	87.3	83	12.7	.007 (1)	.933

Table 5. Results of the alternation in the variable (h). Internal factors

	Vernacular		Hybrid		Standard		χ^2 value (df)	Significance
	N	%	N	%	N	%		
Stress								
Stressed	458	75.5	86	14.2	63	10.4		
Unstressed	542	75.6	113	15.8	62	8.6	1.599 (2)	.449
Word position								
Initial	301	77.0	57	14.6	33	8.4		
Internal	699	74.9	142	15.2	92	9.9	.820 (2)	.664
Word frequency								
Low/medium	322	76.8	53	12.6	44	10.5		
High	678	74.9	146	16.1	81	9.0	3.183 (2)	.204

around 12–13% ($\chi^2(2)$=.150, p=.928). With respect to the glottal variable, a clear stratification pattern can be observed: radio professionals use interdialectal and standard forms most frequently (19.6% and 12.6%, respectively), followed by individuals with a moderate degree of exposure to the public (12.9% and 8.4%), and, finally, by those with less of a presence in radiophonic media (4.5% and 0.6%) ($\chi^2(4)$=54.224, $p<$.001).

According to these results, the initial hypothesis is clearly validated in the case of gender, but only partially in the case of individuals' degree of public contact, since social differences result significant only in one of the linguistic variables. This different behaviour of the two variables surely has to do with the greater prestige enjoyed by both the interdialectal and standard variants of variable (h), as described above.

Chapter 5. Sociophonetic variation in a context of dialect contact

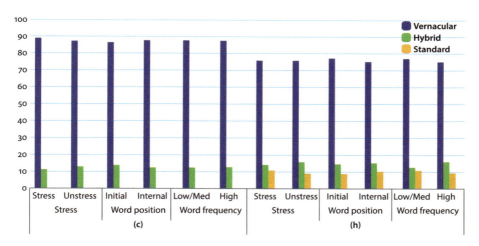

Figure 3. Percentages regarding stress, word position and word frequency for the variants of (c) and (h)

Table 6. Results of the social stratification of (c)

	Vernacular		Hybrid		χ^2 value (df)	Significance
	N	%	N	%		
Gender						
Men	475	89.5	56	10.5		
Women	358	84.8	64	15.2	4.599 (1)	.033*
Degree of public contact						
High	374	87.8	52	12.2		
Medium	380	87.0	57	13.0		
Low	79	87.8	11	12.2	0.150 (2)	.928

Table 7. Results of the social stratification of (h)

	Vernacular		Hybrid		Standard		χ^2 value (df)	Significance
	N	%	N	%	N	%		
Gender								
Men	585	79.9	92	12.6	55	7.5		
Women	415	70.1	107	18.1	70	11.8	17.220 (2)	<.001***
Degree of public contact								
High	415	67.8	120	19.6	77	12.6		
Medium	439	78.7	72	12.9	47	8.4		
Low	146	94.8	7	4.5	1	0.6	54.224 (4)	<.001***

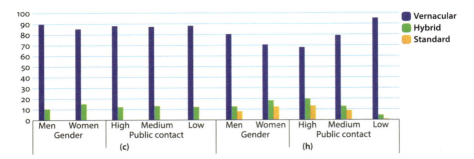

Figure 4. Percentages regarding gender and degree of public contact for the variants of (c) and (h)

5. Conclusions

This study was intended as a contribution towards gaining a better understanding of two changes in progress, through the analysis of certain linguistic and social variables thought to intervene in the organisation of change during the transition and embedding stages. The main characteristic of the variables analysed, (c) and (h), is that both have interdialectal variants alternating with vernacular and standard variants. Due to the special nature of interdialectalisms, the researchers wanted to learn whether these hybrid forms behaved in the same way as the other two variants. The results show that none of the phonetic variants seem to be sensitive to any of the linguistic constraints, meaning that these variants apparently move freely and unpredictably through the linguistic structure of the dialect.

The results also show that the social variables do indeed play a relevant role, since the differences are statistically significant in almost all cases. The innovative variants of (c) and (h) are more frequent among women than men, thus supporting the hypothesis that women are leading the changes towards the abandonment of the vernacular norm and the adoption of salient linguistic forms from other prestige norms. They similarly support the hypothesis that women tend to use the most prestigious linguistic forms in the community more than men. With regard to the degree of public contact, varying behaviour has been observed. For variable (c), no significant differences were observed between groups. In the case of (h), those who work in the world of radio broadcasting make use of the standard and interdialectal forms more often than those who work in less public professions. Ordinary people, who do participate in the change affecting variable (c), hardly do so in the case of (h).

Concerning interdialectalisms (the pseudo-standard forms), it may be concluded that hybrid forms arising from the imperfect learning of a second dialect, as is the case for the intermediate variants of (c), are more frequently used by individuals from all social groups than those arising from the deliberate aim of individuals to express a dual cultural identity, as is the case for the intermediate variants of (h). On the other hand, these hybrid variants show a stratification pattern similar to that of the standard variants (the only exception is found in the "degree of public contact" factor corresponding to variable (c)).

In order to better understand the linguistic and social meaning of the changes examined here, two complementary analyses should be carried out. First of all, a crosstabulation of linguistic variables would be convenient to determine whether there is any interaction. Such analysis has the disadvantage of focusing the study on very specific and local aspects of change. Nevertheless, the information revealed could shed light on the direction of change in the language structure. Secondly, an analysis of individual informants would also be important, since a previous study (Almeida 2019) observed that there is also a significant degree of variation within speakers with a high and medium degree of contact with the public. These differences may be linked to the type of radio programme and the personal attitudes of individuals regarding the way they stylise their speech.

References

Almeida, Manuel. 1992. Mecanismos sociolingüísticos del cambio fonético [Sociolinguistic mechanisms of phonetic change]. In José Antonio Bartol-Hernández, Juan Felipe García-Santos & Javier de Santiago-Guervós (eds.), *Estudios filológicos en homenaje a Eugenio de Bustos Tovar*, 51–60. Salamanca: Universidad de Salamanca.

Almeida, Manuel. 2011. Restricciones sociolingüísticas en un caso de alternancia (morfo)fonológica: /d/ intervocálica en una comunidad de habla canaria [Sociolinguistic constraints in a case of (morpho)phonological alternance: Intervocalic /d/ in a Canarian speech community]. *Lingüística Española Actual* XXXIII(1). 29–53.

Almeida, Manuel. 2019. Language hybridism: On the origin of interdialectal forms. In Juan Andrés Villena-Ponsoda, Francisco Díaz-Montesinos, Antonio Manuel Ávila-Muñoz & Matilde Vida-Castro (eds.), *Language variation – European perspectives VII*, 9–26. Amsterdam & Philadelphia, PA: John Benjamins.

Almeida, Manuel. 2020. The role of interdialectal forms in the formation of koinai. In Massimo Cerruti & Stavroula Tsiplakou (eds.), *Intermediate language varieties: Koinai and regional standards in Europe*, 183–201. Amsterdam & Philadelphia, PA: John Benjamins.

Almeida, Manuel & Carmen Díaz-Alayón. 1989. *El español de Canarias* [The Spanish spoken in the Canary Islands]. Santa Cruz de Tenerife.

Almela, Ramón, Pascual Cantos, Aquilino Sánchez, Ramón Sarmiento & Moisés Almela. 2005. *Frecuencias del español. Diccionario y estudios léxicos y morfológicos* [Spanish frequencies: Dictionary and lexical and morphological studies]. Madrid: Universitas.

Alvar, Manuel & Antonio Quilis. 1966. Datos acústicos y geográficos sobre la "ch" adherente de Canarias [Acoustic and geographic data on adherent "ch" in the Canary Islands]. *Anuario de Estudios Atlánticos* 12. 337–343.

Bailey, Charles. 1982. *On the yin and yang nature of language*. Ann Arbor, MI: Karoma.

Bell, Allan. 1982. This isn't the BBC: Colonialism in New Zealand English. *Applied Linguistics* 3. 246–258.

Bell, Allan. 2001. Back in style: Reworking audience design. In Penelope Eckert & John R. Rickford (eds.), *Style and sociolinguistic variation*, 139–169. Cambridge: Cambridge University Press.

Bybee, Joan. 2003 [2001]. *Phonology and language use*. Cambridge: Cambridge University Press.

Bybee, Joan. 2007. *Frequency of use and the organization of language*. Oxford & New York, NY: Oxford University Press.

Cerruti, Massimo & Stavroula Tsiplakou (eds.). 2020. *Intermediate language varieties: Koinai and regional standards in Europe*. Amsterdam & Philadelphia, PA: John Benjamins.

Chambers, J.K. & Peter Trudgill. 2004 [1980]. *Dialectology*. Cambridge: Cambridge University Press.

Coupland, Nikolas. 1996. Hark, hark the lark: Multiple voicing in DJ talk. In David Graddol, Dick Leith & Joan Swann (eds.), *English: History, diversity and change*, 325–330. London & New York, NY: Routledge & Open University.

Cutillas-Espinosa, Juan Antonio & Juan Manuel Hernández-Campoy. 2006. Nonresponsive performance in radio broadcasting: A case study. *Language Variation and Change* 18(3). 317–330.

Cutillas-Espinosa, Juan Antonio & Juan Manuel Hernández-Campoy. 2007. Script design in the media: Radio talk norms behind a professional voice. *Language & Communication* 27(2). 127–152.

Cutillas-Espinosa, Juan Antonio, Juan Manuel Hernández-Campoy & Natalie Schilling-Estes. 2010. Hypervernacularisation and speaker design: A case study. *Folia Linguistica* 44(1). 31–52.

Díaz-Peralta, Marina. 2001. *La expresión de futuro en el español de Las Palmas de Gran Canaria* [Expression of the future in the Spanish spoken in Las Palmas de Gran Canaria]. Las Palmas de Gran Canaria: Cabildo de Gran Canaria.

Eckert, Penelope. 1989. The whole woman: Sex and gender differences in variation. *Language Variation and Change* 1(3). 245–267.

Fasold, Ralph W. 1990. *The sociolinguistics of language*. Oxford: Basil Blackwell.

Fernald, Anne, Daniel Swingley & John P. Pinto. 2001. When half a word is enough: Infants can recognize spoken words using partial phonetic information. *Child Development* 72(4). 1003–1015.

Gogolin, Ingrid. 2001. The linguistic marketplace. In Rajend Mesthrie (ed.), *The Cambridge handbook of sociolinguistics*, 612–613. Cambridge: Cambridge University Press.

Guy, Gregory R. 2011. Language, social class, and status. In Rajend Mesthrie (ed.), *The Cambridge handbook of sociolinguistics*, 159–185. Cambridge: Cambridge University Press.

Hall-Lew, Lauren, Rebecca Starr & Elizabeth Coppock. 2012. Style-shifting in the U.S. Congress: The vowels of "Iraq(i)". In Juan Manuel Hernández-Campoy & Juan Antonio Cutillas-Espinosa (eds.), *Style-shifting in public: New perspectives on stylistic variation*, 45–63. Amsterdam & Philadelphia, PA: John Benjamins.

Hernández-Campoy, Juan Manuel. 2016. *Sociolinguistic styles*. Malden, MA: Wiley-Blackwell.

Hernández-Campoy, Juan Manuel & Juan Antonio Cutillas-Espinosa. 2010. Speaker design practices in political discourse: A case study. *Language and Communication* 30(4). 297–309.

Hernández-Campoy, Juan Manuel & Juan Antonio Cutillas-Espinosa (eds.). 2012. *Style-shifting in public: New perspectives on stylistic variation*. Amsterdam & Philadelphia, PA: John Benjamins.

Hernández-Campoy, Juan Manuel & José María Jiménez-Cano. 2003. Broadcasting standardisation: An analysis of the linguistic normalisation process in Murcian Spanish. *Journal of Sociolinguistics* 7(3). 321–347.

Labov, William. 1982 [1966]. *The social stratification of English in New York City*. Washington, DC: Center for Applied Linguistics.

Labov, William. 2001. *Principles of linguistic change. Volume II: Social factors*. Oxford: Blackwell.

Lakoff, Robin. 1975. *Language and woman's place*. New York, NY: Harper & Row.

Laver, John. 1994. *Principles of phonetics*. Cambridge: Cambridge University Press.

Marslen-Wilson, William D. & Alan Welsh. 1978. Processing interactions and lexical access during word recognition in continuous speech. *Cognitive Psychology* 10(1). 29–63.

Moya-Corral, Juan Antonio & Emilio J. García-Wiedemann. 1995. *El habla de Granada y sus barrios* [The dialect of Granada and its local areas]. Granada: Universidad de Granada.

Pitt, Mark A. & Arthur G. Samuel. 1990. The use of rhythm in attending to speech. *Journal of Experimental Psychology: Human Perception and Performance* 16(3). 564–573.

Sankoff, David & Suzanne Laberge. 1978. The linguistic market and the statistical explanation of variability. In David Sankoff (ed.), *Linguistic variation: Models and methods*, 239–250. New York, NY: Academic Press.

Sclafani, Jennifer. 2018. *Talking Donald Trump: A sociolinguistic study of style, metadiscourse, and political identity*. London & New York, NY: Routledge.

Selinker, Larry. 1972. Interlanguage. *International Review of Applied Linguistics (IRAL)* X(3). 209–232.

Siegel, Jeff. 2012 [2010]. *Second dialect acquisition*. Cambridge: Cambridge University Press.

Soukup, Barbara. 2011. Austrian listeners' perceptions of standard-dialect style-shifting: An empirical approach. *Journal of Sociolinguistics* 15(3). 347–365.

Stemberger, Joseph P. & Rebecca Treiman. 1986. The internal structure of word-initial consonant clusters. *Journal of Memory and Language* 25(2). 163–180.

Trudgill, Peter. 1974. *The social differentiation of English in Norwich*. Cambridge: Cambridge University Press.

Trudgill, Peter. 1978 [1975]. Sex, covert prestige and linguistic change in the urban British English of Norwich. In Barry Thorne & Nancy Henley (eds.), *Language and sex: Difference and dominance*, 88–104. Rowley: Newbury House Publishers.

Trudgill, Peter. 1983. *On dialect: Social and geographical perspectives*. Oxford: Blackwell.

Trudgill, Peter. 1986. *Dialects in contact*. Oxford: Blackwell.

Trudgill, Peter. 1989. Interlanguage, interdialect and typological change. In Susan Gass, Carolyn Madden, Dennis Preston & Larry Selinker (eds.), *Variation in second language acquisition: Psychological issues*, 244–253. Clevedon: Multilingual Matters.

Trudgill, Peter. 1990. *The dialects of England*. Oxford: Blackwell.

Van de Velde, Hans, Marinel Gerritsen & Roeland van Hout. 1996. The devoicing of fricatives in standard Dutch: A real-time study based on radio recordings. *Language Variation and Change* 8(2). 149–175.

Villena-Ponsoda, Juan Andrés. 2000. Identidad y variación lingüística: Prestigio nacional y lealtad vernacular en el español hablado en Andalucía [Identity and linguistic variation: National prestige and vernacular loyalty in the Spanish spoken in Andalusia]. In Georg Bossong & Francisco Báez de Aguilar-González (eds.), *Identidades lingüísticas en la España autonómica*, 107–150. Frankfurt am Main: Vervuert. Madrid: Iberoamericana.

Villena-Ponsoda, Juan Andrés & Matilde Vida-Castro. 2020. Variation, identity and indexicality in southern Spanish: On the emergence of a new variety in urban Andalusia. In Massimo Cerruti & Stavroula Tsiplakou (eds.), *Intermediate language varieties: Koinai and regional standards in Europe*, 149–182. Amsterdam & Philadelphia, PA: John Benjamins.

Vitevich, Michael S. 2002. Influence of onset density on spoken-word recognition. *Journal of Experimental Psychology: Human Perception and Performance* 28(2). 270–278.

Wang, Jingtian, David Friedman, Walter Ritter & Michael Bersick. 2005. ERP correlates of involuntary attention capture by prosodic salience in speech. *Psycophysiology* 42(1). 43–55.

Weinreich, Uriel, William Labov & Marvin I. Herzog. 1968. Empirical foundations for a theory of language change. In W.P. Lehman & Yakov Malkiel (Eds.), *Directions for historical linguistics*, 95–195. Austin, TX: University of Texas.

Yaeger-Dror, Malcah. 1993. Linguistic analysis of dialect "correction" and its interaction with cognitive salience. *Language Variation and Change* 5(2). 189–224.

Yanes, Julio. 2013. La locución radiofónica en Canarias durante el franquismo [Radio locution in the Canary Islands during the Franco regime]. *Revista Internacional de Historia de la Comunicación* 1(1). 155–175.

Zhang, Qing. 2012. 'Carry shopping through to the end': Linguistic innovation in a Chinese television program. In Juan Manuel Hernández-Campoy & Juan Antonio Cutillas-Espinosa (eds.), *Style-shifting in public: New perspectives on stylistic variation*, 205–224. Amsterdam & Philadelphia, PA: John Benjamins.

Zipf, George K. 1965 [1935]. *The psychology of language: An introduction to dynamic philology*. Cambridge, MA: The MIT Press.

CHAPTER 6

Nuclear pitch accents in the assertive speech prosody of Acapulco, Mexico
Between lowland and highland Spanish

Pedro Martín-Butragueño
El Colegio de México, Mexico

This chapter studies certain aspects of assertive intonation in Acapulco, Mexico, using sociolinguistic interviews from the *Corpus oral del español de México*. It presents acoustic and phonetic analysis that focuses on the nuclear syllable and considers the type of boundary tone, tonal movement, syllable duration and the position of the tonal peak, while examining the effects of information structure, age, gender and educational level. The results show that information structure and age are significant in the distribution of nuclear pitch accents. The conclusions suggest a retraction pattern of the most prominent tonal configurations and the grouping of the prosody of Acapulco with central Mexican Spanish, although some degree of prosodic residue from the coast can also be observed.

Keywords: intonation, socioprosody, geoprosody, vernacular speech, Mexican Spanish

1. Introduction

The historical importance of Acapulco de Juárez, Mexico, is well known, especially its role as a gateway to the Pacific Ocean during the colonial era. During more recent times, since the mid-twentieth century, this port city has become known as an important tourist enclave – a development that has generated numerous opportunities for employment –, and it has maintained a close relationship with central Mexico. At present, Acapulco has a population of 779,566 (according to INEGI data for 2020; see also INEGI 2021: 17). Dialectologists have always regarded Acapulco as one of the most important enclaves on the west coast of North American Spanish (Lipski 2004: 303–304), and its linguistic features have generally been considered to fit the profile of lowland Spanish (see Section 2 below). However, little research has been conducted on this linguistic variety and its internal variation.

https://doi.org/10.1075/silv.31.06mar
© 2024 John Benjamins Publishing Company

The city is similarly not included in the *Atlas lingüístico de México* 'Linguistic atlas of Mexico' (Lope-Blanch 1990–2000), although this volume does include records of nearby towns and villages, such as Iguala, Chilpancingo, Tixtla, Ometepec, Cruz Grande, Tres Palos, Tecpan de Galeana, Petatlán, La Unión and Ciudad Altamirano. These could all be taken as relevant points of comparison in research, since they are all located in Guerrero, the same state as Acapulco. Nevertheless, a sociolinguistic reference study as well as research in general on the linguistic variety of Acapulco could prove incredibly useful for future research on the region. Current works on the Spanish of Acapulco include Reyes-Taboada (2014) regarding /-s/ and Martín-Butragueño (forthcoming), which analyses intonation in a discourse completion task (henceforth, DCT).

The latter of these two works as well as the present study form part of the research that bases on the *Corpus oral del español de México* 'Oral corpus of Mexican Spanish', or COEM (Martín-Butragueño et al. 2015). The COEM documents small sociolinguistic samples of fifteen cities across Mexico. The fieldwork has included reading tests, DCTs and sociolinguistic interviews among other research methods. Table 1 shows some of the results obtained by Martín-Butragueño (forthcoming) from the rather limited DCT data, presented so as to be comparable to the results of the present study, which analyses a broader set of data obtained from the sociolinguistic interviews. See the observations in (1) below for the phonetic description of the nuclear pitch accents.

Table 1. Distribution of nuclear pitch accents in assertive statements from a discourse completion task conducted in Acapulco. $N=54$. (Adapted from Martín-Butragueño forthcoming, Table 2)

Pattern	F (%)	Pitch accent	F (%)
Flat	29.7	L*	24.1
		H*	5.6
Rising	70.4	L+H*	24.1
		L+¡H*	46.3

As is evident in Table 1, nuclear rising pitch accents are predominant in the DCT. The results of the analysis detailed in the following pages, presented below in Table 2, show a similar distribution, though a higher percentage of rising cases can be observed.

2. Between central Mexico and the coast

This study assumes that the prosody of Acapulco is located between two large areas of influence: on the one hand are the "coastal" or "lowland" varieties, with linguistic forms that may be reminiscent of those of the Caribbean basin (cf. Moreno de Alba 2001; Lipski 2004; Moreno-Fernández 2020, etc.), and on the other are the varieties of central Mexico, their frequent features including certain types of tonal rises in the nuclear syllable even in assertive statements with broad focus (Mendoza-Vázquez 2014; Martín-Butragueño & Mendoza-Vázquez 2018; Martín-Butragueño 2019; Mendoza-Vázquez 2021). Regarding the first, the use of traditional dialect along a large part of the Pacific coast (Lope-Blanch 1996; Martín-Butragueño 2023) suggests that the vernacular (or traditional) variety of Acapulco also includes certain lowland elements. As regards the second, the central megalopolitan varieties are increasingly influencing the varieties occurring in the rest of the country, and Acapulco is unlikely to be an exception (Martín-Butragueño 2020a).

In light of the results obtained by Martín-Butragueño (forthcoming) in the analysis of the DCT, presented above in Table 1, the hypothesis for this study is that the sociolinguistic interviews confirm the tendency of intonational patterns in Acapulco speech to show similarity to the varieties of central Mexico. Any patterns of variation or change observed in Acapulco prosody should also show such similarity.

3. Methodology: The use of interviews in socioprosody

In order to test the hypothesis, this study analyses the ten sociolinguistic interviews with individuals that are registered in the COEM.[1] More specifically, it analyses the characteristics of the nuclear pitch accents in 200 assertive statements (10 participants × 20 cases each) based on various phonetic labels and acoustic measurements, which are contrasted with a number of linguistic and social variables. For the most part, the data were selected sequentially, beginning in the middle of each sound recording. The standard format of the original recordings was WAV, stereo (later converted to monaural), 44,100 Hz, 16-bit.

For the purpose of this analysis, the participants are stratified by educational level (4 with a low educational level, i.e. secondary education or lower, 6 with

---

1. The fieldwork for Acapulco was performed between 2012 and 2015 by Stefany Olivar, Laura Herrera and Alberto Montoya. The interviews were subsequently catalogued, transcribed and reviewed by Stefany Olivar, Joyce Avelar, Lorena Gamper and Carmen Aguilar.

a medium–high educational level, i.e. higher than secondary education); age (3 young speakers: 20–34 years, 3 middle-aged speakers: 35–54 years, 4 older speakers: 55 years and over); and gender (5 men, 5 women). Given the small sample size, the analysis contained in the following pages should be considered a case study.

The dependent variable in this analysis is the type of nuclear pitch accent, transcribed by means of an autosegmental-metrical notation system of the Sp_ToBi type (Beckman et al. 2002; Face & Prieto 2007; Estebas-Vilaplana & Prieto 2008; Prieto & Roseano 2010; Hualde & Prieto 2015, etc.). The analysis distinguishes between the following phonetic variants:

(1) Nuclear pitch accents
    a. L*: flat low or falling tonal movement from the previous point of measurement
    b. H*: relatively flat high or very slightly rising tonal movement (<1.5 semitones (st)) from the previous point of measurement
    c. L+H*: moderately rising tonal movement (≥ 1.5 st and <3.0 st) from the previous point of measurement
    d. L+¡H*: clearly rising tonal movement (≥ 3.0 st) from the previous point of measurement

The phonetic notation of (1) is supported by several acoustic measurements. The tonal peaks and valleys and the tonal movement in the nuclear and the final syllable (see Figure 3), as well as the duration of these and the temporal position of the peak have all been measured (see Martín-Butragueño & Mendoza-Vázquez 2018).

The analysis studies the effect of a number of linguistic and sociolinguistic factors on nuclear pitch accent: the type of boundary tone (Tables 3 and 6), the type of tonal peak alignment (Tables 7 and 8), the informative function of the segment in which the nuclear syllable is located (Table 9), and the participants' age (Tables 10–12), gender, and educational level.

The acoustic analysis was performed using Praat (Boersma & Weening 1992–2021), and certain processes relating to sound editing were carried out using Adobe Audition (Adobe 2021). Tonal movements were calculated in hertz (Hz) and in semitones (st), their duration was calculated in milliseconds (ms) and their intensity in decibels (dB). The last measure was only used as an auxiliary tool to establish the syllabic divisions. Descriptive statistical processing was performed using Stata/MP 17 (StataCorp 1985–2021), and multivariate regression analysis using Language Variation Suite (Scrivner & Díaz-Campos n.d., 2016).

The use of interviews in socioprosody is deemed relevant since they provide more spontaneous material than various types of questionnaires. In addition, interviews as a basis for research represent a methodology that has offered excel-

Chapter 6. Nuclear pitch accents in the assertive speech prosody of Acapulco, Mexico

lent results in previous sociolinguistic research. Thus, the findings of this study are based on a proven methodology, and similar tools to those used in studies on other linguistic variables can be employed.

4. Results

Table 2 shows the general distribution of the different nuclear pitch accents in the present study. Flat patterns only occur in 50 cases, that is, in 25.0% of the data, and are subdivided into L* (22.0%) and H* (3.0%). Despite the low recurrence of the H* pitch accent, it should still be viewed as separate, as it often shows a slight rise, in contrast to the more obviously falling pattern of L* (see Figure 3). Rising patterns, on the other hand, are much more common, appearing a total of 150 times, that is, in 75% of the data. The two variants considered in this regard, L+H* and L+¡H*, appear in different proportions: the moderate rise of L+H* occurs 48 times (24.0%), while the clear rise of L+¡H* occurs 102 times (51.0%). In other words, nuclear early rising pitch accents predominate in assertive statements from Acapulco, the most prevalent being those with clear rise above +3.0 st.

Table 2. Distribution of nuclear pitch accents in assertive statements from sociolinguistic interviews conducted in Acapulco. $N = 200$

Pattern	F (%)	Pitch accent	F (%)
Flat	50 (25.0)	L*	44 (22.0)
		H*	6 (3.0)
Rising	150 (75.0)	L+H*	48 (24.0)
		L+¡H*	102 (51.0)

Figure 1 is an example of an assertive statement with an L* nuclear pitch accent. Such figures show the oscillogram at the top and the spectrogram in the middle, on which are marked the Fo line, or melodic trajectory (darker points) and the intensity line (lighter points). Below this are noted the transcription, breaks, and pitch accents and boundary tones. After the peak reached in the first prosodic word, *me gusta* 'I like it', the utterance shows a progressive tonal declination that includes a section of creaky (laryngealised) voice ([m̰] in -*me*-) and a voiceless final. The number "1" separates two prosodic words, and the number "4" marks the right border of the phonological utterance. See below for boundary tones labelled "L%".

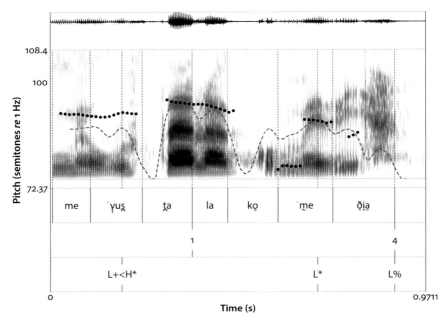

Figure 1. *[...] me gusta la comedia* 'I like comedy' (AC–005–C00–1JM–12). Example of an assertive statement with an L* nuclear pitch accent

Figure 2, on the other hand, is an example of an L+¡H* nuclear pitch accent. The tonal peak of the utterance is maintained through to the final syllable, which begins with high tonality and ends voiceless.

The four phonetic nuclear pitch accents considered in this study have been combined with three boundary tones (Table 3): L% for falling or low, !H% for medium, and HL% for a complex boundary that remains high at first and then falls. Some of the !H% boundary tones observed raise doubts as to whether they really do mark final intonational phrases, even though this is suggested by the context. As for the cases of HL%, despite the focus being on assertive statements, some suggest the activation of a secondary meaning, such as irony, complaint, obviousness, etc. It should be noted that no rising boundaries (H%) were observed. Overall, the role of !H% and HL% in the sample is largely residual, and the relationship between boundary tone and nuclear pitch accent is not significant ($p = .840$), probably due to the general and homogeneous pre-eminence of L% in all nuclear pitch accents. L% represents 183 cases, that is, it occurs in 88.5% of the data. Nevertheless, as shown below (Table 8), the relationship between boundary tone and position of the tonal peak is significant.

Chapter 6. Nuclear pitch accents in the assertive speech prosody of Acapulco, Mexico

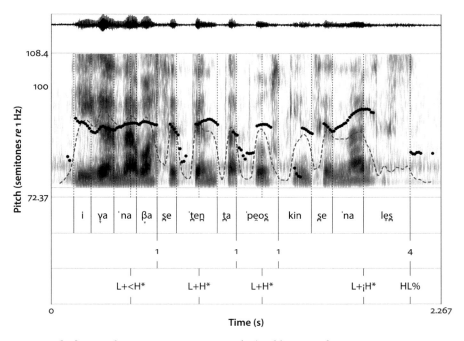

Figure 2. *[...] y ganaba setenta pesos quincenales* 'and he earned seventy pesos every two weeks' (AC-010-C11-2MM-12). Example of an assertive statement with an L+¡H* nuclear pitch accent[2]

Table 3. Distribution of phonetic nuclear pitch accents and boundary tones. *N* = 200

	L% (%)	!H% (%)	HL% (%)	Total (%)
L*	41 (93.2)	0 (0.0)	3 (6.8)	44 (22.0)
H*	6 (100.0)	0 (0.0)	0 (0.0)	6 (3.0)
L+H*	44 (91.7)	2 (4.2)	2 (4.2)	48 (24.0)
L+¡H*	92 (90.2)	3 (2.9)	7 (6.9)	102 (51.0)
Total (%)	183 (91.5)	5 (2.5)	12 (6.0)	200

$\chi^2 = 2.7473$; *d.f.* = 6; *pr.* = 0.840.
Cramér's *V* = 0.0829.

---

[2]. The boundary tone in this example has been labelled HL% because the tonal peak is reached within the final syllable (+23 ms from its beginning). The F0 remains high for a while (about 64 ms), and this sustain is clearly perceived by the author.

The phonetic behaviour of the four nuclear pitch accents (L*, H*, L+H* and L+¡H*) reveals interesting facts. Table 4 shows the average measurements in semitones of the tonal movements observed when comparing the tonal valley of the prenuclear syllable with the tonal peak associated[3] with the nucleus (in Spanish, the last stressed syllable in an intonational phrase) (a), and the tonal peak with the utterance-final Fo value (b), omitting cases of devoicing and creaky voice (see below for comments on such cases). Hence, Table 4 includes the measurements of 195 nuclei and 157 boundaries, out of a total of 200 data at each position. These measurements involve a certain degree of simplification, as only the tonal peak and the final tonal point are compared, regardless of the specific type of boundary tone. To facilitate the calculation, the initial reference point is given a score of 0.0, which then results in the figures for the distances for (a) and (b).

Table 4. Average tonal movements in st (only modal voice). $N = 195$ nuclei, 157 boundaries

Pitch accent	Reference point	Peak (a)	Utterance-final point (b)
L*	0.0	−0.1	−2.5
H*	0.0	1.3	−2.9
L+H*	0.0	2.4	−3.4
L+¡H*	0.0	5.6	−4.6

Figure 3 maps the data in Table 4. As can be observed, the distances in (a) increase when comparing the pitch accents from top to bottom, whereas those in (b) decrease. Regarding (a), only L* shows a very slight fall at the peak (−0.1 st), while H*, L+H* and L+¡H* all rise, with each of the three rising by an average of approximately twice that of the previous one. As for (b), all four pitch accents always fall on average, and the higher the previous tonal peak, the greater these falls are.

Cases of devoicing and more sporadic cases of creaky voice, classified together as "weak" from here on, are also revealing, as Table 5 shows. Only 5 nuclei fall into this category, and all are L*-type. On the other hand, of the total boundaries, 21.5% are weak, the proportion being greater the less prominence the nuclear pitch accent shows. Thus, 40.9% of L* cases are linked to weak boundaries, compared to 13.7% of L+¡H* cases. The proportion of weak cases at the boundary, classified as "L"-type, is therefore a good predictor of nuclear pitch accent.

---

3. For the concepts of association and alignment, see Gussenhoven (2004: 148–152): generally speaking, a pitch accent is associated with a tone-bearing unit (in Spanish, typically a stressed syllable), while a boundary tone is aligned with the edge of a prosodic unit.

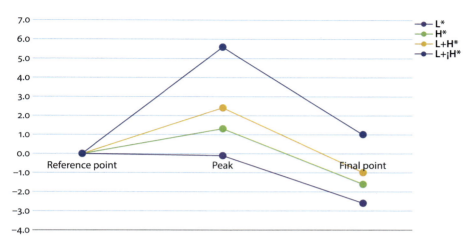

Figure 3. Configuration in st of the four nuclear pitch accents

Table 5. Weak cases (devoicing and creaky voice) at the nucleus and the boundary

Nuclear pitch accent	Total	Weak nucleus	Weak boundary	Weak boundary (%)
L*	44	5	18	40.9
H*	6	0	2	33.3
L+H*	48	0	9	18.8
L+¡H*	102	0	14	13.7
Total	200	5	43	21.5

Two further important aspects in the description of this linguistic material are the duration of the nuclear and final syllables as well as the position of the tonal peak with respect to the nuclear syllable.

Table 6 presents the average length of nuclear syllables and syllables appearing in juncture position. The greater the prominence of the nuclear syllable (that is, the higher the pitch, in this case), the greater its duration, which ranges between 188 ms for L* and 220 ms for L+H*, although the differences are not substantial, since this corresponds to only 32 ms. As for the junctures, the syllables that align L% and HL% last about the same (190 ms and 191 ms), even though the expectation would have been for a longer duration of the relatively complex patterns of HL%. !H% presents the longest syllables, which could confirm that they do not mark final intonational phrases. In general, nuclear syllables have a longer duration than final syllables (209 ms vs. 191 ms).

Table 6. Average length of nuclear syllables according to their pitch accent, and of final syllables according to their boundary tone

Pitch accent (nuclear syllables)	Average length (ms)	Boundary tone (final syllables)	Average length (ms)
L*	188	L%	190
H*	191	!H%	233
L+H*	209	HL%	191
L+¡H*	220		
General average	209	General average	191

The phonetic position of the tonal peak with regard to the nuclear syllable is similarly interesting (Table 7), as early and very early peaks (cf. Martín-Butragueño & Mendoza-Vázquez 2018) constitute 94.0% of cases. In each case, the distance between the tonal peak and the right edge of the nuclear syllable was measured. The results are grouped into four classes: (a) delayed peaks, when the peak occurs beyond the nuclear syllable, that is, in the final syllable, (b) early peaks aligned exactly on the right edge of the nuclear syllable, (c) early peaks reached near the end of the nuclear syllable, specifically within the 15.0% (as an arbitrary partition) corresponding to the final part of the length of the syllable, and (d) very early peaks, when the peak is reached before these final 15.0%.

The relationship between peak position and specific pitch accent is not significant ($\chi^2 = 12.4148$, $d.f. = 9$, $pr. = 0.191$, Cramér's $V = 0.1438$), but the relationship between peak position and general type of pitch accent is (flat vs. rising, Table 7). It must be considered that the abundance of very early peaks in the flat types (80.0%) derives precisely from the falling character of the melody in many of those cases. The most interesting fact regarding this relationship is probably that 56.0% of rising pitch accents also show a very early peak.

Table 7. Position of the tonal peak in relation to the flat or rising type of pitch accent

Pitch accent type	Delayed	Early (=0.0%)	Early (<15.0%)	Very early	Total
Flat	3 (6.0)	2 (4.0)	5 (10.0)	40 (80.0)	50 (25.0)
Rising	9 (6.0)	18 (12.0)	39 (26.0)	84 (56.0)	150 (75.0)
Total	12 (6.0)	20 (10.0)	44 (22.0)	124 (62.0)	200

$\chi^2 = 10.2475$; $d.f. = 3$; $pr. = 0.017$.
Cramér's $V = 0.2264$.

A notable finding is that the relationship between the alignment of the tonal peak and the type of boundary tone is also significant (Table 8), although this may be due, in part, to the cases of HL%, since the delayed peaks have almost

Chapter 6. Nuclear pitch accents in the assertive speech prosody of Acapulco, Mexico   129

always been interpreted as part of the boundary tone. On the other hand, the !H% boundaries are usually linked to very early peaks, while the L% boundaries appear to be more distributed, though these also occur more frequently with very early peaks.

Table 8. Tonal peak position and boundary tone

Boundary tone	Delayed	Early (=0.0%)	Early (<15.0%)	Very early	Total
L%	1 (0.6)	20 (10.9)	43 (23.5)	119 (65.0)	183 (91.5)
!H%	0 (0.0)	0 (0.0)	1 (20.0)	4 (80.0)	5 (2.5)
HL%	11 (91.7)	0 (0.0)	0 (0.0)	1 (8.3)	12 (6.0)
Total	12 (6.0)	20 (10.0)	44 (22.0)	124 (62.0)	200

$\chi^2 = 166.9463$; $d.f. = 6$; $pr. = 0.000$.
Cramér's $V = 0.6460$.

The informative function in which the nucleus participates as part of the nuclear configuration has a significant effect in relation to pitch accent (Table 9). The most frequent pitch accent in all cases, for broad foci (BF), narrow foci (NF), contrastive foci (CF) and others, is L+¡H* (see examples in (2)). Although L* is the second most frequent pitch accent for BF, it only occurs in a limited number of cases for NF and CF. All 6 cases of H* occur in BF, as do two out of every three cases of L+H*. In other words, pitch accents are not fully specialised in a single type of focus (cf. Martín-Butragueño & Mendoza-Vázquez 2018). Although L* is more typical of BF, the geoprosodic effect of choosing L+¡H*, seconded by L+H*, is above the informative effect. This fact is extremely important, as discussed below in Sections 6 and 7.

Contrarily, it should be noted that the relationship between informative function and position of the tonal peak is not significant ($\chi^2 = 7.4556$, $d.f. = 9$, $pr. = 0.590$, Cramér's $V = 0.1115$).

Table 9. Nuclear pitch accents and informative function. $N = 200$

Pitch accent	BF (%)	NF (%)	CF (%)	Other functions (%)	Total (%)
L*	35 (79.6)	7 (15.9)	1 (2.3)	1 (2.3)	44 (22.0)
H*	6 (100.0)	0 (0.0)	0 (0.0)	0 (0.0)	6 (3.0)
L+H*	32 (66.7)	13 (27.1)	3 (6.3)	0 (0.0)	48 (24.0)
L+¡H*	59 (57.8)	20 (19.6)	19 (18.6)	4 (3.9)	102 (51.0)
Total (%)	132 (66.0)	40 (20.0)	23 (11.5)	5 (2.5)	200

$\chi^2 = 17.8732$; $d.f. = 9$; $pr. = 0.037$.
Cramér's $V = 0.1726$.

In (2), three examples with different types of foci are noted. (2a) shows a case of BF, (2b) a case of NF, and (2c) a case of CF. In all three, the nuclear syllable (*gran-, to-, frí-*) is given the pitch accent L+¡H*.

(2) a. *Mi necesidad en aprender era muy **grande***
'My need to learn was great' (AC–004–Coo–1AH–12)

  b. *– ¿Y aquí qué le gusta cocinar?*
*– Pues de **todo***
'– And what do you like to cook here?
– Well, everything' (AC–007–Coo–1MM–12)

  c. *Aquí el calorcito, allá está el **frío***
'Here the warm weather, there is the cold' (AC–005–Coo–1JM–12)

Educational level is not significant when crossing low and medium–high educational level with pitch accent (χ^2 = 0.3101, *d. f.* = 3, *pr.* = 0.958, Cramér's V = 0.0394). Likewise, no significant effects can be observed when the pitch accents are grouped in any other way, i.e. as flat vs. rising or as most prominent (L+¡H*) vs. the others. The same applies to the crossing between educational level and position of the tonal peak.

Gender does not show a significant relationship either. The crossing between gender and pitch accents is not significant (χ^2 = c.1301, *d. f.* = 3, *pr.* = 0.988, Cramér's V = 0.0255), neither is the crossing between gender and flat vs. rising pitch accents, nor that between gender and prominent vs. non-prominent pitch accents. The crossing of gender with position of the tonal peak is also not significant, although it is close to being so (χ^2 = 6.7034, *d. f.* = 3, *pr.* = 0.082, Cramér's V = 0.1831), with men presenting a greater number of very early peaks than women (54.0% vs. 46.0%).

The most relevant social variable in the Acapulco sample is age. Table 10 shows that the crossing between age group and pitch accents is close to significance, with a greater presence of the clearly rising L+¡H* pitch accent in older people, while the more moderately rising L+H* and the low flat or falling L* are more common among middle-aged and young people.

Table 10. Nuclear pitch accents and three age groups. N = 200

Pitch accent	Young (%)	Middle-aged (%)	Older (%)	Total (%)
L*	17 (38.6)	14 (31.8)	13 (29.6)	44 (22.0)
H*	3 (50.0)	1 (16.7)	2 (33.3)	6 (3.0)
L+H*	18 (37.5)	16 (33.3)	14 (29.2)	48 (24.0)
L+¡H*	22 (21.6)	29 (28.4)	51 (50.0)	102 (51.0)
Total (%)	60 (30.0)	60 (30.0)	80 (40.0)	200

χ^2 = 11.1037; *d. f.* = 6; *pr.* = 0.085.
Cramér's V = 0.1666.

Chapter 6. Nuclear pitch accents in the assertive speech prosody of Acapulco, Mexico 131

The crossing between age and flat vs. rising pitch accents is not significant ($\chi^2 = 3.8889$, *d. f.* = 2, *pr.* = 0.143, Cramér's V = 0.1394); nevertheless, the crossing between age and prominent (L+¡H*) vs. non-prominent pitch accents is, as shown in Table 11, which also has a Cramér's V of 0.2270. The distribution observed emphasises the pre-eminence of L+¡H* among older people, whereas middle-aged and especially young people exhibit less occurrences of the more prominent pitch accent and a greater number of the other three variants.

Table 11. Nuclear pitch accents (prominent vs. non-prominent) and three age groups. N = 200

Pitch accent	Young (%)	Middle-aged (%)	Older (%)	Total (%)
Prominent	22 (21.6)	29 (28.4)	51 (50.0)	102 (51.0)
Others	38 (38.8)	31 (31.6)	29 (29.6)	98 (49.0)
Total (%)	60 (30.0)	60 (30.0)	80 (40.0)	200

$\chi^2 = 10.3075$; *d. f.* = 2; *pr.* = 0.006.
Cramér's V = 0.2270.

The relationship between age and position of the tonal peak is significant only when considering the two rising pitch accents (Table 12). Very early peaks are the most common pattern for all age groups, the second most common being early peaks reached during the final 15.0% of the syllable. Older people show the highest percentages for both, at 41.7% and 38.5%, respectively. This circumstance may contribute to the significance of the cross tabulation with respect to χ^2.

Table 12. Tonal peak position and age group (rising pitch accents). N = 150

Tonal peak position	Young (%)	Middle-aged (%)	Older (%)	Total (%)
Delayed	0 (0.0)	0 (0.0)	9 (100.0)	9 (6.0)
Early (= 0.0%)	5 (27.8)	7 (38.9)	6 (33.3)	18 (12.0)
Early (<15.0%)	12 (30.8)	12 (30.8)	15 (38.5)	39 (26.0)
Very early	23 (27.4)	26 (31.0)	35 (41.7)	84 (56.0)
Total (%)	40 (26.7)	45 (30.0)	65 (43.3)	150

$\chi^2 = 13.2298$; *d. f.* = 6; *pr.* = 0.040.
Cramér's V = 0.2100.

5.   A multivariate analysis

A multivariate analysis helps to better delineate some of the facts that have so far been examined separately. For this purpose, having considered the descriptive results (Tables 2–12), the prominent or non-prominent character of the pitch accent was taken as the dependent variable (that is, L+¡H* vs. all others). The independent variables are the following: (a) the very early position of the tonal peak vs. all others, (b) BF's informative function vs. all others, (c) the age of the participants, older vs. young and middle-aged, (d) their gender, men vs. women, and (e) their educational level, low vs. medium–high. A stepwise regression (Table 13) was performed by means of the application Language Variation Suite (Scrivner & Díaz-Campos n.d., 2016), in order to establish a multivariate model for prominent pitch accents (L+¡H*).

Table 13. Variation related to nuclear pitch accents: Stepwise regression. Application value=L+¡H*. $N = 200$

Initial and Final Model – LRT (Log Likelihood Ratio) criterion

Stepwise Model Path – Analysis of Deviance Table

Initial Model: Pitch accent type ~ Educational level + Age + Gender + Tonal peak position + Informative function

Final Model: Pitch accent type ~ Age + Informative function

	Step	D.f.	Deviance	Resid. D.f.	Resid. Dev.	AIC
1				194	259.2974	282.3374
2	Gender	1	0.05171087	195	259.3491	278.5491
3	Educational level	1	0.04428135	196	259.3933	274.7533
4	Tonal peak position	1	2.77632848	197	262.1697	273.6897

The model in Table 13 rejects any thoughts that position of the tonal peak, educational level and gender could play a significant role in the selection of the most prominent pitch accents (L+¡H*). Nevertheless, it does identify two significant effects in the following order: (a) the participant not belonging to the oldest age group disadvantages the use of L+¡H* (estimate = −0.8820, z-value = −2.920, pr. < 0.01), and (b) the pitch accent not occurring in BF favours the use of L+¡H* (*estimate* = 0.7737, *z-value* = 2.467, *pr.* < 0.05). In other words, regarding L+¡H*, age > information structure, or, more precisely, older people > NF, CF (and other functions). Of course, this does not mean that there are no other relevant aspects, as, for example, L+¡H* is also fairly common with BF. These, however, are all variable trends and not categorical specialisations.

Model Summary

Call: glm(formula = Pitch accent type ~ Age + Informative function, family = binomial,
data = plotData(), na.action = na.omit)

Deviance Residuals:

Min	1Q	Median	3Q	Max
−1.6604	−0.9478	0.7620	1.0912	1.4259

Coefficients:

	Estimate	Std. Error	z-value	Pr(>|z|)
(Intercept)	0.3145	0.2533	1.241	0.2144
Age: not older	−0.8820	0.3020	−2.920	0.0035**
Informative function: not BF	0.7737	0.3136	2.467	0.0136*

Signif. codes: 0 '***' 0.001 '**' 0.01 '*' 0.05 '.' 0.1 ' ' 1

(Dispersion parameter for binomial family taken to be 1)

Null deviance: 277.18 on 199 degrees of freedom

Residual deviance: 262.17 on 197 degrees of freedom

AIC: 268.17

Number of Fisher Scoring iterations: 4

6.   In search of vernacular prosody

There is a group of 18 cases where a so-called "coastal accent" or "lowland accent" is apparently easily perceived, at least by a number of speakers from Mexico City. Crossing this set of cases with information structure, educational level and gender does not produce significant results, neither does crossing it with age group, although this does produce results close to significance ($\chi^2 = 5.4029$, $d.f. = 2$, $pr. = 0.067$, Cramér's $V = 0.1644$). The example in Figure 4 helps to explain the characteristics of these "coastal" utterances.

The Fo (thick dark line) in Figure 4 shows two delayed pitch accents in the pre-nucleus and a slight fall in the prenuclear syllable (*mo-*) that continues in the final syllable (*-da*), giving rise to a falling boundary (L%). The nuclear syllable (*-li-*) lasts 157 ms, exhibits a pitch rise of +3.2 st, and is participating in a case of NF. The tonal peak in this nuclear syllable is reached at 116 ms, that is, at 26.1% before the end of the syllable, meaning it falls within the category of very early peaks.

The analysis of the co-occurrence of prominent pitch accents and very early peaks indicates promising results: 13 out of the 18 "coastal" utterances are L+¡H* and 11 present very early peaks, with 8 combining both characteristics. However,

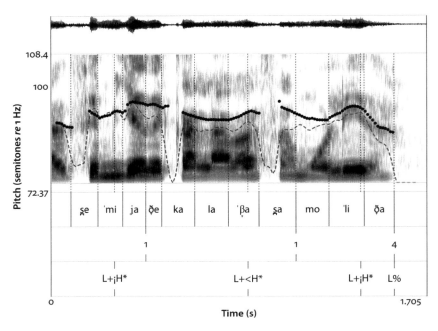

Figure 4. *[…] semilla de calabaza molida* 'ground pumpkin seed' (AC–001–C11–2AM–12). Example of a "coastal" utterance[4]

these proportions are similar to those of the overall sample, and a clear pattern cannot yet be identified. A perception test is required to establish the meaning of the facts.[5]

7. Towards a discussion

The data set analysed in this chapter shows remarkable internal homogeneity. On the one hand, the majority of pitch accents present a rising structure, albeit to varying degrees, and are largely accompanied by falling boundaries. Many also exhibit early or very early tonal alignment. On the other hand, neither educational level nor gender present significant patterns that suggest intra-community differentiation.

---

4. L+<H* represents a delayed pitch accent. The difference between L+<H* and L+¡<H* is phonetic: L+<H* shows a moderate rise (≥1.5 st and <3.0 st) and L+¡<H* a clear rise (≥3.0 st). See Ortega (2019) for a discussion of various Caribbean pitch accents, with some cases similar to figure 4.

5. An additional statistical test considered the crossing between the position of the tonal peak (very early vs. all others) and age, gender and educational level for only the L+H* and L+¡H* pitch accents. However, no significant results were observed.

Two factors have, however, emerged as meaningful. First, information structure shows a significant relationship with clearly rising pitch accents and foci that are not BF, that is, mainly NF and CF. Most interestingly, many cases of BF also exhibit rising pitch accents in the nuclear syllable, a finding that coincides with previous analysis conducted on the speech prosody of central Mexico (Martín-Butragueño & Mendoza-Vázquez 2018). The second factor that has proved to be of great relevance is age. The most prominent nuclear pitch accents (L+¡H*) occur less frequently at lower ages, a fact that also coincides with the results of previous research on central Mexico. In the present results, although one can only speak of a stratification by age and not of a change in progress under way in Acapulco, the pattern does indeed correspond to that observed, for example, in Mexico City, where it has been suggested that a change is indeed under way regarding a retraction of the most prominent pitch accents (Martín-Butragueño 2011, 2020b).

In relation to the hypothesis of this study, the data from Acapulco allow for the contrast of two historically, geographically and socially significant components: central varieties and lowland varieties. At least to a certain extent, the Acapulco data are compatible with the levelling, de-dialectalisation and retraction processes affecting the most salient features observed in central Mexican Spanish. These processes are being promoted by the central megalopolis, with Mexico City at its core (Martín-Butragueño 2020a), and are affecting other Mexican varieties – and perhaps all other varieties of North American Spanish as well – in various ways and to varying degrees (cf. Congosto Martín & Martín-Butragueño forthcoming). In the field of speech prosody, this relationship between central Mexico and other regions can be observed in the rising pitch of the tonal nucleus and in final devoicing. Furthermore, as has been stated, clearly rising pitch accents occur least frequently among the youngest speakers of Acapulco, a finding that would be compatible with the idea of a retraction of the more marked features. The role of early and very early tonal peaks, on the other hand, is unclear, since, although they have been documented in different central Mexican varieties (Martín-Butragueño & Mendoza-Vázquez 2018) and in situations of linguistic contact (Olivar forthcoming), they have been observed very frequently in the data from Acapulco.

Contrarily, several possible cases of prosodic residue that may be linked to "coastal" speech are also present, although establishing the role of these elements will require substantial further research. An option would be to analyse the entirety of the recordings collected during the 1970s in the state to which Acapulco belongs, Guerrero, and within the framework of the *Atlas lingüístico de México* 'Linguistic atlas of Mexico' (Lope-Blanch 1990–2000). Such analysis would serve two purposes: it would consider the geographical environment and provide a real-time image of the linguistic records.[6]

8. Conclusions

Several facts must be highlighted. Firstly, the results obtained here are compatible with those obtained in a previous study based on a DCT (Martín-Butragueño forthcoming). As a methodological reflection, DCTs tend to offer a generally appropriate picture, whereas sociolinguistic interviews confirm the analysis and offer a detailed picture based on a comparatively more spontaneous type of speech. In line with this, the data from the interviews show a higher proportion of rising pitch accents, which suggests a certain stylistic differentiation between the DCT and the sociolinguistic interviews, with the DCT presenting a slightly more careful and the interviews a slightly more casual style.

Secondly, certain linguistic aspects emerged as significant. The most significant is that the majority of the nuclear pitch accents in assertive utterances from Acapulco exhibit a tonal rise, which may be either insignificant, moderate or prominent. Furthermore, many of these rising pitch accents show early or very early alignment of the tonal peak with respect to the nuclear syllable. Regarding information structure, there is a significant correlation between pitch accents with clearer rises and NF and CF. Nevertheless, this relationship is far from categorical, as many cases of BF include rising nuclear pitch accents as well, and some cases of NF and CF lack such a tonal rise.

The interview participants analysed in this study show homogeneous behaviour. However, age has been found to be significant, with older people presenting more prominent nuclear pitch accents and younger people showing a tendency to use less prominent pitch accents. It is premature to establish whether this is a stratification by age or an ongoing change, but the retraction observed is similar to that proposed in connection with central Mexican Spanish, based on stratification data and the behaviour of various immigrant groups (Martín-Butragueño 2011, 2020b).

The linguistic findings and sociolinguistic patterns observed in the Acapulco data substantiate the prosodic grouping of this variety of Spanish with those of central Mexico. However, the data also exhibit certain elements that have been informally called "coastal", the distribution of which requires further analysis in other data from Acapulco as well as from various nearby towns.

---

6. I am grateful to Hugo Morales for the information that, at GIADI–1, Daniel Hernández-Bejarano (2021) presented a paper on the nuclear configuration of Costa Chican intonation, but I am unaware of its surely very interesting content.

Acknowledgments

I thank the two anonymous reviewers for their comments, the editors – Antonio Ávila and Matilde Vida – for their continual attention to word limits, and Weselina Gacinska for her stylistic review of the manuscript. It is a privilege to participate in the tribute to such an outstanding researcher as Juan Villena.

References

Adobe. 2021. *Adobe Audition*. Version 14.4.0.38. Adobe. https://www.adobe.com/mx/products/audition.html. (13 May, 2022.)

Beckman, Mary E., Manuel Díaz-Campos, Julia Tevis McGory & Terrell A. Morgan. 2002. Intonation across Spanish, in the Tones and Break Indices framework. *Probus* 14. 9–36.

Boersma, Paul & David Weening. 1992–2021. *Praat. Doing phonetics by computer*. Version 6.1.38. Amsterdam: University of Amsterdam. https://www.fon.hum.uva.nl/praat/. (13 May, 2022.)

Congosto-Martín, Yolanda & Pedro Martín-Butragueño (eds.). Forthcoming. *La entonación del español americano septentrional: Estudios geoprosódicos* [Intonation in septentrional American Spanish: Geoprosodic studies]. Bern: Peter Lang.

Estebas-Vilaplana, Eva & Pilar Prieto. 2008. La notación prosódica del español: Una revisión del Sp_ToBI [The prosodic notation of Spanish: A review of Sp_ToBI]. *Estudios de Fonética Experimental* 17. 263–283.

Face, Timothy L. & Pilar Prieto. 2007. Rising accents in Castilian Spanish: A revision of Sp-ToBI. *Journal of Portuguese Linguistics* 6(1). 117–146.

Gussenhoven, Carlos. 2004. *The phonology of tone and intonation*. Cambridge: Cambridge University Press.

Hernández-Bejarano, Daniel. 2021. Los patrones entonativos del habla costachiquense del Estado de Guerrero: Un estudio preliminar sobre la configuración nuclear [The intonation patterns of the Costa Chican spoken in the state of Guerrero: A preliminary study on nuclear configuration]. *Primer Encuentro Internacional del Grupo de Investigación en Análisis del Discurso Oral y Escrito (GIADI)*. Querétaro: Universidad Autónoma de Querétaro.

Hualde, José Ignacio & Pilar Prieto. 2015. Intonational variation in Spanish: European and American varieties. In Sónia Frota & Pilar Prieto (eds.), *Intonation in Romance*, 350–391. Oxford: Oxford University Press.

INEGI (Instituto Nacional de Estadística y Geografía). 2020. *México en cifras [...] Acapulco de Juárez, Guerrero* [Mexico in numbers [...] Acapulco de Juárez, Guerrero]. https://www.inegi.org.mx/app/areasgeograficas/. (23 September, 2021.)

INEGI (Instituto Nacional de Estadística y Geografía). 2021. *Panorama sociodemográfico de Guerrero. Censo de población y vivienda 2020* [Sociodemographic panorama of Guerrero. 2020 population and housing census]. Aguascalientes City: INEGI. https://www.inegi.org.mx/contenidos/productos/prod_serv/contenidos/espanol/bvinegi/productos/nueva_estruc/702825197858.pdf. (23 September, 2021.)

Lipski, John M. 2004. *El español de América* [The Spanish of America], 3rd edn. Madrid: Cátedra.

Lope-Blanch, Juan M. (dir.). 1990–2000. *Atlas lingüístico de México* [Linguistic atlas of Mexico]. Mexico City: El Colegio de México, Universidad Nacional Autónoma de México & Fondo de Cultura Económica.

Lope-Blanch, Juan M. 1996. México. In Manuel Alvar (dir.), *Manual de dialectología hispánica: El español de América* [Manual of Spanish dialectology: The Spanish of America], 81–89. Barcelona: Ariel.

Martín-Butragueño, Pedro. 2011. Estratificación sociolingüística de la entonación circunfleja mexicana [Sociolinguistic stratification of Mexican circumflex intonation]. In Pedro Martín-Butragueño (ed.), *Primer encuentro de cambio y variación lingüística: Realismo en el análisis de corpus orales*, 93–121. Mexico City: El Colegio de México.

Martín-Butragueño, Pedro. 2019. *Fonología variable del español de México. II: Prosodia enunciativa, tomo I* [The variable phonology of Mexican Spanish. II: Enunciative prosody, book I]. Mexico City: El Colegio de México.

Martín-Butragueño, Pedro. 2020a. Building the megalopolis: Dialectal leveling and language contact in Mexico City. In Andrew Lynch (ed.), *The Routledge handbook of Spanish in the global city*, 234–274. London & New York, NY: Routledge.

Martín-Butragueño, Pedro. 2020b. Historia de dos medidas: Contacto entonativo en la ciudad de México [A history of two measures: Intonational contact in Mexico City]. In María Ángeles Soler-Arechalde & Julio Serrano (eds.), *Contacto lingüístico y contexto social. Estudios de variación y cambio*, 403–460. Mexico City: Universidad Nacional Autónoma de México.

Martín-Butragueño, Pedro. 2023. El español en México [Spanish in Mexico]. In Rocío Caravedo & Francisco Moreno-Fernández (eds.), *Dialectología hispánica / The Routledge handbook of Spanish dialectology*, 304-318. London & New York, NY: Routledge.

Martín-Butragueño, Pedro. Forthcoming. Características principales de la entonación del español en el puerto de Acapulco, México: Elementos adicionales para una geoprosodia [The principal intonational characteristics of the Spanish spoken in the port of Acapulco, Mexico: Further elements for a geoprosody]. In Yolanda Congosto-Martín & Pedro Martín-Butragueño (eds.), *La entonación del español americano septentrional: Estudios geoprosódicos*. Bern: Peter Lang.

Martín-Butragueño, Pedro, Érika Mendoza-Vázquez & Leonor Orozco-Vaca (coords.). 2015. *Corpus oral del español de México* [Oral corpus of Mexican Spanish]. https://lef.colmex .mx/corpus_oral_del_espanol_de_mexico.html. (13 May, 2022.)

Martín-Butragueño, Pedro & Érika Mendoza-Vázquez. 2018. Prosodic nuclear patterns in narrow and broad focus utterances: Pragmatic and social factors in Central Mexican Spanish. In Melanie Uth & Marco García (eds.), *Focus realization in Romance and beyond*, 131–172. Amsterdam & Philadelphia, PA: John Benjamins.

Mendoza-Vázquez, Érika. 2014. *La impresión de un tono: Estudio sociolingüístico de la entonación en Cuapiaxtla, Tlaxcala* [The impression of a tone: A sociolinguistic study of intonation in Cuapiaxtla, Tlaxcala]. Mexico City: El Colegio de México dissertation.

Mendoza Vázquez, Érika. 2021. Entonación de los enunciados aseverativos en el español de la Ciudad de México entre los años 1960 y 1970 [Intonational patterns of statements in Central Mexican Spanish. Approach to period 1960–1970]. *Anuario de Letras. Lingüística y Filología* 9(2). 5–41.

Moreno de Alba, José G. 2001. *El español en América* [Spanish in America], 3rd edn. Mexico City: Fondo de Cultura Económica.

Moreno-Fernández, Francisco. 2020. *Variedades de la lengua Española* [Varieties of the Spanish language]. London & New York, NY: Routledge.

Olivar, Stefany. Forthcoming. *Algunos aspectos en el estudio de la entonación del español en contacto con el náhuatl de San Miguel "Canoa", Puebla* [Certain aspects in the study of intonation of the Spanish in contact with the Nahuatl of San Miguel "Canoa", Puebla]. Mexico City: El Colegio de México dissertation.

Ortega, Alex. 2019. Patrones entonativos en el español de Riohacha: un estudio sobre bilingües y monolingües [Intonational patterns in Riohacha Spanish: a study on bilinguals and monolinguals]. Mexico City: El Colegio de México dissertation.

Prieto, Pilar & Paolo Roseano (eds.). 2010. *Transcription of intonation of the Spanish language*. Munich: Lincom.

Reyes-Taboada, Verónica. 2014. La variabilidad del segmento /s/ en posición implosiva: Estudio comparativo entre residentes del puerto de Acapulco y migrantes a la ciudad de México [The variability of the /s/ segment in the implosive position: A comparative study between residents of the port of Acapulco and migrants to Mexico City]. In Pedro Martín-Butragueño & Leonor Orozco-Vaca (eds.), *Argumentos cuantitativos y cualitativos en sociolingüística. Segundo coloquio de cambio y variación lingüística*, 199–220. Mexico City: El Colegio de México.

Scrivner, Olga & Manuel Díaz-Campos. (n.d.). *Language Variation Suite (LVS)*. https://languagevariationsuite.shinyapps.io/Pages/. (25 September, 2021.)

Scrivner, Olga & Manuel Díaz-Campos. 2016. Language Variation Suite: A theoretical and methodological contribution for linguistic data analysis. *Proceedings of the Linguistic Society of America* 1. 1–15.

StataCorp. 1985–2021. *Stata/MP 17.0 for Mac*. College Station, TX: StataCorp LLC. https://www.stata.com. (13 May, 2022.)

CHAPTER 7

Little words, small moves

Clitic placement and syntactic change

Stavroula Tsiplakou
Open University of Cyprus, Cyprus

This paper explores clitic placement in two different varieties of Greek, Standard Modern Greek and Cypriot Greek, and it is argued that, under heavy influence from the standard variety, the Cypriot variety is undergoing change as regards a core property of its syntax, namely the placement of pronominal object clitics, since alongside structures where object clitics appear in second position in the clause, they also tend to appear in the immediately preverbal position, as in Standard Greek, the roofing standard for the Cypriot koine. An overview of existing studies is provided, after which the argument is made for competing grammars; the availability in the Cypriot koine of the Standard Greek as well as the Cypriot clitic placement strategy is accounted for on the basis of successful second dialect acquisition.

Keywords: Cypriot Greek, Standard Greek, clitic, diglossia, diaglossia, koine, interface, bidialectalism

1. Introduction

This paper examines syntactic change in the Cypriot Greek koine and advergence to the syntax of Standard Greek, focusing on an area of Cypriot Greek syntax where advergence appears to be at work, namely clitic placement. Cypriot Greek is a southeastern Greek variety (Trudgill 2003; Tsiplakou 2006) that emerged from the Hellenistic Greek koine along with the other Modern Greek dialects around the 11th century (Browning 1983; Horrocks 1997; Holton et al. 2019). Cypriot Greek has long stood in a diglossic relationship to Standard Modern Greek. Following the Turkish invasion of 1974 and the forced movement of Greek-speaking populations southward, most local subvarieties of Cypriot Greek have been subjected to massive levelling (Tsiplakou et al. 2006; Tsiplakou & Kontogiorgi 2016; Tsiplakou & Armostis 2020). Concomitantly, a Cypriot koine

https://doi.org/10.1075/silv.31.07tsi
© 2024 John Benjamins Publishing Company

has emerged, which shows advergence (Mattheier 1996) to Standard Greek in phonology, morphology, vocabulary, and partly in syntax. Pronominal object clitic placement is the principal structural aspect of Cypriot Greek grammar where the strong influence of the standard variety has yielded dialect change; changes in Cypriot Greek clitic placement are therefore the focus of this paper. It must be noted that this "exceptional", standard-like clitic placement (or unexpected proclisis; Pappas 2014; Tsiplakou et al. 2016; Leivada et al. 2017; Tsiplakou 2017, 2019; Tsiplakou & Armostis 2020; Grohmann et al. 2021) is one of the facets of the koine that gives it its mixed, hybrid flavour, and may to some extent account for the accrual of covert (or even overt) prestige (Rowe & Grohmann 2013) to this intermediate, compromise variety (Trudgill 1986; Hinskens et al. 2005; Kerswill 2013; Cerruti & Tsiplakou 2020)

2. Clitics in Greek

2.1 Three types of clitic placement

As regards pronominal object clitic placement, Modern Greek dialects belong to three groups (Condoravdi & Kiparsky 2001; Revithiadou 2006; Revithiadou & Spyropoulos 2020):

1. Standard Greek (and Italiot Greek;[1] see Rohlfs 1977; Manolessou 2005; Chatzikyriakidis 2010), where *proclisis* obtains, i.e. pronominal object clitics appear immediately to the left of the verb if the verb form inflects for tense (with the indirect object clitic preceding the direct object); *enclisis* obtains, i.e. pronominal object clitics appear immediately to the right of the verb, in imperatives, which have aspect and agreement but not tense features, and in gerunds, which have none of these features (in these cases the ordering of indirect and direct object is free):

(1) a. **to** ˈepçases
it.SG.ACC catch.PAST.PERF.2SG
'You caught it.'

b. ˈpçase **to**
catch.PERF.2SG it.SG.ACC
'Catch it.'

c. ˈpçanodas **to**
catching it.SG.ACC
'catching it'

2. Pontic Greek varieties, spoken around the Black Sea and vestigially in Northern Greece (Papadopoulos 1955; Drettas 1997; Chatzikyriakidis 2010, 2012), where *enclisis* obtains across the board, irrespective of tense and agreement features on the verb or of what types of constituents precede the verb:

(2) a. 'ekser   **aton**
       know.PAST.IMPERF.1SG **him.SG.ACC**
       'I knew him.'

    b. ðo   **m**   a'vuto   to   vi'vlion
       give.2SG **me.SG.GEN** this.SG.ACC the.SG.ACC book.SG.ACC
       'Give me this book.'

    c. ci   kser   **aton**
       NEG know.PRES.2SG **him.SG.ACC**
       'I don't know him.'

    d. 'pios   en'doken   **aton**
       who.SG.NOM hit.PAST.PERF.3SG **him.SG.ACC**
       'Who hit him?'   (Chatzikyriakidis 2010: 235–236)

    e. esi   c   e'pices e'cino do 'ipa   **se**
       you.NOM NEG did.2SG this.ACC what tell.PAST.PERF.1SG **you.SG.ACC**
       'You did not do what I told you.'

    f. 'ipe   **me**   na 'leɣo **se**   po'la
       tell.PAST.PERF.3SG **me.ACC** MOD tell **you.SG.ACC** many.PL.ACC
       'He told me to tell you many things.'
                     (Papadopoulos 1955: 172, in Chatzikyriakidis 2010: 236)

3. Cypriot Greek (and Cappadocian Greek;[2] see Janse 1998), which displays clitic-second effects (Wackernagel, or, more accurately, Tobler-Mussafia effects; Tobler 1875; Wackernagel 1892; Mussafia 1898; Anderson 2005), since they appear after the first constituent in the clause (Agouraki 2001; Tsiplakou 2006; Chatzikyriakidis 2010, 2012; Mavrogiorgos 2013; Neokleous 2015). Clitic-second effects obtain when the first element in the clause is (a) the

---

1. Below are some examples from Italiot Greek (Chatzikyriakidis 2010: 91):

(i)   **ton**   ga'pa
      him.ACC love.PRES.3SG
      'S/he loves him.'

(ii) 'grafe   **to**
      write.2SG **it.ACC**
      'Write it.'

(iii) pul'onta **o**
      selling **it.ACC**
      'by selling it...'

verb, (b) some element in CP or below, e.g. the mood marker [na], the future marker ['enːa], the negation marker [en], *wh-* expressions, preverbal focus clefts and most complementisers (in the latter case the clitic must be immediately to the left of the verb, hence the descriptive term "proclisis"):

(3) a. 'epcaes   **to**
   take.PAST.PERF.2SG **it**.SG.ACC
   'You took it.'

  b. pcas   **to**
   take.PERF.2SG **it**.SG.ACC
   'Take it.'

  c. 'pcano^{n}das **to**
   taking   **it**.SG.ACC
   'taking it'

  d. na / 'enːa **to**   'pcais
   MOD / FUT **it**.SG.ACC take.PERF.2SG
   'You should/will take it.'

  e. en **to**   'epcaes
   NEG **it**.SG.ACC take.PAST.PERF.2SG
   'You didn't take it.'

  f. pços   **to**   'epcaen
   who.NOM **it**.SG.ACC take.PAST.PERF.2SG
   'Who took it?'

This pattern of clitic placement is quite similar to that of Medieval Cypriot. Pappas (2004) examined clitic placement in the two Medieval Cypriot chronicles, Leontios Machairas' Ἐξήγησις τῆς γλυκείας χώρας Κύπρου, ἡ 'ποῖα λέγεται Κρόνακα, τουτἔστιν Χρονικόν [Recital concerning the Sweet Land of Cyprus entitled Cronaca, that is to say Chronicle] (Dawkins 1932) and Georgios Voustronios' Διήγησις Κρόνικας Κύπρου ... [Recital of the Chronicle of Cyprus...] (Kechagioglou 1997). He found that in Medieval Cypriot Greek, clitic-second effects obtain quite consistently. Some of his findings are summarised in Table 1.

---

2. Below are some examples of clitic-second effects in Cappadocian (adapted from Janse 1998: 261; data from Dawkins 1916):

(i)   as **to**   fa'γo m
   FUT **he**.ACC eat.PERF.1SG INTERR
   'Will I eat him?'

(ii)   ti   **to**   'pices
   what.ACC **he**.ACC do.PAST.PERF.2SG
   'What did you do to him?'

Table 1. Clitic placement in the Medieval Cypriot chronicles (adapted from Pappas 2004: 85)

Text→ Factor↓	Makhairas Cl-V	Makhairas V-Cl	Voustronios Cl-V	Voustronios V-Cl
Initial	0	103	0	105
Clitic doubling	0	9	0	6
Function word	43	2	58	1
Fronted constituent	1	10	0	4
Subject	0	23	0	6
Temporal adverb	1	4	0	3
Gerund	0	13	0	6
Imperative	0	2	0	2
Infinitive	0	0	0	0
Total	45	166	58	133

As Pappas (2004: 86) aptly notes, in Medieval Cypriot there appears to be "a clear-cut distinction in pronoun placement between 'function word', which is associated with categorically preverbal pronouns, and all other factors, which are associated with categorical postverbal placement". Proclisis/clitic-second placement obtains with the mood marker [na], the future marker ['enːa], the negation marker [en], *wh-* expressions, etc.:

(4) a. τὰ   χαρτιά,   τά   τοῦ ἔδωκεν...
          the.PL.ACC paper.PL.ACC which.PL.ACC **him**.SG.GEN gave.PAST.PERF.3SG
          'the papers which he gave him...'
     b. νὰ **τοῦ**   δώσουν θάνατο
          MOD **him**.SG.GEN give.PERF death.SG.ACC
          'to give him death...'   (Makhairas § 313)

In all other cases enclisis obtains: in (5a) the clitic appears after the verb, which is preceded by the co-ordinating conjunction; in (5b) the clitic appears after the verb, which is preceded by the subject; and in (5c), the clitic appears after the verb, which is preceded by a PP (data from Pappas 2004: 86):

(5) a. καὶ ἔσφιξε   **τον**
          and force.PAST.PERF.3SG **him**.SG.ACC
          'and he forced him...'   (Makhairas § 315)
     b. ὁ   κουβερνούρης   ἐμήνυσέν   **το**
          the.SG.ACC governor.SG.ACC message.PAST.PERF.3SG **it**.SG.ACC
          'the governor sent word...'   (Makhairas § 313)

c. κατὰ   τὸ   συνήθιν   ἔδωκεν   **του**
following the.SG.ACC custom.SG.ACC give.PAST.PERF.3SG **him**.SG.GEN
τον
it.SG.ACC
'according to custom, he gave him [the prisoner] to him...'

(Makhairas § 313)

2.2 Exceptional clitic placement

Recent research indicates that the clitic-second pattern described above may be in a state of shift and that clitics appear preverbally with constituents other than such function words in contemporary Cypriot Greek. In fact, proclisis–enclisis alternation has been claimed to obtain with the subordinating conjunction [ja'ti]/[epi'ði] 'because' (Chatzikyriakidis 2010, 2012; Grohmann et al. 2017), the complementiser [oti] 'that' (Chatzikyriakidis 2010, 2012), preverbal subjects, clitic left-dislocated objects, and even with the co-ordinating conjunction [tʃe] 'and' (Tsiplakou 2009a, b):

(6) a. epi'ði   ene'vriases   **me**   en   'kamno   'tipota
    because anger.PAST.PERF.2SG **me**.SG.ACC NEG do.PRES.1SG nothing
   b. epi'ði   **me**   ene'vriases en   'kamno   'tipota
    because **me**.SG.ACC NEG   anger.PAST.PERF.2SG do.PRES.1SG nothing
    'Because you made me angry, I am doing nothing.'

(Chatzikyriakidis 2010: 214)

(7) a. 'ipen   'oti e'θcavasen   **to**
    said.3SG that read.PAST.PERF.3SG **it**.SG.ACC
   b. 'ipen   'oti **to**   e'θcavasen
    said.3SG that **it**.SG.ACC read.PAST.PERF.3SG
    'S/he said that s/he read it.'   (Chatzikyriakidis 2010: 170)

(8) o ce'malis   'itan   'telos   'paⁿdon 'tutos   o 'turkos
   the.SG.NOM Kemal.SG.NOM was.PAST.3SG anyway this.SG.NOM the.SG.NOM
   o me'θistakas   tʃ   'ercetun   tʃe
   Turk.SG.NOM   the.NOM   drunkard.NOM   and come.PAST.IMPF.3SG
   mas   efo'itʃazen
   and **us**.PL.ACC scare.PAST.IMPF.3SG
   'Anyway, Kemal was this Turkish drunkard, and he would come and scare us.'

Proclitic structures may also be utterance initial, not preceded by any element in the C field:

(9) e'ɣo   pa'ʎːa   ðen mi'lusa   tin   cipria'ci
    I.SG.NOM in the past NEG speak.PAST.IMPF.1SG the.SG.ACC Cypriot.SG.ACC
    ði'alekto   **tin**   eθe'orun   'ðiɣman
    dialect.SG.ACC   **her.SG.ACC** consider.PAST.IMPF.1SG   sign.SG.ACC
    amorfo'ʃas
    illiteracy.SG.GEN
    'In the past I did not speak the Cypriot dialect; I used to consider it a sign of lack of education.'

(10) a. en   'efaes   'tipota
         NEG eat.PAST.PERF.2SG nothing
         'You didn't eat anything.'
     b. 'oi   'efaa   to   ko'topulːo   mu   **to**
         NEG eat.PAST.PERF.1SG the.SG.ACC chicken.SG.ACC my.SG.ACC **it.SG.ACC**
         'efaa   'olo
         eat.PAST.PERF.1SG all.SG.ACC
         'No, I ate my chicken. I ate it all.'   (Tsiplakou 2019: 987)

(11) **ta**   ekat'aferes   stavrulːa   'ivres
     them.CL.ACC make.PAST.PERF.2SG Stavroula.VOC find.PAST.PERF.2SG
     to
     it.SG.ACC
     'Did you make it, Stavroula? Did you find it?'

(12) 'ekamnen   **to**   se   'alːo   'maθima   **to**
     do.PAST.IMPF.3SG **it.SG.ACC** in   other.SG.ACC class.SG.ACC **it.SG.ACC**
     'ekamnen   se 'alːo   'maθima
     do.PAST.IMPF.3SG in other.SG.ACC class.SG.ACC
     'He used to do **it** in another class; he used to do **it** in another class.'
                                                        (Tsiplakou & Armostis 2020: 210)

(13) **ta**   'valan   tʃa'me e kaman   **ta**
     them.PL.ACC put.PAST.PERF.3PL there   make.PAST.PERF.3PL **them.PL.ACC**
     ja'li
     glass.SG.ACC
     "They put them there, they got them to be crystal-clean."
                                                        (Leivada et al. 2017)

As can be seen from (11)–(13), proclisis may alternate with enclisis, and this for no apparent pragmatic reason; it would seem that the two structures are syntactically and functionally equivalent.

3. Sociolinguistic studies of clitic placement in Cypriot Greek

A significant number of sociolinguistic studies have been conducted to date, all attesting to the spread of exceptional clitic placement in Cypriot Greek. They also largely converge in terms of the rate of the spread, despite the fact that data were collected using different methodological tools. In addition, experimental psycholinguistic studies indicate that unexpected proclisis occurs in the grammar of children. In Tsiplakou et al. (2016), data were collected from sociolinguistic interviews. The number of participants was 57 (28 female and 29 male), and their ages ranged from 26 to 90. The study examined different variables that have a dialectal and a standard-like[3] variant, namely standard-like palatal [c] and [ç] vs. Cypriot palatoalveolar [tʃ] and [ʃ], standard-like periphrastic present and past perfect vs. Cypriot simple past, and standard-like unexpected proclisis vs. enclisis. Results are shown in Figure 1:

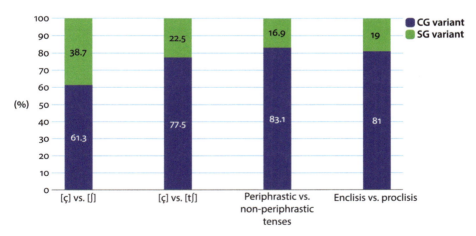

Figure 1. Palatals, periphrastic tenses and proclisis in the Cypriot Greek koine (from Tsiplakou et al. 2016: 17)

---

3. As is noted in Tsiplakou and Armostis (2020: 208), "[w]e opt for describing the variants that are identical to the Standard Greek ones as standard(-like) precisely because their occurrence does not necessarily signal a switch to the standard variety, but rather some type of style-shifting within the Cypriot Greek register continuum, to which they arguably belong"; cf. the discussion on competing grammars below.

As can be observed in Figure 1, unexpected proclisis occurs at a rather high 19%. The principal innovators are young, educated women, while younger, uneducated men show a distinct preference for the Cypriot variants, including clitic-second effects (Tsiplakou et al. 2016: 19).

Leivada et al. (2017) examined data from a small corpus of spontaneous conversations between five female participants of different ages and educational levels. Again, as can be seen in Figure 2, proclisis occurred at a rather high rate, in 62 out of 363 utterances:

Figure 2. Cypriot and standard-like variants in the speech of five female participants (from Leivada et al. 2017)

Recording Area	Phonology tʃ	Phonology c	Morphology -u	Morphology -ak	Syntax Enclisis	Syntax Proclisis	Other utterances (not featuring the variants under examination)
1	21	15	4	0	39	9	906
2	52	5	8	2	79	12	841
3	40	3	8	4	99	13	680
4	36	7	20	7	88	9	751
5	35	18	14	10	58	19	906
Total	184	48	54	23	363	62	4084

Figure 3 shows the results per participant, from two different recordings:

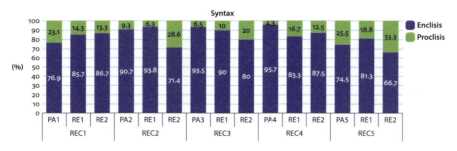

Figure 3. Proclisis and enclisis in two different recordings of the speech of five female participants (PA: Participant, RE(C): Recording; from Leivada et al. 2017)

Figure 4 shows the use of Cypriot variants per participant, also providing their educational level:

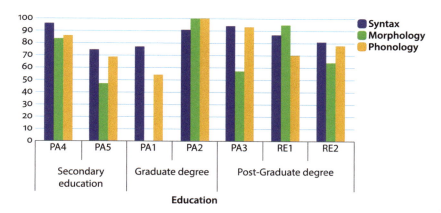

Figure 4. Use of Cypriot variants per participant; educational level is indicated for each participant (from Leivada et al. 2017)

Given that there is both *inter-* and *intra-*speaker variation in clitic placement and that educational level does not seem to consistently predict a preference for the more standard-like variants, Leivada et al. (2017) argue that it is not so much the case that each speaker places herself on a different point in the Cypriot dialect continuum but rather that the data point to a hybrid grammar, also since the two variants are functionally, i.e. pragmatically, equivalent (cf. (11)–(13) above as well as the discussion on code-mixing below).

Pappas (2014) presents the results of a grammaticality judgement task (in the form of a Magnitude Estimation Test) for proclisis in 10 different morphosyntactic environments, namely (a) with temporal [aˈfu] 'since', (b) with causal [aˈfu] 'since', (c) with emphatic negation [ˈentʃe], which invariably triggers enclisis, (d) with [epiˈði] 'because', (e) with [jaˈti] 'because', (f) with [jaˈti] 'why', (g) with [ˈoti] 'that', (h) with focused preverbal subjects with contrastive focus, (i) with focused preverbal subjects with informational focus, and (j) with non-focused preverbal subjects. The test was completed by 38 participants (24 female, 14 male) whose ages ranged between 19 and 47.

Pappas notes that the lack of a distinct preference for proclisis or enclisis in some syntactic environments points to the fact that "it is impossible to dismiss these patterns as accidents of performance or the result of dialect mixing. They clearly constitute aspects of competence in Cypriot grammar" (Pappas 2014: 204).

In more recent work, Papanicola and Armostis (2020, 2021) have explored the acceptability of unexpected proclisis through a questionnaire-based grammaticality judgement task. Participants were asked to rate structures with unexpected proclisis in different syntactic environments, namely proclisis preceded by a topicalised subject, proclisis with a topicalised, clitic left-dislocated (CLLD) object,

Table 2. Clitic placement in different syntactic environments (adapted from Pappas 2014: 203)

Environment	Magnitude estimation test
[a'fu]	enclisis
['entʃe]	enclisis
['oti]	no preference
[epi'ði]	enclisis (?)
[ja'ti]	no preference
[ja'ti] wh	proclisis
subj. contrastive	no preference
subj. informational	proclisis
subj. neutral	enclisis

proclisis with the coordinating conjunction [tʃe] 'and', and proclisis after interjections.[4] Moreover, the questionnaire tested for proclisis with direct objects in accusative, with direct objects in genitive, with direct and indirect objects, and with ethical/benefactive/malefactive genitive clitics, i.e. clitics that are not arguments. In addition, the behaviour of 1st/2nd vs. 3rd person clitic pronouns was investigated to examine whether person and number make a difference. Sociolinguistic parameters included gender and age.[5]

The questionnaire items were presented in the form of short scenarios or dialogues, and participants were asked to rate proclitic structures as more or less "natural" Cypriot Greek. The number of participants was 74 (50 female and 24 male) with an age range from 19 to 62. Results indicate that the case, person and number of the clitic were not predictive factors for proclisis, nor were most of the syntactic environments examined (see Papanicola & Armostis 2020, 2021). On the whole, unexpected proclisis was rated as fairly "natural" in the dialect, as is shown in Figure 5, where the highest percentages concentrate around points 4, 5 and 6.

---

4. These studies did not test for the environments tested in Pappas (2014), as some of them invariably trigger enclisis, e.g. [a'fu] 'since' and emphatic negation ['entʃe], and some of them necessarily trigger proclisis, e.g. [ja'ti] "why", being a *wh*- word and preverbal foci; the differential behaviour of preverbal focused subjects in Pappas (2014) may be attributed to the difficulty posed for participants to interpret the subjects as focused, since the sole clue is intonation, and to distinguish between informational and contrastive focus. Nonmatrix clauses with [ja'ti]/[epi'ði] 'because' and ['oti] 'that' were also not included, as these are well-known sites of variation between proclisis and enclisis.

5. Educational level was not included, as all but two participants were university graduates.

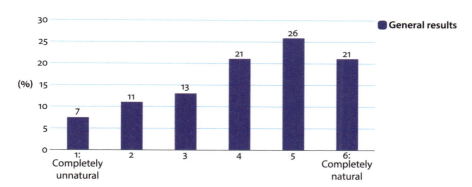

Figure 5. General results of evaluating the naturalness of utterances with unexpected proclisis (Papanicola & Armostis 2021: 1021)

Moreover, female subjects found proclisis more natural than male subjects did (the odds was 1.676 times that of male subjects, $b = 0.516$, Wald $\chi2(1) = 86.872$, $p < .0005$), as is also shown in Figure 6.[6]

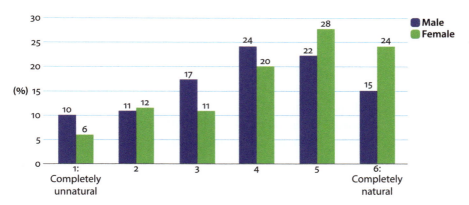

Figure 6. Comparison of male and female responses regarding the evaluation of the naturalness of utterances with unexpected proclisis (Papanicola & Armostis 2021: 1022)

Studies in child language acquisition also confirm that exceptional clitic placement is on its way to becoming a part of the grammar of Cypriot Greek and that the preference for proclisis may well be conditioned by sociolinguistic factors. A series of studies by the Cyprus Acquisition Team (CAT), involving large num-

---

6. Papanicola (2021) provides a more fine-tuned account of proclisis involving, among other things, larger numbers of participants, oral data and the consideration of register as a factor significantly affecting proclisis or enclisis. The data in these studies confirm that proclisis is no longer "unexpected" or "exceptional" in the grammar of Cypriot Greek.

bers of children, tested for proclisis-enclisis alternation in nonmatrix clauses introduced by [ja'ti] 'because' through an experimental production task (Grohmann 2011, 2014; Grohmann et al. 2017). A striking finding was that children initially acquire enclisis, but that proclisis increases with the onset of schooling. A possible explanation, couched within Grohmann's Socio-Syntax of Development Hypothesis (Grohmann 2011), is that enclisis is fully acquired early on (as there is no omission or misplacement of clitics), but that proclisis also emerges with schooling, which in Cyprus' diglossic context involves maximisation of exposure to Standard Greek (see, e.g. Tsiplakou et al. 2018).

4. Competing grammars and the nature of the competition

4.1 Code-mixing and/or competing grammars?

It is quite clear that instances of exceptional clitic placement such as the ones discussed here cannot be treated as code-switching, as, assuming there is dialect alternation between Standard and Cypriot Greek, such alternation is *intra-* and not *inter*sentential. Moreover, as is well-known, code-switching performs pragmatic functions: it is a contextualisation cue (Gumperz 1982) or an indexical of social negotiations (Myers-Scotton 2000), i.e. it indexes an aspect of the content or the context of the interaction (a change in topic or a shift in footing or alignment among participants, etc.). Auer (1999) distinguishes between discourse-oriented and participant-oriented code-switching, the former typically indexing changes such as shifts in topic, agreements, disagreements, repairs or other changes in conversational dynamics, and the latter usually indicating something about the identity or status of the interlocutor(s). It is obvious from the data presented above that the switches do not perform any such functions. It might, however, be tempting to treat such cases of exceptional clitic placement as a type of *intra*sentential switching or code-mixing between Standard and Cypriot Greek, with the mixing involving different linguistic levels, i.e. Standard Greek syntax co-occurring with Cypriot morphology, phonology and lexis; this is the case in all of the examples above, where the only aspect of Standard Greek grammar in the mix is the placement of the clitic, the rest of the utterance being in Cypriot Greek.

As to the unavailability of specific discursive, pragmatic or social functions associated with proclisis, this is hardly unexpected for code-mixing. Poplack's pioneering study showed, among other things, that the degree of bilingualism affects the type of language alternation, and that "balanced bilingualism" is strongly associated with a preference for code-mixing (Poplack 2000: 230). Poplack argues that code-switching may be used as a discourse strategy to achieve certain interactional effects at specific points during a conversation [...] this use is characteristic only of certain types of code-switching, which we call 'emblematic', including tags, interjections, idiomatic expressions, and even individual noun switches. On the other hand, a generalized use of intra-sentential code-switching may represent instead an overall discourse MODE. The very fact that a speaker makes alternate use of both codes itself has interactional motivations and implications beyond any particular effects of specific switches [...] More important, there is no need to require any social motivation for this type of code-switching, given that, as a discourse mode, it may itself form part of the repertoire of a speech community. It is then the choice (or not) of this mode which is of significance to participants rather than the choice of switch points. (Poplack 2000: 254–255)

Similarly, Myers-Scotton (2000: 145 ff.) defines such code-mixing as "overall switch" and notes that this is often the *unmarked* choice between bilinguals, and that it "could be thought of as a type of interaction similar to monolingual language usage" (Myers-Scotton 2000: 148), i.e. presumably as akin to register or style-shifting among monolinguals. Moreover, Auer (1999; see also Auer 2014; Auer & Hakimov 2020) argues that code-mixing is often the stage prior to the emergence of "fused lects", where elements from two codes/varieties/languages are part of the same system, often with different grammatical functions assigned to elements from each code, but with both codes constituting a single grammar. It is therefore tempting to hypothesise that unexpected proclisis is not a micro-transition, a micro-switch outside the Cypriot dialect continuum and into the standard variety, and this for no apparent reason, but rather that such cases are instances of style-shifting within the same, single continuum – or, in other words, that they are instances of a "competing" grammatical structure within Cypriot Greek.

The structural properties of code-mixing, as discussed in the relevant literature, appear to confirm this point. Recall that, according to the Equivalence Constraint, "[...] switches will tend to occur at points in discourse were juxtaposition of L1 and L2 elements does not violate a syntactic rule of either language" (Poplack 2000: 586). Clearly, the position of clitics is such a "conflict site" (cf. Poplack & Meechan 1998; see MacSwan 1999, 2014 for Minimalist reformulations of the constraint) between the grammar of the two varieties, such that it is difficult to argue for a mix between the two syntactic systems resulting in syntactically hybrid structures. It is therefore more plausible to argue that in cases of unexpected proclisis, the syntactic structure is that of Standard Greek; Cypriot phonological, morphological and lexical features in the utterance can then be taken as an indication of the degree of integration of the Standard Greek structure into the Cypriot Greek grammar. Thus, exceptional clitic placement looks more like an output of competing grammars (see Kroch 1994; Kroch & Taylor 1997, 2000; Lightfoot

1999; Yang 2002; Fruehwald & Wallenberg 2013; and Tsiplakou 2009a, b; 2014a, b; Grohmann et al. 2017; Leivada et al. 2017; Papanicola 2021 for Cypriot Greek). Whether there is genuine optionality or free variation in the selection of the one rule or the other (as is argued for in Grohmann et al. 2021), or whether there is stylistic or sociolinguistic differentiation at work (Papanicola & Armostis 2020, 2021), the fact remains that the competing grammatical rule is not extraneous to the Cypriot Greek grammatical system, for the reasons outlined above.

This necessarily leads the discussion to the issue of bidialectal acquisition and the nature of bidialectalism. Auer (2005, 2011) has argued that in standard-cum-dialect situations the standard language and the dialects are acquired naturalistically, while in diglossic situations, where the transition to type C diaglossia has not taken place, intermediate varieties form a continuum between dialect and norm (cf. Bellman 1998). In type C diaglossia we may expect varying degrees of acquisition of the extraneous variety, i.e. gradient bidialectalism, depending on possible differences in the acquisition processes but also on the properties of the grammatical phenomena in question (Grohmann et al. 2017; Tsiplakou 2017, 2019). It is therefore worth looking more closely at the structural properties of clitic placement in the two varieties, in an attempt to explore whether these facilitate bidialectal acquisition.

4.2   Approaches to clitic placement in Standard and Cypriot Greek

Most approaches to clitic placement in Standard and Cypriot Greek take on board the analysis proposed by Sportiche (1996) that clitics head their own phrasal projections, Clitic Phrases; the clitic moves there from the VP. The presence of XP^ yields Clitic Left Dislocation (CLLD), the presence of XP* yields Clitic Doubling, and languages parametrise as to whether XP^ or XP* are overt or not, etc.:

(14)   [CP C [ClP XP^ Cl [IP I [VP V XP*]]]]

Other approaches are inspired by the proposal in Bošković (2001), whereby clitic placement is primarily a syntactic operation that is, however, filtered by phonology in case the output is ungrammatical. To account for the differences in clitic placement in otherwise closely related South Slavic languages such as Bulgarian, Macedonian and Serbian/Croatian, where patterns such as the following obtain:

(15)   a.   Dade   **mi**   go.
           give.PAST.3SG **me.**DAT **it.**ACC
           'S/he gave me it.'   (Bulgarian)

b. **Mi   go**   dade.
   me.DAT **it**.ACC give.PAST.3SG
   'S/he gave me it.'   (Macedonian)

c. Ana **mu   ga**   daje.
   Ana **me**.DAT **it**.ACC give.PAST.3SG
   'Ana gave me it.'   (Serbian/Croatian)

Bošković assumes that first AgrDO and then AgrIO merge with VP:

(16)   [AgrIOP mi+go+dade [AgrDOP go+dade [[VP dade]]]

He proposes (simplifying somewhat) that the difference between Macedonian and Bulgarian depends on whether higher or lower copies are deleted (Bošković 2001:185). Serbian/Croatian Wackernagel effects are accounted for by assuming that the higher copies of the clitics are licenced within the Intonational Phrase comprising the clitics and the preceding element; phonology filters out the unwanted lower copies produced by syntax (Bošković 2001:65).

Both of the analyses above have been taken on board for Greek. Terzi (1999) suggests that clitics appear under FP (which is akin to Sportiche's Clitic Phrase; cf. also Uriagereka 1995):[7]

(17)   [CP C [NegP Neg [MoodP M [FP ClDAT ClACC [TP T / Agr [VP]]]]]]

Terzi assumes that in gerunds and imperatives the V ends up in MoodP and CP respectively (cf. Rivero & Terzi 1995), which yields Standard Greek postverbal cli-

---

7. As is well-known, similar variation exists in Spanish varieties, both synchronically and diachronically. Medieval Spanish displayed Tobler-Mussafia clitic placement (see, e.g. Rivero 1991; Bouzouita 2008), as do varieties such as Galician (Uriagereka 1995):

(i)   Que **te**   dixo   Heliseus?
      What **you**.SG.ACC say.PAST.PERF.3SG Heliseus
      'What did Heliseus tell you?'   (Medieval Spanish, in Bouzouita 2008:222)

(ii) Oyol   Ruben
      heard.PAST.PERF.3SG **it**.SG.ACC Ruben
      'Ruben heard it.'   (Medieval Spanish, in Bouzouita 2008:222)

(iii) Ouvimo-**lo**.
      hear.PRES.1PL **it**.SG.ACC
      'We hear it.'   (Galician, Uriagereka 1995:95)

(iv) Quen **o**   ten   ouvido?
      who   **it**.SG.ACC have.3SG heard
      'Who has heard it?'   (Galician, Uriagereka 1995:95)

(v)   Non **o**   ten   ouvido.
      NEG **it**.SG.ACC have.3SG heard
      'S/he hasn't heard it.'   (Galician, Uriagereka 1995:95)

tics with gerunds and imperatives; she assumes that in Cypriot Greek, the verb needs to move to MoodP or CP, which yields postverbal clitics; the verb cannot move up if MoodP or NegP are filled, which yields proclisis, or rather clitic-second effects. Agouraki (1993, 1997, 2001) also assumes that clitics appear in ClP:

(18) [CP C [FocP Foc [ClP Cl [IP I [VP]]]]]   (Agouraki 1993: 47, 51)

She assumes that Cypriot Greek has an additional syntactic requirement for a filled C (Agouraki 1997, 2001), which results in verb raising to C unless C is filled by a *wh*-element or (oddly) negation. These assumptions combined yield Cypriot Greek clitic-second effects (see Chatzikyriakidis 2010 and Papanicola 2021 for discussion).

Revithiadou (2006) follows Bošković (2001) in assuming that syntax produces more than one copy for clitics, and phonology filters the outputs based on different hierarchies of prosodic constraints for Standard and Cypriot Greek as well as other dialects (see also Revithiadou & Spyropoulos 2008, 2020). Finally, mixed approaches are adopted by Mavrogiorgos (2010, 2013) and Neokleous (2015). Mavrogiorgos (2010, 2013) suggests that proclisis in Tobler-Mussafia languages in general, and in Cypriot Greek in particular, obtains as a result of verb movement for phonological reasons. He assumes that the basic structure is proclisis, that the order *wh-* / MOD / FUT / NEG – Clitic – Verb simply follows from the syntactic positions of the above and, crucially, that the rearrangement of the clitic-verb complex takes place at the phonological level, with the verb raising when the above elements do not exist to satisfy the phonological requirement that the clitic form an intonational phrase with a preceding element. A similar mixed approach is adopted by Neokleous (2015), who observes that typically developing children may produce structures with simultaneous proclisis and enclisis. The difference between child and adult grammars is that in the latter the phonological requirement that the clitic form an intonational phrase with a preceding element has been established, and this leads to the deletion/filtering out of lower clitic copies or verb raising in the absence of preceding elements (Neokleous 2015: 43–44).

4.3   The Interface Hypothesis

If we assume, as we have done so far, that exceptional clitic placement involves the introduction of a novel, competing rule in the grammar of Cypriot Greek, it is worth exploring which structural properties of the Cypriot Greek system facilitate the innovation and, concomitantly, allow for successful bidialectal acquisition, which is arguably the reason for emergent grammatical competition. Tsiplakou (2017, 2019) has argued that this may be captured successfully by the Interface Hypothesis (Tsimpli & Sorace 2006; Sorace & Serratrice 2009; Montrul 2011; Sorace 2011; White 2011; Tsiplakou 2014a, b; Lozano 2016). According to the Interface

Hypothesis, for structural phenomena related to different interfaces (e.g. syntax-phonology, syntax-semantics, syntax-pragmatics, syntax-discourse) second language acquisition ranges from perfect to incomplete. Tsimpli and Sorace (2006) suggest that phenomena involving "narrow", i.e. grammar-internal interfaces, such as syntax-phonology or syntax-semantics, make for easier and more complete acquisition, while phenomena pertaining to the syntax-pragmatics or syntax-discourse interface are harder to acquire (see also Slabakova 2011). Tsiplakou (2017, 2019) has shown on the basis of quantitative data that Standard Greek *ex situ* focus movement is notoriously hard to acquire for Cypriot Greek speakers, but that Standard Greek clitic placement is fully acquired, and that the difference can be attributed to the fact that acquiring the syntax of focus also requires acquiring the relevant information structures and pragmatic/discourse properties. In contrast, at least according to existing analyses of the differences in clitic placement between the two varieties of Greek in question, the consensus is that in both varieties the clitic is generated preverbally in Clitic Phrase (or T), and in Cypriot Greek the verb moves higher either for semantic reasons (Agouraki, Terzi) or due to a phonological requirement (Revithiadou, Mavrogiorgos, Neokleous).[8] In both cases clitic placement pertains to interfaces that are "grammar-internal" (Tsimpli & Sorace 2006), which predicts successful second dialect acquisition and which may account for the seeping of Standard Greek clitic placement into the Cypriot Greek koine in the form of a competing grammatical rule.

5. Conclusions

This paper examined exceptional clitic placement in Cypriot Greek and the suggestion was made that this is due to a competing grammatical rule from Standard Greek, the roofing standard of the Cypriot Greek koine. It attempted to show that exceptional clitic placement is a result of full bidialectal acquisition of this particular aspect of the grammar of the standard variety, which in turn can be accounted for on the basis of the Interface Hypothesis. As regards the effects of bidialectalism on language change, the argument was made that bidialectalism is a gradient phenomenon, with levels and rates of bidialectal acquisition depending, among other things, on the area of the grammar and the structural properties of the grammatical phenomena involved.

---

8. Note that the semantic and pragmatic properties of the clitics are otherwise identical in both varieties: they encode familiarity and/or specificity, they topicalise associated DP doubles, and they are incompatible with focused DP doubles (see also Papanicola 2021).

Acknowledgments

Studies summarised and reviewed in this paper were carried out for the purposes of the research project *From Diglossia to Diaglossia* (P.I.: Stavroula Tsiplakou; funded by the Open University of Cyprus).

References

Agouraki, Yoryia. 1993. *Spec-head licensing: The scope of the theory*. London: University College London dissertation.

Agouraki, Yoryia. 1997. On the enclisis/proclisis alternation. *Second International Conference on Greek Linguistics* 2. 393–404.

Agouraki, Yoryia. 2001. The position of clitics in Cypriot Greek. In Angela Ralli, Brian D. Joseph & Mark Janse (eds.), *Proceedings of the first international conference of Modern Greek Dialects and Linguistic Theory*, 1–18. Patras: University of Patras.

Anderson, Stephen R. 2005. *Aspects of the theory of clitics*. Oxford: Oxford University Press.

Auer, Peter. 1999. From code-switching via language mixing to fused lects: Toward a dynamic typology of bilingual speech. *International Journal of Bilingualism* 3. 309–332.

Auer, Peter. 2005. Europe's sociolinguistic unity, or: A typology of European dialect/standard constellations. In Nicole Delbecque, Johan van der Auwera & Dirk Geeraerts (eds.), *Perspectives on variation: Sociolinguistic, historical, comparative*, 7–42. Berlin & New York, NY: De Gruyter.

Auer, Peter. 2011. Dialect vs. standard: A typology of scenarios in Europe. In Bernd Kortmann & Johan van der Auwera (Eds.), *The languages and linguistics of Europe* (The World of Linguistics 1), 485–500. Berlin & New York, NY: De Gruyter.

Auer, Peter. 2014. Language mixing and language fusion: When bilingual talk becomes monolingual. In Juliane Besters-Dilger, Cynthia Dermarkar, Stefan Pfänder & Achim Rabus (eds.), *Congruence in contact-induced language change. Language families, typological resemblance, and perceived similarity*, 294–334. Berlin & New York, NY: De Gruyter.

Auer, Peter & Nikolay Hakimov. 2020. From language mixing to fused lects: The process and its outcomes. *International Journal of Bilingualism* 25(2). 361–368.

Bellman, Günter. 1998. Between base dialect and standard language. *Folia Linguistica* 32. 23–34.

Bouzouita, Miriam. 2008. At the syntax-pragmatics interface: Clitics in the history of Spanish. In Robin Cooper & Ruth M. Kempson (eds.), *Language in flux: Dialogue coordination, language variation, change and evolution*, 221–263. London: College Publications.

Bošković, Željko. 2001. *On the nature of the syntax-phonology interface: Cliticization and related phenomena*. Amsterdam: Elsevier Science.

Browning, Robert. 1983. *Medieval and Modern Greek*. Cambridge: Cambridge University Press.

Cerruti, Massimo & Stavroula Tsiplakou. 2020. *Intermediate language varieties. Koinai and regional standards in Europe* (Studies in Language Variation 24). Amsterdam & Philadelphia, PA: John Benjamins.

Chatzikyriakidis, Stergios. 2010. *Clitics in four dialects of modern Greek: A dynamic account*. London: King's College London dissertation.

Chatzikyriakidis, Stergios. 2012. A dynamic account of the Cypriot Greek clitic positioning system. *Lingua* 122(6). 642–672.

Condoravdi, Cleo & Paul Kiparsky. 2001. Clitics and clause structure. *Journal of Greek Linguistics* 2. 1–39.

Dawkins, Richard M. 1916. *Modern Greek in Asia Minor; a study of the dialects of Sílli, Cappadocia and Phárasa, with grammar, texts, translations and glossary*. Cambridge: Cambridge University Press.

Dawkins, Richard M. (ed.). 1932. *Leontios Makhairas: Recital concerning the sweet land of Cyprus entitled 'Chronicle'*. Oxford: Oxford University Press.

Drettas, Georges. 1997. *Aspects pontiques* [Pontic aspects]. Paris: ARP.

Fruehwald, Josef & Joel C. Wallenberg. 2013. Optionality is stable variation is competing grammars. *Paper presented at the 25th Scandinavian Conference of Linguistics, Formal Ways of Analyzing Variation (FWAV) Workshop*. University of Iceland.

Grohmann, Kleanthes K. 2011. Some directions for the systematic investigation of the acquisition of Cypriot Greek: A new perspective on production abilities from object clitic placement. In Esther Rinke & Tanja Kupisch (eds.), *The development of grammar: Language acquisition and diachronic change*, 179–203. Amsterdam & Philadelphia, PA: John Benjamins.

Grohmann, Kleanthes K. 2014. CAT research on object clitic placement: Where we are now. In Kleanthes K. Grohmann & Theoni Neokleous (eds.), *Developments in the acquisition of clitics*, 1–40. Newcastle-upon-Tyne: Cambridge Scholars Publishing.

Grohmann, Kleanthes K., Elena Papadopoulou & Charalambos Themistocleous. 2017. Acquiring clitic placement in bilectal settings: Interactions between social factors. *Frontiers in Communication* 2(8).

Grohmann, Kleanthes K., Maria Kambanaros, Evelina Leivada & Natalia Pavlou. 2021. On "free" grammatical variation in a mixed lect: Clitic placement in Cypriot Greek. *Zeitschrift für Sprachwissenschaft* 39(3). 275–298.

Gumperz, John J. 1982. Conversational code-switching. In John J. Gumperz (ed.), *Discourse strategies*, 59–99. Cambridge: Cambridge University Press.

Hinskens, Frans L. M. P., Peter Auer & Paul Kerswill. 2005. The study of dialect convergence and divergence: Conceptual and methodological considerations. In Peter Auer, Frans Hinskens & Paul Kerswill (eds.), *Dialect change. The convergence and divergence of dialects in contemporary societies*, 1–48. Cambridge: Cambridge UP.

Holton, David, Geoffrey Horrocks, Marjolein Janssen, Tina Lendari, Io Manolessou & Notis Toufexis. 2019. The Cambridge Grammar of Medieval and Early Modern Greek. Cambridge: Cambridge University Press.

Horrocks, Geoffrey. 1997. *Greek: A history of the language and its speakers*. London: Longman.

Janse, Mark. 1998. Cappadocian clitics and the syntax-morphology interface. In Brian D. Joseph, Geoffrey C. Horrocks & Irene Philippaki-Warburton (eds.), *Themes in Greek linguistics II*, 257–281. Amsterdam & Philadelphia, PA: John Benjamins.

Kechagioglou, Giōrgos (ed.). 1997. Διήγησις Κρονίκας Κύπρου – Τζώρτζης (Μ)πούστρους *(Γεώργιος Βο(σ)τρ(υ)νός ή Βουστρώνιος)* [Recital of the Chronicle of Cyprus – Tzortzis (M)poustrous (Georgios Vo(s)tr(y)nos or Voustronios)]. Nicosia: Centre for Scentific Research.

doi Kerswill, Paul. 2013. Koineization. In Jack K. Chambers & Natalie Schilling (eds.), *The handbook of language variation and change*, 2nd edn., 519–536. Oxford: Wiley-Blackwell.

Kroch, Anthony. 1994. Morphosyntactic variation. In Katherine Beals (ed.), *Papers from the 30th Regional Meeting of the Chicago Linguistics Society: Parasession on variation and linguistic theory*, 180–201. Chicago, IL: Chicago Linguistic Society.

Kroch, Anthony S. & Ann Taylor. 1997. Verb movement in Old and Middle English: Dialect variation and language contact. In Ans van Kemenade & Nigel Vincent (eds.), *Parameters of morphosyntactic change*, 297–325. Cambridge: Cambridge University Press.

Kroch, Anthony S. & Ann Taylor. 2000. Verb-Object order in Early Middle English. In Susan Pintzuk, George Tsoulas & Anthony Warner (eds.), *Diachronic syntax: Models and mechanisms*, 132–163. Oxford: Oxford University Press.

Leivada, Evelina, Elena Papadopoulou & Natalia Pavlou. 2017. Functionally equivalent variants in a non-standard variety and their implications for Universal Grammar: A spontaneous speech corpus. *Frontiers in Psychology* 8.

Lightfoot, David. 1999. *The development of language: Acquisition, change, and evolution*. Oxford: Wiley-Blackwell.

doi Lozano, Cristóbal. 2016. Pragmatic principles in anaphora resolution at the syntax-discourse interface: Advanced English learners of Spanish in the CEDEL2 corpus. In Margarita Alonso-Ramos (ed.), *Spanish learner corpus research: State of the art and perspectives*, 236–265. Amsterdam & Philadelphia PA: John Benjamins.

MacSwan, Jeff. 1999. *A minimalist approach to intrasentential code switching*. New York, NY: Garland Press.

MacSwan, Jeff. 2014. Programs and proposals in codeswitching research. In Jeff MacSwan (ed.), *Grammatical theory and bilingual codeswitching*, 1–33. Cambridge, MA: MIT Press.

Manolessou, Io. 2005. The Greek dialects of Southern Italy: An overview. *KAMPOS: Cambridge Papers in Modern Greek* 13. 103–125.

Mattheier, Klaus J. 1996. Varietätenkonvergenz. Überlegungen zu einem Bausteineiner Theorie der Sprachvariation [Variety convergence. Considerations for a component theory of language variation]. In Peter Auer, Frans Hinskens & Klaus J. Mattheier (eds.), *Convergence and divergence of dialects in Europe* (Sociolinguistica 10), 31–52.

doi Mavrogiorgos, Marios. 2010. *Clitics in Greek. A minimalist account of proclisis and enclisis*. Amsterdam & Philadelphia, PA: John Benjamins.

doi Mavrogiorgos, Marios. 2013. Enclisis at the syntax-PF interface. In Christine Meklenborg Salvesen & Hans Petter Helland (eds.), *Challenging clitics*, 27–54. Amsterdam & Philadelphia, PA: John Benjamins.

doi Montrul, Silvina. 2011. Multiple interfaces and incomplete acquisition. *Lingua* 121(4). 591–604.

doi Mussafia, Adolfo. 1898. Enclisi o proclisi del pronome personale atono qual oggetto [Enclisis or proclisis of the unstressed personal pronoun as object]. *Romania* 27. 145–6.

Myers-Scotton, Carol. 2000. Code-switching as indexical of social negotiations. In Li Wei (ed.), *The bilingualism reader*, 137–165. London: Routledge.

Neokleous, Theoni. 2015. The L1 acquisition of clitic placement in Cypriot Greek. *Lingua* 161. 27–47.

Papadopoulos, Anthimos A. 1955. *Ιστορική Γραμματική της Ποντικής Διαλέκτου* [Historical grammar of the Pontic dialect]. Athens: Committee for Pontic Studies.

Papanicola, Evanthi. 2021. *Η θέση των κλιτικών στη σύγχρονη κοινή κυπριακή: δομικές και κοινωνιογλωσσολογικές παράμετροι* [Clitic placement in the contemporary Cypriot Greek Koine: Structural and sociolinguistic parameters]. Latsia: Open University of Cyprus dissertation.

Papanicola, Evanthi & Spyros Armostis. 2020. Η θέση των κλιτικών στη σύγχρονη κοινή κυπριακή: δομικές και κοινωνιογλωσσολογικές παράμετροι [Clitic placement in the contemporary Cypriot Greek Koine: Structural and sociolinguistic parameters]. *Studies in Greek Linguistics* 40. 675–689.

Papanicola, Evanthi & Spyros Armostis. 2021. Clitic placement in Cypriot Greek. In Theodoros Markopoulos, Christos Vlachos, Argiris Archakis, Dimitris Papazachariou, George J. Xydopoulos & Anna Roussou (eds.), *Proceedings of the 14th International Conference on Greek Linguistics*, 1013–1026. Patras: University of Patras.

Pappas, Panayiotis A. 2004. *Variation and morphosyntactic change in Greek: From clitics to affixes*. New York, NY: Palgrave Macmillan.

Pappas, Panayiotis A. 2014. Exceptional clitic placement in Cypriot Greek: Results from an MET study. *Journal of Greek Linguistics* 14(2). 190–211.

Poplack, Shana. 2000. Sometimes I'll start a sentence in Spanish y termino en español: Toward a typology of code-switching. In Li Wei (ed.), *The bilingualism reader*, 221–256. London: Routledge.

Poplack, Shana & Marjory Meechan. 1998. How languages fit together in code-mixing. *International Journal of Bilingualism* 2. 127–138.

Revithiadou, Anthi. 2006. Prosodic filters on syntax: An interface account of second position clitics. *Lingua* 116. 79–111.

Revithiadou, Anthi & Vassilios Spyropoulos. 2008. Greek object clitic pronouns: A typological survey of their grammatical properties. *STUF – Language Typology and Universals* 61. 39–53.

Revithiadou, Anthi & Vassilios Spyropoulos. 2020. Cliticisation in Greek: A contrastive examination and cross-linguistic remarks. In Michalis Georgiafentis, Giannoula Giannoulopoulou, Maria Koliopoulou & Angeliki Tsokoglou (eds.), *Contrastive studies in morphology and syntax*, 225–244. London: Bloomsbury Academic.

Rivero, María Luisa. 1991. Clitic and NP climbing in Old Spanish. In Héctor Campos & Fernando Martínez-Gil (eds.), *Current studies in Spanish linguistics*, 241–282. Washington, DC: Georgetown University Press.

Rivero, María Luisa & Arhonto Terzi. 1995. Imperatives, V-movement and logical mood. *Linguistics* 31. 301–332.

Rohlfs, Gerhard. 1977. *Grammatica storica dei dialetti italo-greci* [Historical Grammar of the Italo-Greek Dialects]. München: Beck.

Rowe, Charlie & Kleanthes K. Grohmann. 2013. Discrete bilectalism: Towards co-overt prestige and diglossic shift in Cyprus. *International Journal of the Sociology of Language* 142. 119–142.

Slabakova, Roumyana. 2011. Which features are at the syntax–pragmatics interface? *Linguistic Approaches to Bilingualism* 1(1). 89–93.

Sorace, Antonella. 2011. Pinning down the concept of "interface" in bilinguals. *Linguistic Approaches to Bilingualism* 1(1). 1–33.

Sorace, Antonella & Ludovica Serratrice. 2009. Internal and external interfaces in bilingual language development: Beyond structural overlap. *International Journal of Bilingualism* 13(2). 195–210.

Sportiche, Dominique. 1996. Clitic constructions. In Laurie Zaring & Johan Rooryck (eds.), *Phrase structure and the lexicon*, 213–277. Dordrecht: Kluwer Academic Publishers.

Terzi, Arhonto. 1999. Clitic combinations, their hosts and their ordering. *Natural Language and Linguistic Theory* 17. 85–121.

Tobler, Adolf. 1875. Review of J. Le Coultre, De l'ordre des mots dans Chrétien de Troyes [Review of J. Le Coultre, On word order in Chrétien de Troyes]. In Adolf Tobler (ed.), *Vermischte Beiträge zur französischen Grammatik*, vol. 5, 395–414. Leipzig: Hirzel.

Trudgill, Peter J. 1986. *Dialects in contact*. Oxford: Blackwell Publishing.

Trudgill, Peter J. 2003. Modern Greek dialects: A preliminary classification. *Journal of Greek Linguistics* 4. 45–63.

Tsimpli, Ianthi M. & Antonella Sorace. 2006. Differentiating interfaces: L2 performance in syntax-semantics and syntax-discourse phenomena. In David Bamman, Tatiana Magnitskaia & Coleen Zaller (eds.), *BUCLID 30: Proceedings of the annual Boston University Conference on Language Development*, 653–664. Somerville, MA: Cascadilla Press.

Tsiplakou, Stavroula. 2006. Cyprus: Language situation. In Keith Brown (ed.), *Encyclopedia of language and linguistics*, 2nd edn., 337–339. Oxford: Elsevier.

Tsiplakou, Stavroula. 2009a. Code-switching and code-mixing between related varieties: Establishing the blueprint. *The International Journal of Humanities* 6. 49–66.

Tsiplakou, Stavroula. 2009b. Γλωσσική εναλλαγή, ανταγωνιστικές γραμματικές και διαγλώσσα: ακόμα μια διάσταση του «κυπριακού» [Language alternation, competing grammars and interlanguage: Another facet of the "Cyprus problem"]. In Georgios Giannakis, Mary Baltazani, George Xydopoulos & Anastasios Tsangalidis (eds.), *Proceedings of the 8th International Conference on Greek Linguistics*, 1195–1209. Ioannina: University of Ioannina.

Tsiplakou, Stavroula. 2014a. How mixed is a 'mixed' system? The case of the Cypriot Greek koine. *Linguistic Variation* 14. 161–178.

Tsiplakou, Stavroula. 2014b. Does convergence generate stability? The case of the Cypriot Greek koiné. In Kurt Braunmuller, Steffen Höder & Karoline Kühl (eds.), *Stability and divergence in language contact. Factors and mechanisms*, 165–177. Amsterdam & Philadelphia, PA: John Benjamins.

Tsiplakou, Stavroula. 2017. Imperfect acquisition of a related variety? Residual clefting and what it reveals about (gradient) bilectalism. *Frontiers in Communication* 2.

Tsiplakou, Stavroula. 2019. Διαφορές στην κατάκτηση των δομών εστίασης και της σύνταξης των κλιτικών: κατανοώντας τον διδιαλεκτισμό [Differences in the acquisition of focus structures and the syntax of clitics: Understanding bidialectalism]. *Studies in Greek Linguistics* 39. 985–998.

Tsiplakou, Stavroula, Andreas Papapavlou, Pavlos Pavlou & Marianna Katsoyannou. 2006. Levelling, koineization and their implications for bidialectism. In Frans Hinskens (ed.), *Language variation – European Perspectives. Selected papers from the Third International Conference on Language Variation in Europe (ICLaVE 3), Amsterdam, June* 2005, 265–276. Amsterdam: John Benjamins.

Tsiplakou, Stavroula, Elena Ioannidou & Xenia Hadjioannou. 2018. Capitalizing on language variation in Greek Cypriot education. *Linguistics and Education* 45. 62–71.

Tsiplakou, Stavroula & Marilena Kontogiorgi. 2016. Διαδικασίες διαλεκτικής ισοπέδωσης στη σύγχρονη κυπριακή [Processes of dialect levelling in contemporary Cypriot Greek]. *Studies in Greek Linguistics* 36. 451–464.

Tsiplakou, Stavroula & Spyros Armostis. 2020. Survival of the oddest. In Massimo Cerruti & Stavroula Tsiplakou (eds.), *Intermediate language varieties. Koinai and regional standards in Europe* (Studies in Language Variation 24), 203–230. Amsterdam & Philadelphia, PA: John Benjamins.

Tsiplakou, Stavroula, Spyros Armostis & Dimitris Evripidou. 2016. Coherence 'in the mix'? Coherence in the face of language shift in Cypriot Greek. *Lingua* 172–173. 10–25.

Uriagereka, Juan. 1995. Aspects of the syntax of clitic placement in Western Romance. *Linguistic Inquiry* 26(1). 79–123.

Wackernagel, Jacob. 1892. Über ein Gesetz der indogermanischen Wortstellung [On a law concerning Indo-European word order]. *Indogermanische Forschungen* 1. 333–436.

White, Lydia. 2011. Second language acquisition at the interfaces. *Lingua* 121(4). 577–590.

Yang, Charles. 2002. Grammar competition and language change. In David Lightfoot (ed.), *Syntactic effects on morphological change*, 367–380. Oxford: Oxford University Press.

CHAPTER 8

After dialectalisation
An overview of ongoing processes of convergence in Italian

Massimo Cerruti
University of Turin, Italy

This paper provides an overview of ongoing processes of convergence in the Italian language. It focuses on regional varieties of Italian, which essentially are the result of the so-called dialectalisation of the standard language and are nowadays affected by extensive processes of vertical and horizontal convergence. It considers the "downward" convergence of the standard usage towards sub-standard varieties, the "upward" convergence of sub-standard varieties towards the standard usage, and the supra-regional use, i.e. "horizontal" diffusion, of linguistic features originally confined to distinct geographic areas. The overall picture suggests that differences persist between regional varieties of Italian, though they are becoming increasingly less pronounced.[1]

Keywords: Italian, Italo-Romance dialects, regional variation, vertical convergence, horizontal convergence

1. Introduction

The Italo-Romance dialect–standard constellation has several features in common with those of most other languages in Europe: it results from a previous situation of diglossia, consists of various intermediate layers between the base dialects and the standard variety, and is experiencing a progressive loss of base dialects (see, e.g. Auer et al. 1996; Auer 1998, 2005; Auer et al. 2005; Cerruti & Tsiplakou 2020). However, it also presents certain characteristics that are not as common

---

1. This paper examines one of the major scholarly interests of the honoree: the investigation of convergence processes in dialect-standard situations. It is influenced by his research and by insight gained from discussions that the author has had with him at various ICLaVE conferences.

https://doi.org/10.1075/silv.31.08cer
© 2024 John Benjamins Publishing Company

in Europe, one being that, in most areas of the Italo-Romance domain, primary dialects (to use Coseriu's 1980 terminology) are still to be deemed *Abstand* languages. To this day, the majority of the Italo-Romance dialects show structural distance from both each other and standard Italian, such that they may be considered languages in their own right (cf. Maiden & Parry 1997; Berruto 2018a). The intermediate layers between the base dialects and the standard variety are therefore understood to be divided into two separate continua: the dialect continuum and the standard language continuum.

Certain structural characteristics of Italo-Romance dialects are reflected in the respective regional varieties of Italian, as the latter have, in essence, resulted from a process of dialectalisation (or "dialectisation", cf. Berruto 2005: 83) of the standard language. It was essentially the transfer of linguistic features from Italo-Romance dialects to the standard language that prompted the emergence of regional varieties of Italian,[2] which currently still differ at all linguistic levels (i.e. phonetics/phonology, morphology, syntax, and lexis; cf. Cerruti 2011). At present, however, these regional varieties are mainly undergoing processes of convergence, a fact that may lead to a substantial reduction in variation within the standard language in future.

Section 2 of this paper provides a brief outline of the long-standing contact between Italo-Romance dialects and Italian. Section 3 and 4 focus on the regional varieties of Italian, with the former detailing processes of vertical convergence and the latter processes of horizontal convergence. Section 5 draws conclusions regarding the current extent of regional variation in Italian.

2.   Italian and Italo-Romance dialects

There is evidence for the transfer of linguistic features from Italo-Romance dialects to the standard language dating back to as early as the sixteenth century, when the standard norm of Italian was first codified and established. However, actual contact between Italo-Romance dialects and Italian was limited until at least the end of the nineteenth century. Prior to this, Italo-Romance dialects and Italian had always had strictly separate and seldom-overlapping domains of use: the former were almost exclusively used in everyday conversation, whereas the latter was used mainly in writing and formal contexts. The population was gen-

---

2. Although Italo-Romance dialects and standard Italian have also undergone many similar developments independently of one another, meaning that, in several cases, the distinction between contact-induced features and intrinsic features is far from clear cut (for examples, see Cerruti 2011).

erally socialised in an Italo-Romance dialect and only a minority also had a command of Italian (fewer than 3% according to De Mauro 1976: 43; about 10% according to Castellani 1982).

The relationship between Italo-Romance dialects and Italian began to change towards the end of the nineteenth century. Following the political unification of Italy in 1861 and as a result of the socio-economic changes that occurred between the nineteenth and twentieth centuries, Italian spread increasingly across speakers and situations. Many speakers of Italo-Romance dialects gradually shifted to Italian, the national language, which thus progressively extended its reach to informal situations. Both Italo-Romance dialects and Italian therefore began to be used in everyday conversation, increasing the degree of contact between the two. The retention of substratum features prompted the emergence of regional varieties of Italian. These took form during the years between the two world wars (De Mauro 1976: 143–144) and became the native varieties of the generations born in the following decades.[3] It was between 1950 and 1970 that the first generations of native speakers of Italian were born and that a "shift from a mainly dialect-speaking to a mainly Italian-speaking community" took place (Berruto 2018a: 500).

Nowadays, "40%–45% of Italian people are monolingual in Italian; about 25% are Italian/dialect bilingual with Italian dominance; [and] a very small number (1–5%?) are still monolingual in dialect" (Berruto 2018a: 500). The majority of the population thus consists of native speakers of Italian, although they are in actual fact native speakers of a certain regional variety, or, more precisely, of a certain socio-geographic variety of Italian. Every regional variety has its own social varieties that differ in some respect; for example, the varieties of poorly educated, elderly speakers are more affected by substratum interference than those of the highly educated and young. Furthermore, the majority of the population uses a regional variety in both informal and formal situations (occasionally switching to and from an Italo-Romance dialect, especially in the latter). Some regional features of Italian show both social and stylistic markedness, as they are restricted to uneducated varieties and casual speech, whereas others are insensitive to socio-stylistic variation, as they are used regularly even by educated speakers in writing and formal speech (cf. Cerruti 2011).

The extensive spread of Italian during the twentieth century resulted in the decline of Italo-Romance dialects, which experienced an increasing loss of speak-

---

3. Some scholars are of the opinion that the distribution of the regional varieties of Italian matches either the regions of Italy or a varying number of macroregions (e.g. North-West, North-East, Centre, South, Islands). Others consider it to match the distribution of the main Italo-Romance dialect groups in Italy (in this respect, see the map in Pellegrini 1977). Such issue is discussed, *inter alia*, in Cerruti (2009: 25–32).

ers and domains. Today, Italo-Romance dialects are used only by a minority of the population and almost exclusively in informal and in-group interactions, in which, moreover, they are mainly drawn on in the context of code-switching to and from Italian (cf. ISTAT 2017). Nonetheless, behaviour still differs from region to region and between social groups. For example, among highly educated, young speakers living in urban settings – especially in North-West Italy –, Italo-Romance dialects mostly occur in tag switches and one-word switches and only fulfil expressive, symbolic and folkloric functions. Conversely, among poorly educated, elderly speakers living in small towns and villages – especially in North-East and Southern Italy –, they are fluently used in both bilingual and monolingual speech and serve their original function of languages for communication (cf. Moretti 2006; Berruto 2006; D'Agostino 2012; Dal Negro & Vietti 2011).

However, Italo-Romance dialects have lost speakers and domains of use to a much greater extent than linguistic features. Over the past six to seven decades, the substitution of dialect features with Italian features has mostly concerned vocabulary, characterised by the adoption of loanwords for new concepts. A lesser degree of substitution has been observed regarding phonetics/phonology, morphology and syntax (cf. Berruto 2006). As a result, the Italo-Romance dialects have maintained most of their structural characteristics.

3. Vertical convergence

The range of varieties of contemporary Italian, as well as that of most other European languages (see, e.g. Auer 2005), is mainly affected by processes of convergence. On the vertical dimension, two principal dynamics can be observed: the "downward" convergence of the standard usage towards sub-standard varieties and the "upward" convergence of sub-standard varieties towards the standard usage. Downward convergence has led to the emergence of a new standard variety, i.e. neo-standard Italian (cf. Berruto 2012; Cerruti et al. 2017; Ballarè 2020), which differs slightly across regions. It consists of (a) a nationwide shared core of originally sub-standard features that have come to be used and accepted even in formal and educated speech, and (b) a number of regionally marked vernacular features that have become part of the standard usage in distinct geographic areas. At the same time, upward convergence is leading to the obsolescence of several sub-standard features. These are becoming increasingly disused even among poorly educated speakers and no longer tend to be transmitted across generations. Some of these features are common to all regional varieties, whereas others (i.e. those resulting from substratum interference) are region-specific. Downward convergence can also be referred to as "restandardisation" (Berruto 2012; cf. "destandardisation" and "demotisation", Auer & Spiekermann 2011; Auer 2017) and, where region-specific features are concerned, upward convergence can be referred to as "de-dialectalisation" (Cerruti 2017). Both dynamics appear to affect every regional variety of Italian.

The regular occurrence of regionally marked vernacular features in neo-standard usage is particularly evident in phonetics/phonology. Neither the traditional normative model(s) for pronunciation nor the so-called "modern neutral" model (Canepari 1999) is currently used by any socially or geographically defined group of speakers. In addition, several regionally marked features have been found to be insensitive to social and stylistic variation, even characterising the pronunciation of educated speakers in careful speech styles (cf. Crocco 2017). By way of example, (1) presents five different utterances of the same sentence, taken from the read speech section of a corpus of spoken Italian (CLIPS). The pronunciation of a professional speaker (opting for the aforementioned "modern neutral" model) is contrasted with the read speech of four university students from different regions. It is apparent that regional features do emerge, such as the low-mid front unrounded vowel in a stressed syllable in Milan, the intervocalic voiceless velar fricative in Florence, the slight lenition of the intervocalic voiceless velar plosive in Rome, and the intervocalic voiceless alveolar sibilant in Rome and Naples.[4]

(1)   Standard: [u'mːeze di va'kantsa 'pasːa iŋ 'fretːa]
      Milan: [u'mːeze di va'kantsa 'pasːa iŋ 'frɛtːa]
      Florence: [u'mːeze di va'xantsa 'pasːa iŋ 'fretːa]
      Rome: [u'mːese di va'ʞantsa 'pasːa iŋ 'fretːa]
      Naples: [u'mːese di va'kantsa 'pasːa iŋ 'fretːa]
                  un mese di vacanza passa in fretta
                  (orthographic transcription)
      'a one-month vacation passes quickly'   (CLIPS Corpus, Crocco 2017: 99–100)

Regional features can also be found in morphology and syntax. An example is provided in Figure 1, where a number of morphosyntactic regional features of Turinese Italian are arranged on a four-value implicational scale (a slightly reduced version of the scale provided in Cerruti 2009: 238–239). These features were observed in a translation test from the local Italo-Romance dialect into Italian. A sample of Turinese speakers was asked to each translate a set of sentences that included dialect features with regionally marked counterparts in Italian (cf.

---

4. Yet not all the regional features typical of these areas are used. A selection process has indeed occurred, steered by the interplay of manifold factors (including the influence exerted by Italian orthography; cf. Crocco 2017: 106–109).

Cerruti 2009: 44–45). Certain regional features occurred frequently both among highly and poorly educated informants as well as among elderly and young informants. More specifically, features 1 through 5 were observed in more than 50% of cases across all social groups (with only one exception). The same five features have also been found to occur regularly in so-called "model texts" (Ammon 2015: 58–59), e.g. in spoken media, novels, newspapers and magazines (cf. Regis 2006; Cerruti 2014: 301; Cerruti & Regis 2014: 89; Regis 2017: 152–166). They can therefore be considered part of the regional standard usage.

Figure 1 may also indicate the progressive loss of several sub-standard regional features. The synchronic implicational patterns could be interpreted as the reflection of a diachronic process of de-dialectalisation that is less advanced among poorly educated, elderly speakers and more advanced among highly educated, young speakers. The former group still presents a significant number of sub-standard regional features, with these occurring in more than 25% of cases at the least, whereas the latter presents the lowest number of these features, their use being limited to fewer than or equal to 25% of cases. Overall, however, the group of individuals presenting the least sub-standard regional features is that of highly educated speakers in general. This shows that a number of regional features are becoming increasingly rare among highly educated, young speakers and are losing ground even among poorly educated, elderly speakers.[5]

The same can be observed for other regional varieties of Italian. Figure 2 presents the results of a translation test analogous to the one described above. A sample of speakers living in Caserta was asked to translate a set of sentences from the local Italo-Romance dialect into Italian. The regional features observed in the translations are arranged on a binary implicational scale (a slightly reduced version of the scale provided in De Ninno 2019: 137). A plus sign indicates that a certain feature was observed in more than 50% of cases, and a minus sign indicates a frequency of less than or equal to 50%. As with Turinese Italian, the implicational patterns in Figure 2 may be interpreted as reflections of both restandardisation and de-dialectalisation processes. In Caserta Italian, however, generational differences appear to outweigh educational differences, with young speakers showing the most minus signs and elderly speakers the most plus signs.

The processes affecting a given regional variety of Italian can also show conflicting tendencies. An example is the use of the compound past and simple past in Sicilian Italian. In Table 1, the meanings expressed by the compound and simple past in this regional variety are compared with those expressed by the same tenses in the local Italo-Romance dialect, i.e. Sicilian, and in standard Italian. The

---

5. This is the result of a selection process steered by internal, external and extra-linguistic factors (see, e.g. Cerruti & Regis 2014; Regis 2017: 167–171).

Figure 1. Morphosyntactic features of Turinese Italian: A four-value implicational scale (adapted from Cerruti 2009: 238–239).

3 = a certain feature occurred in more than 75% of cases, 2 = in more than 50%, 1 = in more than 25%, 0 = in equal to or fewer than 25%

	Elderly, poorly educated	Elderly, highly educated	Young, poorly educated	Young, highly educated
1. focus adverbial *solo più* (lit. 'only more')	3	3	3	3
2. *già* ('already') used as backchecking marker	3	3	3	3
3. 3sg *lui, lei* / pl *loro* (lit. 'him, her' / 'them') used as personal and reflexive pronouns	3	3	3	3
4. *fare che*+inf (lit. 'do that'+INF) expressing imminence and/or modality	2	2	2	2
5. progressive periphrasis *essere qni/lì che*+V/a+INF (lit. 'to be here/there that'+V/'to'+INF)	1	2	2	2
6. Ø preV negation with postV negative quantifier *niente* ('nothing')	2	1	1	0
7. progressive periphrasis *essere dietro a*+INF (lit. 'to be behind to'+INF)	2	1	0	0
8. doubly filled complementizer	2	0	0	0
9. Ø preV negation with postV negative quantifiers (≠ *niente* 'nothing')	2	0	0	0
10. *c'è* ('there is') in plural existential constructions	2	0	0	0
11. 2sg *te* (lit. 'you' as object pronoun) used as object and subject pronoun	1	0	0	0
12. *si* used as 1 pl reflexive clitic pronoun	1	0	0	0
13. V-pronouns agreeing with the gender of the addressee	1	0	0	0
14. progressive periphrasis *essere in cammino a*+INF (lit. 'to be on the way to'+INF)	0	0	0	0
15. lack of agreement with a plural postV subject (verb ≠ *c'è* 'there is')	0	0	0	0
16. 1sg *me* (lit. 'me') used as object and subject pronoun	0	0	0	0

Figure 2. Morphosyntactic features of Caserta Italian: A binary implicational scale (adapted from De Ninno 2019:137). + = a certain feature occurred in more than 50% of cases, − = in less than 50% of cases

	Elderly, less educated	Elderly, more educated	Young, less educated	Young, more educated
1. phasal adverbs in preverbal position (e.g. *lui già mi conosce* 'he already knows me')	+	+	+	+
2. possessive adjectives in postnominal position (e.g. *il ragazzo mio* 'my boyfriend')	+	+	+	+
3. *che* + V + *a fare?* (lit. 'what + V + to do?'; e.g. *che ridi a fare?* 'why are you laughing?')	+	+	+	+
4. *vicino a* ('to', lit. 'near to') + personal pronouns (e.g. *dillo vicino a me* 'say it to me')	+	+	+	+
5. transitive use of intransitive verbs (e.g. *l'ho telefonato* 'I phoned him')	+	+	−	−
6. overextension of the imperfect subjunctive (e.g. *chi l'avesse detto* 'who knew?')	+	+	−	−
7. differential object marking with post-V proper nouns (e.g. *chiamo a Luca* 'I call Luca')	+	+	−	−
8. *non me ne tiene* ('I don't want to', lit. 'it doesn't take of it to me')	−	−	−	−
9. progressive periphrasis *stare a* + INF (lit. 'stay to + INF')	−	−	−	−
10. *a* + content clauses (e.g. *è bello a vederti* 'it's good to see you')	−	−	−	−
11. possessive enclitic pronouns (e.g. *casma* 'my house')	−	−	−	−
12. differential object marking with post-V common nouns (e.g. *chiamo al dottore* 'I call the doctor')	−	−	−	−
13. *a* + object of comparison (e.g. *è alto come a me* 'he's tall as me')	−	−	−	−
14. *a* + personal pronouns for inalienable possession (es. *lui è padre a me* 'he's my father')	−	−	−	−

semantic functions associated with the use of these tenses in the two local varieties result from the analysis of a collection of semi-structured interviews and translations (from the ALS Corpus, cf. Amenta 2020). Bertinetto (1986) has been taken as a benchmark for standard Italian.

Table 1. Compound past and simple past: A comparison between Sicilian, Sicilian Italian and standard Italian (adapted from Amenta 2020: 74, 109)

	Sicilian		Sicilian Italian		Standard Italian	
	Compound past	Simple past	Compound past	Simple past	Compound past	Simple past
Aorist	−	+	+	+	+	+
Recent past	−	+	+	+	+	−
Persistent result	+	+/−	+	+/−	+	−
Experiential	+	+/−	+	−	+	−
Inclusive	+	+/−	+	−	+	−

As is apparent from Table 1, the use of the compound past in Sicilian is limited to the expression of certain functions; it is outcompeted by the use of the simple past in aoristic contexts, e.g. (2), and when referring to recent past events. It is also worth noting that the use of the simple past to denote persistent result, experientiality and inclusivity appears to be a fairly recent innovation in Sicilian (cf. Amenta 2020: 72), providing evidence for the acknowledged language vitality of Italo-Romance dialects (see Section 2 above). On the other hand, the use of the compound past in Sicilian Italian encompasses all semantic functions, including the aoristic, e.g. (3), thus conforming to the tendency in standard Italian to turn the compound past into a general-purpose perfective tense (cf. Squartini & Bertinetto 2000: 422–426). Regarding the use of the simple past, Sicilian Italian lies halfway between Sicilian and standard Italian, revealing a possible conflict between two opposing tendencies, i.e. the generalisation of the simple past vs. the marginalisation thereof, the former being modelled on the grammar of Sicilian and the latter on that of standard Italian.

(2) *avevo quattordici anni* **quannu me cugnatu appi l'incidenti**
[…] vent'anni fa[6]
'I was fourteen **when my brother-in-law had the accident**
[…] twenty years ago' (ALS Corpus, Palermo, Amenta 2020: 66)

---

6. Italian words are in italics, Sicilian words are highlighted in bold.

(3) *nel 1938 mi hanno chiamato sotto le armi*
    'in 1938 they called me (lit. 'they have called me') into the army'
    (ALS Corpus, Agrigento, Amenta 2020: 111)

In Sicilian Italian, the tendency to generalise the simple past is more noticeable among poorly educated, elderly speakers, whereas the tendency to generalise the compound past clearly prevails among highly educated, young speakers (see also Alfonzetti 1997: 29–39). More generally, such conflicting tendencies reflect two opposing vertical dynamics, i.e. convergence towards Italo-Romance dialects and convergence towards the standard usage. The former, which resists the de-dialectalisation of Italian, can mostly be observed in the varieties of the older generations (especially in those of poorly educated individuals), who are generally native and active speakers of Italo-Romance dialects. It is thus no coincidence that the process of de-dialectalisation is less advanced among the elderly (and less educated), as described above. On the contrary, convergence towards the standard usage mainly affects the varieties of the younger generations (especially those of highly educated speakers), who are generally socialised in Italian and have an increasingly limited command of Italo-Romance dialects.[7]

Finally, lexis is also influenced by restandardisation and de-dialectalisation. The Italian spoken in a given area tends to be characterised by the coexistence of region-specific and regionally unmarked expressions, the latter being widely used throughout the peninsula. Neo-standard usage allows a certain degree of lexical variation across areas, especially in certain semantic domains (such as food and household items). At the same time, an increasing number of region-specific expressions are becoming socially and/or stylistically marked and are tending towards no longer being transferred from generation to generation (cf. D'Achille & Viviani 2003; Nesi 2013).

4. Horizontal convergence

Contemporary Italian is also affected by processes of horizontal convergence, mainly concerning the inter-regional dimension. The differences between regional varieties are becoming less pronounced, partly due to the supra-regional use of features originally confined to distinct areas. Every regional variety increasingly consists of both "autochthonous" features, i.e. linguistic features essentially resulting from substratum interference, and "allochthonous" features, i.e. linguistic features

---

7. Evidence for the two opposing tendencies described can be found in morphosyntactic phenomena, such as in the variability of subject–verb agreement in existential plural constructions and in the pace of grammaticalisation of progressive periphrasis (cf. Cerruti 2014, 2017).

originating from other geographic areas. The presence of the latter is mostly the result of internal migration, which has reached peaks of over 2 million reallocations per year in the past six decades (cf. Fiaschi & Tealdi 2018: 4–6). These "composite" varieties[8] are especially noticeable in Northern Italy, as the south-to-north migration flows have always been the most significant (see, e.g. Impicciatore & Panichella 2019), and among the younger generations, regardless of whether they were born to immigrant parents (see, e.g. Boario 2017).

The results of recent research also provide valuable insight into the sociolinguistic status of composite utterances. A study carried out in Turin (Fontanot 2019) examined the linguistic behaviour of young speakers with different levels of education in two speech styles, i.e. casual speech (from the KIParla Corpus) and read speech (from CLIPS, also mentioned above), the aim being to explore the social and stylistic diffusion of composite pronunciations. The research showed that a number of features originating from central and southern varieties of Italian also occur among Turinese speakers, e.g. phonosyntactic doubling, as in [a ˈvːɔlte] 'sometimes', [ɔ kːaˈpito] 'I understood', and [e ˈnːɔj] 'and us'; "intrinsic geminates" (Bertinetto & Loporcaro 2005), as in [disperaˈtːsjɔne] 'desperation', [aˈdːzjɛnda] 'company', and [biˈʎːɛtːo] 'ticket'; and intervocalic [b] lengthening, as in [ˈabːile] 'skilled', and [ˈkwɛlːa ˈbːɛlːa] 'that beautiful'.[9] The same phenomena can increasingly be found in other major cities in Northern Italy as well, such as Genoa, Milan and Venice (cf. Fontanot 2019: 77–90).

However, the results show that these features appear to be socially and/or stylistically marked. Composite pronunciations are, to a certain extent, more widespread among less educated speakers and in casual speech. The use of allochthonous features by highly educated speakers and in more careful speech styles is rarer, though attested; see, for example, the occurrence of the central–southern intrinsic geminate [tːs] (in lieu of the autochthonous [ts]) in the read speech of a Milanese university student in (4).

(4) [troˈvava le paˈrɔle aˈdatːe ad ˈoɲi sitwaˈtːsjone]
     'he/she found the proper words to say in any situation'
                                   (CLIPS Corpus, Milan, Fontanot 2019: 81)

Moreover, these two groups of speakers show extensive inter-individual variation. Some speakers categorically use either the autochthonous or the allochthonous variants, whereas others alternate between the two. Among the latter, those who present similar patterns of usage for one variant do not necessarily show similar

---

8. Regional varieties of Italian consisting of both "autochthonous" and "allochthonous" features have been referred to as "composite" since Canepari (1983).

9. The autochthonous variants would be the following: [a ˈvɔlte], [ɔ kaˈpito], [e ˈnɔj]; [disperaˈtsjɔne], [aˈdzjɛnda], [biˈʎɛtːo]; and [ˈabile], [ˈkwɛlːa ˈbɛlːa].

patterns in their use of the other. It is often the case that the two variants themselves do not even present coherent patterns of occurrence in the speech of a single individual. Composite pronunciations can thus be characterised as resulting from "bricolage" (Eckert 2008). In (5) and (6), for example, a Turinese speaker alternates between two allophones of the intrinsic geminate /ʎː/, i.e. the autochthonous variant [lj] and the allochthonous variant [ʎː], when pronouncing the same word in casual speech.

(5) *quando lavori con la fami[ʎː]a è bellissimo, però devi essere una fami[lj]a come la nostra*
'it is wonderful when you work with the family, but it must be a family like ours'　(KIParla Corpus, Turin, Fontanot 2019:39)

(6) *è completamente un altro mondo rispetto all'Ita[lj]a, a Torino [...], perché non è come in Ita[ʎː]a*
'it is a completely different world compared to Italy, to Turin [...], because it's not like in Italy'　(KIParla Corpus, Turin, Fontanot 2019:57)

Of all linguistic levels, pronunciation is most characterised by such a mix of features. However, the coexistence of autochthonous and allochthonous features can also be observed in morphology and syntax. A study based on data from the KIParla Corpus (Cerruti 2018) examined the distribution of eight regionally marked morphosyntactic features of Italian in the speech of students at the University of Bologna. It found that morphosyntactic features originating from central and southern varieties of Italian also occur among students of northern origin, especially in casual speech. Below are examples of central–southern features appearing in spontaneous in-group conversations, i.e. the progressive periphrasis *stare a* + infinitive in (7), the apocopic forms of the infinitives *di'* in (7) and *cresce* in (8), and the overextension of *stare* as a copula in (9). The speakers are from Lombardy (7), Emilia-Romagna (8) and Trentino-Alto Adige (9).[10]

(7) *che stavamo a di', stavam parlando di Grigi*
'what were we talking about? we were talking about Grigi'
(KIParla Corpus, Bologna, Cerruti 2018:22)

(8) *ancora ti deve cresce la barba*
'your beard still has to grow'　(KIParla Corpus, Bologna, Cerruti 2018:22)

(9) *questa in realtà sta praticamente fuori corso*
'actually, she's practically past the prescribed time for completing her degree'
(KIParla Corpus, Bologna, Cerruti 2018:22)

---

10. In northern varieties of Italian, the most common counterparts would be *che stavamo dicendo?* (vs. *che stavamo a di'*, (7)), *crescere* (vs. *cresce*, (8)) and *è* (vs. *sta*, (9)).

The students' speech was examined in three types of interactions: in spontaneous in-group conversations, semi-structured interviews and oral examinations. The relationship between the participants is symmetrical in the former two (student–student interactions) and asymmetrical in the latter (student–professor interactions). Table 2 reports the number of tokens for the above-mentioned eight regionally marked morphosyntactic features of Italian, including the central–southern features occurring in (7), (8) and (9).[11] The allochthonous or autochthonous status of each token is relative to the speaker's provenance. It is apparent that the allochthonous/autochthonous token ratio is higher in student–student interactions than in student–professor interactions, which corroborates the stylistic markedness of composite utterances. Moreover, the ratio differs between spontaneous in-group conversations and semi-structured interviews ($F=0.0054$, $p<.01$). This could suggest that the presence of (at least some) allochthonous features is related to communicative purposes. During in-group conversations, speakers are more concerned with the representation and negotiation of social identities, whereas in semi-structured interviews, speakers focus rather on transmitting information (cf. Cerruti 2018: 21).

Table 2. "Allochthonous" and "autochthonous" morphosyntactic features among university students in Bologna (Cerruti 2018: 21)

	Spontaneous conversations	Semi-structured interviews	Oral examinations
"Allochthonous" tokens	64	7	0
"Autochthonous" tokens	335	109	3
Ratio	0.191	0.064	0

Previous studies on spoken Italian have shown that the supra-regional use of originally region-specific features is often accompanied by changes in the indexicalities of these features (a phenomenon comparable to that of "reallocation", cf. Kerswill & Trudgill 2005); that is, linguistic features that spread beyond their borders frequently shift from being markers of geographic provenance to being markers of social identity (see, e.g. Cortinovis & Miola 2009; Boario 2017). To return to phonetics/phonology, such is the case, for instance, with phonosyntactic doubling among Turinese adolescents. The presence of phonosyntactic doubling in Turin is presumably due to migration flows from Southern Italy, as mentioned above. However, in Turin, this feature appears to be particularly widespread among adolescent communities of practice. These communities comprise both speakers of

---

11. The full list of features is provided in Cerruti (2018: 20–21).

southern and northern origin as well as foreign-origin speakers of various ethnic groups. In (10), for example, phonosyntactic doubling can be observed among two adolescents of Moroccan origin.[12] This feature is mostly used in conversations between members of the same community of practice, indexing a speaker's membership and thus serving as a marker of social identity (cf. Boario 2017).

(10) A: *ma abbiamo allenamento alle sette*
'but we have soccer practice at seven'
B: *sì ma io devo andare a [k:]asa a prendere la roba*
'yes, but I have to go home and get my stuff'
A: *sì ma abiti qua [v:]icino mica*
'yes, but you live right around here'
B: *a che ora te ne devi andare?*
'what time do you have to go?' (Turin, Boario 2017:302)

Lexis, too, is becoming increasingly composite. As mentioned above in Section 3, every regional variety of Italian generally consists of both region-specific and regionally unmarked expressions. The latter often result from the supra-regional spread of lexical features originally confined to distinct areas (see, e.g. Nesi & Poggi-Salani 2013). This can be observed in a comparison of two questionnaire surveys conducted many years apart on almost all the same features – one was conducted in the 1950s (Rüegg 1956), the other in the 2000s (cf. D'Achille & Viviani 2003; Nesi 2013). An example is the spread over time of *l'anno scorso* 'last year'. In the 1950s, this expression was mostly found in Northern Italy, whereas nowadays it is widespread throughout the country and forms part of the standard usage. On the other hand, most of the other variants encountered in the 1950s, e.g. *l'anno trascorso* 'the past year', *l'anno precedente* 'the previous year', *l'anno prima* 'the year before', and *anno* 'year', are still used but are now regionally and/ or socio-stylistically marked (see also Berruto 2018b).

This is also indicative of a north-to-south spread of linguistic features occurring alongside south-to-north processes of feature diffusion. Whereas the latter result mainly from internal migration flows, the former is driven to a greater extent by factors other than migration, including speakers' attitudes. A number of features of northern varieties of Italian have been gaining prestige and functioning as indexicals of standardness (cf. Galli de' Paratesi 1984; De Pascale et al. 2017), which has fostered the spread of these features across the country, particularly within the standard usage. This has affected all linguistic levels but is especially evident in phonetics/phonology. A well-known example is the north-to-south spread of the intervocalic voiced alveolar sibilant. The use of intervocalic

---

12. The Northern Italian variants would be *a* [k]*asa* and *qua* [v]*icino*, respectively.

/z/ is traditionally generalised in northern varieties of Italian, as is the use of inter-vocalic /s/ in southern varieties, while they can contrast in pairs in central varieties such as Florentine (see, e.g. *fuso* ['fuso] 'spindle' vs. *fuso* ['fuzo] 'liquefied'). Under the influence of northern pronunciation, in central varieties, intervocalic /s/ is being used less frequently and the phonemic contrast between /z/ and /s/ in intervocalic position is becoming weaker (cf. Bertinetto & Loporcaro 2005; Calamai 2017). For Florentine, see, for example, the pronunciation [u'mːeze] 'one month' in (1).

5. Conclusions

Overall, differences persist between the regional varieties of Italian, though they are becoming increasingly less pronounced. On the one hand, in distinct geographic areas, the convergence of the standard usage towards sub-standard varieties has led, and continues to lead, to certain regionally marked vernacular features becoming more widespread as part of the regional standard usage. Downward convergence has therefore consolidated some of the extant differences between regional varieties.

On the other hand, regional differentiation has become significantly less pronounced. In various areas, the convergence of sub-standard varieties towards the standard usage has led, and continues to lead, to the obsolescence of several sub-standard regional features. This process is more advanced among young (and highly educated) individuals – who are generally socialised in Italian and have an increasingly limited command of Italo-Romance dialects – and less advanced among elderly (and poorly educated) speakers – who are generally native and active speakers of Italo-Romance dialects. Upward convergence is thus resulting in horizontal, i.e. inter-regional, convergence, as the obsolescence of region-specific features can only lead to regional varieties becoming more similar.

Horizontal convergence is also a process in itself, driven in particular by the supra-regional diffusion of originally region-specific features. This process affects northern, youth, and sub-standard varieties to a greater extent. The presence of central–southern features in northern varieties is, indeed, more prevalent among the younger generations and is in most cases socially and/or stylistically marked. Moreover, the indexical value of these linguistic features tends to shift from being a marker of geographic provenance to a marker of social identity. Horizontal convergence can also be observed, however, in the standard usage, as is the case with a number of northern features that have been gaining prestige and spreading across Italy as indexicals of standardness.

Chapter 8. After dialectalisation **179**

Finally, the obsolescence of sub-standard regional features is opposed by the active influence of Italo-Romance dialects on the speech of older generations and partly counterbalanced by the use of allochthonous features among the younger generations. At present, the use of features originating from different regions is nevertheless subject to extensive inter-individual variation and bricolage, and it seems that co-occurrence patterns are still far from becoming established.

References

Alfonzetti, Giovanna. 1997. 'Ora la luna si nascose, ma prima era bellissima'. Passato prossimo e passato remoto nell'italiano di Sicilia ['The moon has gone into hiding now, but it was really beautiful before'. The compound past and simple past in Sicilian Italian]. In Mari D'Agostino (ed.), *Aspetti della variabilità*, 11–48. Palermo: Centro di studi filologici e linguistici siciliani.

ALS (Atlante Linguistico della Sicilia). http://www.atlantelinguisticosicilia.it. (26 November, 2021.)

Amenta, Luisa. 2020. *Strutture tempo-aspettuali nel siciliano e nell'italiano regionale di Sicilia* [Tense and aspect in Sicilian and Sicilian Italian]. Palermo: Centro di studi filologici e linguistici siciliani.

Ammon, Ulrich. 2015. On the social forces that determine what is standard in a language, with a look at the norms of non-standard language varieties. *Bulletin Suisse de Linguistique Appliquée (VALS-ASLA)* 3. 53–67.

Auer, Peter (ed.). 1998. Dialect levelling and the standard varieties in Europe. *Folia Linguistica* 32.

Auer, Peter. 2005. Europe's sociolinguistic unity, or: A typology of European dialect-standard constellations. In Nicole Delbecque, Johan van der Auwera & Dirk Geeraerts (eds.), *Perspectives on variation. Sociolinguistic, historical, comparative*, 7–42. Berlin & New York, NY: Mouton de Gruyter.

Auer, Peter. 2017. The neo-standard of Italy and elsewhere in Europe. In Massimo Cerruti, Claudia Crocco & Stefania Marzo (Eds.), *Towards a new standard: Theoretical and empirical studies on the restandardization of Italian*, 365–374. Berlin & New York, NY: Mouton de Gruyter.

Auer, Peter, Frans Hinskens & Klaus J. Mattheier (eds.). 1996. Convergence and divergence of dialects in Europe. *Sociolinguistica* 10.

Auer, Peter, Frans Hinskens & Paul Kerswill (eds.). 2005. *Dialect change: Convergence and divergence in European languages*. Cambridge: Cambridge University Press.

Auer, Peter & Helmut Spiekermann. 2011. Demotisation of the standard variety or destandardisation? The changing status of German in late modernity (with special reference to south-western Germany). In Tore Kristiansen & Nikolas Coupland (eds.), *Standard languages and language standards in a changing Europe*, 161–176. Oslo: Novus.

Ballarè, Silvia. 2020. L'italiano neo-standard oggi: Stato dell'arte [Neo-standard Italian today: State of the art]. *Italiano LinguaDue* 12(2). 469–492.

Berruto, Gaetano. 2005. Dialect-standard convergence, mixing, and models of language contact: The case of Italy. In Peter Auer, Frans Hinskens & Paul Kerswill (eds.), *Dialect change: Convergence and divergence in European languages*, 81–95. Cambridge: Cambridge University Press.

Berruto, Gaetano. 2006. Quale dialetto per l'Italia del Duemila? Aspetti dell'italianizzazione e risorgenze dialettali in Piemonte (e altrove) [Which dialect for Italy in the 2000s? Certain aspects of Italianisation and dialect 'resurgences' in Piedmont (and elsewhere)]. In Alberto A. Sobrero & Annarita Miglietta (eds.), *Lingua e dialetto nell'Italia del Duemila*, 101–127. Galatina: Congedo.

Berruto, Gaetano. 2012. *Sociolinguistica dell'italiano contemporaneo. Nuova edizione* [Sociolinguistics of contemporary Italian. Revised edition]. Roma: Carocci.

Berruto, Gaetano. 2018a. The languages and dialects of Italy. In Wendy Ayres-Bennett & Janice Carruthers (eds.), *Manual of Romance sociolinguistics*, 494–525. Berlin & New York, NY: Mouton de Gruyter.

Berruto, Gaetano. 2018b. Tendenze nell'italiano del Duemila e rapporti fra varietà standard e sub-standard [Trends in the Italian of the 2000s and relationships between standard and sub-standard varieties]. *AggiornaMenti* 13. 5–15.

Bertinetto, Pier Marco. 1986. *Tempo, aspetto e azione nel verbo italiano. Il sistema dell'indicativo* [Tense, aspect and aktionsart in the Italian verb: The system of the indicative]. Firenze: Accademia della Crusca.

Bertinetto, Pier Marco & Michele Loporcaro. 2005. The sound pattern of Standard Italian, as compared with the varieties spoken in Florence, Milan and Rome. *Journal of The Phonetic Association* 35. 131–151.

Boario, Anna. 2017. Native speaker–non-native speaker interaction: More than one type of accommodation. *Sociolinguistic Studies* 11(2–3–4). 291–312.

Calamai, Silvia. 2017. Tuscan between standard and vernacular: A sociophonetic perspective. In Massimo Cerruti, Claudia Crocco & Stefania Marzo (eds.), *Towards a new standard: Theoretical and empirical studies on the restandardization of Italian*, 213–241. Berlin & New York, NY: Mouton de Gruyter.

Canepari, Luciano. 1983. *Italiano standard e pronunce regionali* [Standard Italian and regional pronunciations]. Padova: CLEUP.

Canepari, Luciano. 1999. *Il MaPi. Manuale di pronuncia italiana* [MaPi. The Handbook of Italian pronunciation]. Bologna: Zanichelli.

Castellani, Arrigo. 1982. Quanti erano gli italofoni nel 1861? [How many speakers of Italian were there in 1861?]. *Studi Linguistici Italiani* 8. 3–26.

Cerruti, Massimo. 2009. *Strutture dell'italiano regionale. Morfosintassi di una varietà diatopica in prospettiva sociolinguistica* [Structures of regional Italian. Morphosyntax of a diatopic variety in a sociolinguistic perspective]. Frankfurt am Main: Lang.

Cerruti, Massimo. 2011. Regional varieties of Italian in the linguistic repertoire. *International Journal of the Sociology of Language* 210. 9–28.

Cerruti, Massimo. 2014. From language contact to language variation: A case of contact-induced grammaticalization in Italo-Romance. *Journal of Language Contact* 7(2). 288–308.

Cerruti, Massimo. 2017. Morphosyntactic variation: Individual grammar and group grammar in the 'de-dialectalization' of Italian. *Sociolinguistic Studies* 11(2–3–4). 313–339.

Cerruti, Massimo. 2018. Il parlato regionale oggi: un italiano composito? [Regional speech today: A composite Italian?]. *Lingua Italiana d'Oggi* 15. 15–31.

Cerruti, Massimo, Claudia Crocco & Stefania Marzo (eds.). 2017. *Towards a new standard: Theoretical and empirical studies on the restandardization of Italian*. Berlin & New York, NY: Mouton de Gruyter.

Cerruti, Massimo & Riccardo Regis. 2014. Standardization patterns and dialect-standard convergence: A northwestern Italian perspective. *Language in Society* 43(1). 83–111.

Cerruti, Massimo & Stavroula Tsiplakou (eds.). 2020. *Intermediate language varieties. Koinai and regional standards in Europe*. Amsterdam & Philadelphia, PA: John Benjamins.

CLIPS (Corpora e Lessici di Italiano Parlato e Scritto). http://www.clips.unina.it. (26 November, 2021.)

Cortinovis, Enrica & Emanuele Miola. 2009. Chiamami *rappuso*: Il suffisso -*uso* dai dialetti meridionali al linguaggio giovanile torinese [Call me *rappuso*: The spread of the suffix -*uso* from southern dialects to youth varieties in Turin]. *Rivista Italiana di Dialettologia* 33. 195–218.

Coseriu, Eugenio. 1980. "Historische Sprache" und "Dialekt" ["Historical language" and "dialect"]. In Joachim Göschel, Pavle Iviæ & Kurt Kehr (eds.), *Dialekt und Dialektologie*, 106–122. Wiesbaden: Steiner.

Crocco, Claudia. 2017. Everyone has an accent: Standard Italian and regional pronunciation. In Massimo Cerruti, Claudia Crocco & Stefania Marzo (eds.), *Towards a new standard: Theoretical and empirical studies on the restandardization of Italian*, 89–117. Berlin & New York, NY: Mouton de Gruyter.

D'Achille, Paolo & Andrea Viviani (eds.). 2003. *La lingua delle città. I dati di Roma, Latina, L'Aquila e Catania* [The language of the cities. Data from Rome, Latina, L'Aquila and Catania]. Roma: Aracne.

D'Agostino, Mari. 2012. *Sociolinguistica dell'Italia contemporanea* [Sociolinguistics of contemporary Italy]. Bologna: Il Mulino.

Dal Negro, Silvia & Alessandro Vietti. 2011. Italian and Italo-Romance dialects. *International Journal of the Sociology of Language* 210. 71–92.

De Mauro, Tullio. 1976. *Storia linguistica dell'Italia unita* [Linguistic history of unified Italy]. Bari: Laterza.

De Ninno, Maria Antonietta. 2019. *L'italiano regionale campano: Analisi sociolinguistica di alcuni tratti morfosintattici* [Regional Italian in Campania: A sociolinguistic analysis of certain morphosyntactic features]. Turin: University of Turin MA thesis.

De Pascale, Stefano, Stefania Marzo & Dirk Speelman. 2017. Evaluating regional variation in Italian: Towards a change in standard language ideology? In Massimo Cerruti, Claudia Crocco & Stefania Marzo (eds.), *Towards a new standard: Theoretical and empirical studies on the restandardization of Italian*, 118–141. Berlin & New York, NY: Mouton de Gruyter.

Eckert, Penelope. 2008. Variation and the indexical field. *Journal of Sociolinguistics* 12. 453–476.

Fiaschi, Davide & Cristina Tealdi. 2018. Some stylised facts on Italian inter-regional migration. *Discussion Papers del Dipartimento di Economia e Management dell'Università di Pisa* 231, http://www.ec.unipi.it/documents/Ricerca/papers/2018-231.pdf. (20 September, 2021.)

Fontanot, Arianna. 2019. *Aspetti di italiano composito nella pronuncia di giovani torinesi: un'indagine su corpora* [Composite Italian in the pronunciation of young speakers in Turin: a corpus-based analysis]. Turin: University of Turin MA thesis.

Galli de' Paratesi, Nora. 1984. *Lingua toscana in bocca ambrosiana. Tendenze verso l'italiano standard: un'inchiesta sociolinguistica* [The Tuscan language as spoken by the Ambrosians. Tendencies towards standard Italian: a sociolinguistic investigation]. Bologna: Il Mulino.

Impicciatore, Roberto & Nazareno Panichella. 2019. Internal migration trajectories, occupational achievement and social mobility in contemporary Italy. A life course perspective. *Population Space and Place* 25(6). 1–19.

ISTAT. 2017. *L'uso della lingua italiana, dei dialetti e delle lingue straniere* [The use of Italian, dialects and foreign languages]. Roma: Istituto Nazionale di Statistica. https://www.istat.it /it/archivio/207961. (20 September, 2021.)

Kerswill, Paul & Peter Trudgill. 2005. The birth of new dialects. In Peter Auer, Frans Hinskens & Paul Kerswill (eds.), *Dialect change: Convergence and divergence in European languages*, 196–220. Cambridge: Cambridge University Press.

KIParla (Corpus di Italiano Parlato). https://www.kiparla.it. (26 November, 2021.)

Maiden, Martin & Mair Parry. 1997. Introduction. In Martin Maiden & Mair Parry (eds.), *The dialects of Italy*, 1–4. London: Routledge.

Moretti, Bruno. 2006. Nuovi aspetti della relazione italiano-dialetto in Ticino [New aspects of the relationship between Italian and dialect in the Canton of Ticino]. In Alberto A. Sobrero & Annarita Miglietta (eds.), *Lingua e dialetto nell'Italia del Duemila*, 31–48. Galatina: Congedo.

Nesi, Annalisa (ed.). 2013. *La lingua delle città. Raccolta di studi* [The language of the cities. A collection of studies]. Firenze: Franco Cesati.

Nesi, Annalisa & Teresa Poggi-Salani. 2013. "La lingua delle città". Che cos'è e a cosa serve ["The language of the cities". What it is and what it is for]. In Annalisa Nesi (ed.), *La lingua delle città. Raccolta di studi*, 15–45. Firenze: Franco Cesati.

Pellegrini, Giovan Battista. 1977. *Carta dei dialetti d'Italia* [Map of the dialects of Italy]. Pisa: Pacini. https://phaidra.cab.unipd.it/detail/o:318149 (1 June, 2022.)

Regis, Riccardo. 2006. Breve fenomenologia di una locuzione avverbiale: il *solo più* dell'italiano regionale piemontese [A brief phenomenology of an adverbial locution: *Solo più* in Piedmontese Italian]. *Studi di lessicografia italiana* 23. 275–289.

Regis, Riccardo. 2017. How regional standards set in: The case of standard Piedmontese Italian. In Massimo Cerruti, Claudia Crocco & Stefania Marzo (eds.), *Towards a new standard: Theoretical and empirical studies on the restandardization of Italian*, 145–175. Berlin & New York, NY: Mouton de Gruyter.

Rüegg, Robert. 1956. *Zur Wortgeographie der Italienischen Umgangssprache* [On the word geography of colloquial Italian]. Köln: Kölner Romanistische Arbeiten.

Squartini, Mario & Pier Marco Bertinetto. 2000. The simple and compound past in Romance languages. In Östen Dahl (ed.), *Tense and aspect in the languages of Europe*, 403–440. Berlin & New York, NY: Mouton de Gruyter.

Juan Andrés Villena-Ponsoda's publications

1984a. Variación o sistema. El estudio de la lengua en su contexto social: William Labov (I) [Variation or system. The study of language in its social context: William Labov (I)]. *Analecta Malacitana* 7(2). 267–295.

1984b. Variación o sistema. El estudio de la lengua en su contexto social: William Labov (II) [Variation or system. The study of language in its social context: William Labov (II)]. *Analecta Malacitana* 8(1). 3–45.

1987a. *Forma, sustancia y redundancia contextual: El caso del vocalismo del español andaluz* [Form, substance and contextual redundancy: The case of vowels in Andalusian Spanish]. Malaga: Universidad de Málaga.

1987b. Creatividad y mímesis en las ciencias del lenguaje [Creativity and mimesis in the language sciences]. *Analecta Malacitana* 10(2). 423–431.

1988. Perspectivas y límites de la investigación sociolingüística contemporánea (Reflexiones programáticas a propósito del Proyecto de Investigación del sistema de Variedades Vernáculas Malagueñas) [Perspectives and limitations of contemporary sociolinguistic research (programmatic reflexions for the purpose of the Research Project on the Vernacular Varieties System of Malaga)]. *Estudios de Lingüística Universidad de Alicante* 5. 237–274.

1990, with Rafael Gobernado-Arribas, Félix Requena-Santos & José Luis Gómez-Urda. *Familia y red social: Roles, normas y relaciones externas en las familias urbanas corrientes* [Family and social network: Roles, norms and external relationships in ordinary urban families], translation of *Family and social network: Roles, norms and external relationships in ordinary urban families* by Elizabeth Bott. Madrid: Taurus.

1991. Las consecuencias lingüísticas de ser una mujer. Notas para la intervención teórica en el campo de la conexión entre la lengua y el sexo [The linguistic consequences of being a woman. Notes for theoretical intervention in the area that connects language and gender]. In María Isabel Calvo-Ortega (ed.), *La mujer en el mundo contemporáneo. Realidad y perspectivas*, 149–191. Malaga: Diputación Provincial.

1992a. *Fundamentos del pensamiento social sobre el lenguaje. Constitución y crítica de la sociolingüística* [The fundamentals of social thought in the field of language. Constitution and criticism of sociolinguistics]. Malaga: Ágora.

1992b. Manipulación y uso lingüístico comunitario. El caso del español de Andalucía [Manipulation and shared linguistic usage. The case of Andalusian Spanish]. *Analecta Malacitana* 14(1). 343–374.

1992c. Representational procedures and schemes for the University of Malaga Spanish spoken corpus. Pilot report. In *NERC Project* 141, 1–30. Contribution by Universidad de Málaga.

1993a, with Inés Carrasco, Pilar Carrasco, Manuel Galeote & María Isabel Montoya (eds.). *Antiqua et nova Romania. Estudios lingüísticos y filológicos en honor del profesor José Mondéjar* [*Antiqua et nova Romania*. Linguistic and philological studies in honour of the professor José Mondéjar], vol. 1, vol. 2. Granada: Universidad de Granada.

1993b. Conformismo y ciencia del lenguaje. La ideología del neutralismo lingüístico y la posición sociolingüística [Conformism and science of language. The ideology of linguistic neutrality and the sociolinguistic stance]. In Juan Andrés Villena-Ponsoda, Inés Carrasco, Pilar Carrasco, Manuel Galeote & María Isabel Montoya (eds.), *Estudios lingüísticos y filológicos en honor del profesor José Mondéjar*, vol. 1, vol. 2, 89–120. Granada: Universidad de Granada.

1993c. Presentación [Foreword]. In Juan Luis Jiménez-Ruiz (ed.), *Campo léxico y connotación. A propósito de la razón y la inspiración en Bécquer*, 5–6. Alicante: Universidad de Alicante.

1994a, with José María Sánchez-Sáez & Antonio Manuel Ávila-Muñoz. Modelos probabilísticos multinomiales para el estudio del seseo, ceceo y distinción de /s/ y /θ/. Datos de la ciudad de Málaga [Multinomial probabilistic models for the study of seseo, ceceo and the distinction between /s/ and /θ/. Data from the city of Malaga]. *Estudios de Lingüística Universidad de Alicante* 10. 391–436.

1994b, with Manuel Alvar-Ezquerra. *Estudios para un corpus del español* [Studies towards a corpus of Spanish]. Malaga: Universidad de Málaga.

1994c. Pautas y procedimientos de representación del corpus oral español de la Universidad de Málaga. Informe preliminar [Representational standards and procedures for the Spanish oral corpus of the University of Malaga. Preliminary report]. In Manuel Alvar-Ezquerra & Juan Andrés Villena-Ponsoda (eds.), *Estudios para un corpus del español*, 73–101. Malaga: Universidad de Málaga.

1994d. Dimensiones sociales y límites internos en la enseñanza de la lengua española en Andalucía [Social dimensions and internal limitations in Spanish language teaching in Andalusia]. In Manuel Alvar-Ezquerra & Juan Andrés Villena-Ponsoda (eds.), *Estudios para un corpus del español*, 185–216. Malaga: Universidad de Málaga.

1994e. *La ciudad lingüística: Fundamentos críticos de la sociolingüística urbana* [The linguistic city: Crucial foundations of urban sociolinguistics]. Malaga: Universidad de Málaga.

1995. Perspectivas terapéuticas y emancipadoras en la genesis de la investigación variacionista [Therapeutic and emancipatory perspectives in the genesis of variationist research]. In Juan de Dios Luque-Durán & Antonio Pamiés-Beltrán (eds.), *Primer Simposio de historiografía lingüística*, 132–148. Granada: Universidad de Granada.

1996a, with Félix Requena-Santos. Género, educación y uso lingüístico: La variación social y reticular de s/z en la ciudad de Málaga [Gender, education and linguistic use: Social and social network variation of s/z in the city of Malaga]. *Lingüística* 8. 5–52.

1996b. Convergence and divergence of dialects in a standard-dialect continuum. Networks and individuals in Malaga. *Sociolinguistica* 10. 112–137.

1996c. Modelos ideales y pautas de pronunciación en la modalidad lingüística andaluza [Ideal models and standards for pronunciation in the Andalusian linguistic modality]. In Jerónimo de las Heras, Pedro Carbonero, Alberto Costa & Valentín Torrejón (eds.), *La modalidad lingüística andaluza en el aula: Actas de las I Jornadas sobre Modalidad Lingüística Andaluza*, 31–64. Sevilla: Alfar.

Juan Andrés Villena-Ponsoda's publications   **185**

1997a. Convergencia y divergencia dialectales en el continuo sociolingüístico andaluz. Datos del vernáculo urbano malagueño [Dialectal convergence and divergence in the Andalusian sociolinguistic continuum. Data on the urban vernacular of Malaga]. *Lingüística Española Actual* 19. 83–125.

1997b. Sociolingüística andaluza y sociolingüística del andaluz [Andalusian sociolinguistics and sociolinguistics of Andalusian]. In Antonio Narbona & Miguel Ropero (eds.), *El habla andaluza. Actas del congreso del habla andaluza*, 277–347. Sevilla: Universidad de Sevilla.

1999, with Antonio Manuel Ávila-Muñoz. La disolución cultural del sexo [The cultural dissolution of gender]. In María Dolores Fernández de la Torre, Antonia María Medina-Guerra & Lidia Taillefer (eds.), *El sexismo en el lenguaje*, vol. 1, 107–142. Malaga: Diputación Provincial.

2000a. Identidad y variación lingüística: Prestigio nacional y lealtad vernacular en el español hablado en Andalucía [Identity and linguistic variation: National prestige and vernacular loyalty in the Spanish spoken in Andalusia]. In Georg Bossong & Francisco Báez de Aguilar (eds.), *Identidades lingüísticas en la España autonómica*, 107–150. Frankfurt am Main: Vervuert. Madrid: Iberoamericana.

2000b. La lengua y la sociedad en Andalucía [Language and society in Andalusia]. In Antonio Narbona (ed.), *El habla andaluza: Historia, normas y uso*, 89–120. Sevilla: Ayuntamiento de Estepa.

2001. *La continuidad del cambio lingüístico. Tendencias innovadoras y conservadoras de la fonología del español a la luz de la investigación sociolingüística urbana* [The continuity of linguistic change. Innovative and conservative tendencies of Spanish phonology considered through the lens of urban sociolinguistic research]. Granada: Universidad de Granada.

2002a. Tipología de sistemas fonológicos y variación sociolingüística en el español de Andalucía [The typology of phonological systems and sociolinguistic variation in Andalusian Spanish]. In Antonio Martínez (ed.), *Las hablas andaluzas ante el siglo XXI*, 189–213. Almería: Instituto de Estudios Almerienses.

2002b. La reintroducción del realismo en la teoría de la variación del lenguaje: Las redes sociales en la metodología sociolingüística [The re-introduction of realism into the theory of linguistic variation: Social networks in sociolinguistic methodology]. In Miguel Casas & Luis Escoriza (eds.), *VI Jornadas de lingüística*, 229–265. Cádiz: Universidad de Cádiz.

2003a. El valor interpretativo de las redes sociales en la variación lingüística. Datos para una polémica en curso [The interpretative value of social networks in linguistic variation. Data for an ongoing controversy]. In José Luis Girón-Alconchel, Francisco Javier Herrero-Ruiz, Silvia Iglesias-Recuero & Antonio Narbona-Jiménez (eds.), *Estudios ofrecidos al Profesor José Jesús de Bustos Tovar*, vol. 1, 823–836. Madrid: Arco/Libros.

2003b, with Juan Antonio Moya-Corral, Antonio Manuel Ávila-Muñoz & Matilde Vida-Castro. Proyecto de investigación de la formación de dialectos (FORDIAL) [Research project on dialect formation (FORDIAL)]. *Estudios de Lingüística Universidad de Alicante* 17. 607–636.

2003c. Fundamentos semánticos de la variación lingüística [The semantic foundations of linguistic variation]. In *Actas del VIII Simposio de Actualización Científica y Didáctica de Lengua Española y Literatura*, 121–146. Malaga: Diputación Provincial.

2003d. Igualdad y desigualdad social como factores condicionantes de la variación lingüística en el español de Andalucía [Social equality and inequality as conditioning factors of linguistic variation in Andalusian Spanish]. In Antonio Narbona (ed.), *El habla andaluza. El español hablado en Andalucía*, 73–105. Sevilla: Ayuntamiento de Estepa.

2003e. Restricciones de coocurrencia entre las obstruyentes fricativas en los dialectos innovadores del español [Co-occurrence restrictions among fricative obstruents in innovative Spanish dialects]. In Francisco Moreno, Francisco Gimeno, José Antonio Samper, María Luz Gutiérrez, María Vaquero & César Hernández (eds.), *Lengua, variación y contexto. Estudios dedicados a Humberto López Morales*, 907–922. Madrid: Arco/Libros.

2003f. El conflicto entre los principios universales y los modelos ideales de pronunciación: Restricciones de buena formación y de fidelidad en la fonología del español de Andalucía [The conflict between universal principles and ideal models of pronunciation: Markedness and faithfulness constraints in the phonology of Andalusian Spanish]. In Juan Antonio Moya-Corral & María Isabel Montoya (eds.), *Variación lingüística y enseñanza de la lengua española. Actas de las VIII jornadas sobre la enseñanza de la lengua*, 85–105. Granada: Universidad de Granada.

2004a, with Matilde Vida-Castro. The effect of social prestige on reversing phonological changes: Universal constraints on speech variation in Southern European Spanish. In Matts Thelander et al. (eds.), *Language variation in Europe. Papers from the 2nd International Conference on Language Variation and Change in Europe (ICLaVE2). Uppsala University*, 2003, 432–444. Uppsala: University of Uppsala.

2004b. Recensión crítica de Carmen Silva-Corvalán. Sociolingüística y pragmática del español (con ejercicios de comprensión de Andrés Enrique-Arias) [A critical review of Carmen Silva-Corvalán. Sociolinguistics and pragmatics of Spanish (including comprehension exercises by Andrés Enrique-Arias)]. Washington, DC: Georgetown University Press. 2001. Studies in Spanish Linguistics. *Oralia* 7. 298–325.

2004c, with Francisco Díaz-Montesinos. Condicionamientos internos en la variación de los pronombres personales átonos en Los hechos de Don Miguel Lucas de Iranzo [Internal conditioning in the variation of unstressed personal pronouns in Los Hechos de Don Miguel Lucas de Iranzo]. *Revista de Filología Española* 84(1). 95–127.

2005a. How similar are people who speak alike – Social networks and convergence and divergence of dialects. In Peter Auer, Frans Hinskens & Paul Kerswill (eds.), *Dialect change. convergence and divergence in European languages*, 303–334. Cambridge: Cambridge University Press.

2005b, with Juan Antonio Moya-Corral. Corpus orales del español de Andalucía. Los corpus de Málaga, Granada y Jaén [Oral corpora of Andalusian Spanish. The corpora of Malaga, Granada and Jaen]. *Oralia* 8. 189–212.

2005c. Sociolingüística. Perspectivas y límites [Sociolinguistics. Perspectives and limitations]. In Román Reyes (ed.), *Diccionario crítico de ciencias sociales. Terminología científico social*. Madrid: Universidad Complutense. https://webs.ucm.es/info/eurotheo /diccionario/S/index.html. (20 July, 2022.)

2006. Andaluz oriental y andaluz occidental: Estandarización y planificación en ¿una o dos comunidades de habla? [Eastern and western Andalusian: Standardisation and planning in one or two speech communities?]. In Ana María Cestero, Isabel Molina & Florentino Paredes (eds.), *Estudios sociolingüísticos del español de España y América*, 233–254. Madrid: Arco/Libros.

2007a. Redes sociales y variación lingüística: El giro interpretativo en el variacionismo sociolingüístico [Social networks and linguistic variation: The shift in interpretation in sociolinguistic variation]. In Pablo Cano, Isabel Fernández, Miguel González, Gabriela Prego & Monserrat Souto (eds.), *Actas del VI congreso de lingüística general. Vol III. Lingüística y variación de las lenguas (Santiago de Compostela, 3–7 de mayo de 2004)*, 2769–2803. Madrid: Arco/Libros.

2007b. Interacción de los factores internos y externos en la explicación de la variación fonológica. Análisis multivariante del patrón de pronunciación no sibilante [θ] de la consonante fricativa coronal [θ^s] en el español hablado en Málaga [The interaction of the internal and external factors in the explanation of phonological variation. A multivariate analysis of the pattern of the non-sibilant pronunciation [θ] of the coronal fricative consonant [θ^s] in the Spanish spoken in Malaga]. In Juan Antonio Moya-Corral & Marcin Sosinski (eds.), *Las hablas andaluzas y la enseñanza de la lengua. Actas de las XII jornadas sobre la enseñanza de la lengua española*, 69–97. Granada: Universidad de Granada.

2007c. Prólogo [Prologue]. In Matilde Vida-Castro (ed.), *El español hablado en Málaga. Corpus oral para su estudio sociolingüístico, I. Nivel de estudios bajo*, 7–14. Malaga: Sarriá.

2008a. Divergencia dialectal en el español de Andalucía: El estándar regional y la nueva koiné meridional [Dialect divergence in Andalusian Spanish: The regional standard and the new southern koine]. In Hans-Jörg Döhla, Raquel Montero & Francisco Báez de Aguilar (eds.), *Lenguas en diálogo. El iberorromance y su diversidad lingüística y literaria. Ensayos en homenaje a Georg Bossong*, 369–392. Madrid: Iberoamericana. Frankfurt am Main: Vervuert.

2008b. La formación del español común en Andalucía. Un caso de escisión prestigiosa [The development of common Spanish. A case of a prestigious split]. In Esther Herrera & Pedro Martín-Butragueño (eds.), *Fonología instrumental. Patrones fónicos y variación*, 211–253. Mexico City: El Colegio de México.

2008c, with Antonio Manuel Ávila-Muñoz & María de la Cruz Lasarte-Cervantes (eds.). *El español hablado en Málaga II. Corpus oral para su estudio sociolingüístico. Nivel de estudios medio* [The Spanish spoken in Malaga II. An oral corpus for sociolinguistic research. Medium educational level]. Malaga: Sarriá.

2008d. Sociolinguistic patterns of Andalusian Spanish. *International Journal of the Sociology of Language* 193–194. 139–160.

2008e. The Iberian Peninsula/Die iberische Halbinsel. In Ulrich Ammon, Norbert Dittmar, Klaus Mattheier & Peter Trudgil (eds.), *Soziolinguistik/Sociolinguistics. An International Handbook of the Science of Language and Society (HSK)*, vol. 3, 2nd edn., 1802–1810. Berlin & New York, NY: De Gruyter Mouton.

2009a, with María de la Cruz Lasarte-Cervantes, José María Sánchez-Sáez & Antonio Manuel Ávila-Muñoz (eds.). *El español hablado en Málaga III. Corpus oral para su estudio sociolingüístico. Nivel de estudios alto* [The Spanish spoken in Malaga III. An oral corpus for sociolinguistic research. High educational level]. Malaga: Sarriá.

2009b, with Juan Manuel Hernández-Campoy. Standardness and non-standardness in Spain: Dialect attrition and revitalization of regional dialects of Spanish. *International Journal of the Sociology of Language* 196–197. 181–214.

2009c, with Juan Antonio Moya-Corral, José Ramón Gómez-Molina, Francisco Díaz-Montesinos & María Concepción Torres-López. Proyecto para el estudio sociolingüístico del español de España y América (PRESEEA). Proyecto coordinado: Estudio del español de Las Palmas, Lérida, Granada, Madrid-Alcalá, Málaga, Sevilla y Valencia [Project for the sociolinguistic study of Spanish in Spain and America (PRESEEA). Coordinated project: A study of the Spanish of Las Palmas, Lleida, Granada, Madrid-Alcala, Malaga, Seville and Valencia]. In Esteban Montoro & Juan Antonio Moya-Corral (eds.), *El español del siglo XXI. Actas de las XIV jornadas sobre la lengua española y su enseñanza*, 307–321. Granada: Universidad de Granada.

2010a, with Antonio Manuel Ávila-Muñoz. *Variación social del léxico disponible en la ciudad de Málaga* [Social variation in the available vocabulary of the city of Malaga]. Malaga: Sarriá.

2010b, with José María Sánchez-Sáez, Antonio Manuel Ávila-Muñoz & María de la Cruz Lasarte-Cervantes. Problemas de anotación e intercambio en los corpus orales. Estrategias para la transformación de textos etiquetados en documentos XML. El caso de los corpus PRESEEA [Problems of notation and exchange in oral corpora. Strategies for the processing of texts labelled in XML documents. The case of the PRESEEA corpora]. *Oralia* 13. 261–323.

2010c. Community-based investigations: From traditional dialect grammar to sociolinguistic studies. In Peter Auer & Jürgen E. Schmidt (eds.), *Language and space. An International Handbook of Linguistic Variation. Vol. 1. Theory and Methods*, 613–631. Berlin & New York, NY: De Gruyter Mouton.

2011a. Efectos fonológicos de la coexistencia de modelos ideales en la comunidad de habla y en el individuo. Datos para la representación de la variación fonológica del español de Andalucía [The phonological effects of the co-existence of ideal models in the speech community and the individual. Data for the description of phonological variation in Andalusian Spanish]. *Interlingüística* 16. 43–70.

2011b. Sobre la fonología del español de Andalucía. Constricciones sintagmáticas y paradigmáticas sobre la variación de las consonantes obstruyentes [On the phonology of Andalusian Spanish. Syntagmatic and paradigmatic constraints on the variation of obstruent consonants]. In José Jesús de Bustos-Tovar, Rafael Cano-Aguilar, Elena Méndez-García & Araceli López-Serena (coords.), *Sintaxis y análisis del discurso hablado en español. Homenaje a Antonio Narbona*, vol. 2, 1067–1086. Sevilla: Universidad de Sevilla.

2011c, with Francisco Díaz-Montesinos, Antonio Manuel Ávila-Muñoz & María de la Cruz Lasarte-Cervantes. Interacción de factores fonéticos y gramaticales en la variación fonológica: La elision de /d/ intervocálica en la variedad de los hablantes universitarios de la ciudad de Málaga [The interaction of phonetic and grammatical factors in phonological variation: The elision of intervocalic /d/ in the variety spoken by university students from the city of Malaga]. In Yolanda Congosto-Martín & Elena Méndez-García (eds.), *Variación lingüística y contacto de lenguas en el mundo hispánico. In memoriam Manuel Alvar*, 311–359. Frankfurt am Main: Vervuert. Madrid: Iberoamericana.

2012a, with Antonio Manuel Ávila-Muñoz (eds.). *Estudios sobre el español de Málaga. Pronunciación, léxico, sintaxis* [Studies on the Spanish of Malaga. Pronunciation, vocabulary, syntax]. Malaga: Sarriá.

2012b. Patrones sociolingüísticos del español de Andalucía [Sociolinguistic patterns in Andalusian Spanish]. In Juan Andrés Villena-Ponsoda & Antonio Manuel Ávila-Muñoz (eds.), *Estudios sobre el español de Málaga. Pronunciación, vocabulario y sintaxis*, 27–66. Malaga: Sarriá.

2012c, with Matilde Vida-Castro. La influencia del prestigio social en la reversión de los cambios fonológicos. Constricciones universales sobre la variación en el español ibérico meridional. Un caso de nivelación dialectal [The influence of social prestige on the reversal of phonological changes. Universal constraints on variation in southern Iberian Spanish. A case of dialect levelling]. In Juan Andrés Villena-Ponsoda & Antonio Manuel Ávila-Muñoz (eds.), *Estudios sobre el español de Málaga. Pronunciación, léxico, sintaxis*, 67–128. Malaga: Sarriá

2012d, with Antonio Manuel Ávila-Muñoz & José María Sánchez-Sáez. Condicionamiento social de la capacidad léxica individual. Patrones sociolingüísticos del vocabulario disponible en la ciudad de Málaga [Social conditioning of individual lexical capacity. Sociolinguistic patters in the available vocabulary of the city of Malaga]. In Antonio Manuel Ávila-Muñoz & Juan Andrés Villena-Ponsoda, *Estudios sobre el español de Málaga. Pronunciación, vocabulario y sintaxis*, 281–309. Malaga: Sarriá.

2012e. La investigación sociolingüística de la comunidad de habla: El origen inconformista de la dialectología social [Sociolinguistic research on the speech community: The nonconformist origin of social dialectology]. *Revista de Filología* 30. 155–176.

2012f, with Antonio Manuel Ávila-Muñoz & José María Sánchez-Sáez. Patrones sociolingüísticos del vocabulario disponible. Condicionamiento estratificacional de la capacidad léxica en la ciudad de Málaga. Proyecto CONSOLEX [Sociolinguistic patterns in available vocabulary. Stratificational conditioning of lexical capacity in the city of Malaga. The CONSOLEX project.]. In Emilio Ruidrejo, Teresa Solías, Nieves Mendizábal & Sara Alonso (eds.), *Tradición y progreso en la lingüística general*, 409–432. Valladolid: Universidad de Valladolid.

2012g. Estatus, red e individuo. Fundamentos del análisis escalonado de la variación lingüística. Elisión de /d/ en el español de Málaga [Status, network and the individual. Foundations of the scaled analysis of linguistic variation. The elision of /d/ in the Spanish of Malaga]. In José Francisco Val-Álvaro et al. (eds.), *Actas del X Congreso Internacional de Lingüística General*, 953–969. Zaragoza: Universidad de Zaragoza.

2012i, with Andrés Villena-Oliver. Vulnerabilidad cultural y capacidad léxica: Constricciones estructurales y biográficas del vocabulario virtual [Cultural vulnerability and lexical capacity: Structural and biographical constraints on virtual vocabulary]. In Antonio Pamies (ed.), *De lingüística, traducción y lexicofraseología. Homenaje a Juan de Dios Luque Durán*, 199–213. Granada: Comares.

2013. Actos de identidad. ¿Por qué persiste el uso de los rasgos lingüísticos de bajo prestigio social? Divergencia geográfica y social en el español urbano de Andalucía [Acts of identity. Why do linguistic features of low social prestige continue to be used? Geographic and social divergence in Andalusian urban Spanish]. In Rosario Guillén-Sutil & Rosario Millán-Garrido (coords.), *Sociolingüística Andaluza* 16. 173–207. Sevilla: Universidad de Sevilla.

2014a, with Antonio Manuel Ávila-Muñoz. Dialect stability and divergence in southern Spain. Social and personal motivations. In Kurt Braunmüller, Steffen Höder & Karoline Kühl (eds.), *Stability and Divergence in Language Contact. Factors and Mechanisms*, 207–38. Amsterdam: John Benjamins.

2014b. Review of John Bellamy. Language attitudes in England and Austria. A sociolinguistic investigation into perceptions of high and low-prestige varieties in Manchester and Vienna. *Zeitschrift Für Dialektologie und Linguistik* 81. 323–328. Stuttgart: Franz Steiner Verlag. 2012.

2014c. Necrologies. José Mondéjar. *Estudis Romànics* 36. 674–679.

2016a, with Giovanni Caprara & Emilio Ortega-Arjoni la (eds.). *Variación lingüística, traducción y cultura. De la conceptualización a la práctica professional* [Linguistic variation, translation and culture. From conceptualisation to professional practice]. Frankfurt am Main: Peter Lang.

2016b. Variación lingüística y traducción. Por qué el traductor necesita del variacionista [Linguistic variation and translation. Why the translator needs the variationist]. In Giovanni Caprara & Emilio Ortega-Arjonilla (eds.), *Variación lingüística, traducción y cultura. De la conceptualización a la práctica professional*, 15–124. Frankfurt am Main: Peter Lang.

2016c, with Matilde Vida-Castro. Percepción y análisis de pistas en la discriminación alofónica. Fusión y escisión en el estudio sociolingüístico de la ciudad de Málaga. Informe preliminar [The perception and analysis of clues in allophonic discrimination. Mergers and splits in the sociolinguistic study of the city of Malaga]. In Ana María Fernández-Planas (ed.), *53 reflexiones sobre aspectos de la fonética y otros temas de lingüística*, 129–137. Barcelona: Universidad de Barcelona.

2017a, with Juan Antonio Moya-Corral. Análisis comparativo de un cambio fonológico erosivo. Variación de /d/ intervocálica en dos comunidades de habla (Granada y Málaga) [A comparative analysis of an erosive phonological change. The variation of intervocalic /d/ in two speech communities (Granada and Malaga)]. *Boletín de Filología* 51(2). 281–321.

2017b, with Matilde Vida-Castro. Variación, identidad y coherencia en el español meridional. Sobre la indexicalidad de las variables convergentes en el español de Málaga [Variation, identity and coherence in southern Spanish. On the indexicality of the convergent variables in the Spanish of Malaga]. *Lingüística en la Red* 14. 1–32.

 2017c, with Matilde Vida-Castro. Between local and standard varieties: Horizontal and vertical convergence and divergence of dialects in Southern Spain. In Isabelle Buchstaller & Beat Siebenhaar (eds.), *Language Variation – European Perspectives VI*, 125–140. Amsterdam: John Benjamins.

2017d, with Antonio Manuel Ávila-Muñoz & María Clara von Essen. Efecto de la estratificación, la red social y las variables de pequeña escala en la variación léxica. Proyecto de investigación sobre la convergencia del léxico dialectal en la ciudad de Málaga (CONVERLEX) [The effect of stratification, social network and small-scale variables on lexical variation. Research project on the convergence of dialectal vocabulary in the city of Malaga (CONVERLEX)]. In Luis Luque-Toro & Rocío Luque (eds.), *Léxico Español Actual V*, 209–233. Venice: Università Ca' Foscari.

2018. The dilemma of the reliability of geolinguistic and dialectological data for sociolinguistic research. The case of the Andalusian demerger of /θ/. *Acta Lingüistica Lithuanica* 79. 9–36.

2019, with Francisco Díaz-Montesinos, Antonio Manuel Ávila-Muñoz, Matilde Vida-Castro (eds.). *Language Variation – European Perspectives VII*. Amsterdam & Philadelphia, PA: John Benjamins.

2020a, with Matilde Vida-Castro. Variation, identity and indexicality in southern Spanish. On the emergence of a new intermediate variety in urban Andalusia. In Massimo Cerruti & Stavroula Tsiplaklou (eds.), *Intermediate language varieties. Koinai and regional standards in Europe*, 149–182. Amsterdam: John Benjamins.

2020b, with Matilde Vida-Castro & Álvaro Molina-García. El paisaje sociolingüístico urbano de Andalucía. ¿Es el andaluz tan homogéneo como algunos creen? Datos de la ciudad de Málaga [The sociolinguistic urban landscape of Andalusia. Is Andalusian as homogenous as some believe? Data from the city of Malaga]. In Enrique Baena (coord.), *Visiones literarias y lingüísticas del paisaje urbano*, 135–162. Madrid: Marcial Pons.

2022, with Matilde Vida-Castro & Álvaro Molina-García. Coherence in a levelled variety. The case of Andalusian. In Karen B. Beaman & Gregory R. Guy (eds.), *The coherence of linguistic communities. Orderly heterogeneity and social meaning*, 239–257. New York, NY: Routledge.

2023a. El español en España [The Spanish of Spain]. In Francisco Moreno-Fernández & Rocío Caravedo (eds.), *Dialectología Hispánica. The Routledge Handbook of Spanish Dialectology*, 264–280. New York, NY: Routledge.

2023b, with Matilde Vida-Castro & María Isabel Molina-Martos. Variación de la /-s/ postnuclear en español: Patrones sociolingüísticos y geolectales [Variation of post-nuclear /-s/ in Spanish: Sociolinguistic and geolectal patterns]. *Círculo de Lingüística Aplicada a la Comunicación* 94. 23–35.

2023c, with Matilde Vida Castro & María Isabel Molina Martos. Guía PRESEEA de estudio de la /-s/ en coda [PRESEEA's guide to the study of postnuclear /-s/]. *Documentos PRESEEA de investigación*, 1–21. Alcalá: Universidad de Alcalá.

2023d, with Antonio Manuel Ávila-Muñoz & José María Sánchez-Sáez. Individual Lexical Breadth and its associated measures. A contribution to the calculation of individual lexical richness. In Irene Checa-García & Laura Marqués-Pascual (eds.), *Current perspectives on Spanish lexical development*. Berlin & New York, NY: De Gruyter Mouton.

Forthcoming a, with Antonio Manuel Ávila-Muñoz & Yorgos-Sionakidis. Las voces de Málaga. Reconstrucción histórica y archivo sonoro de la Ciudad Lingüística [The voices of Malaga. A historical reconstruction and audio archive of the linguistic city]. Malaga: Universidad de Málaga.

Forthcoming b, with Francisco Díaz Montesinos. ¿Los atlas la aburren o Los atlas le aburren? Distribución del uso de los clíticos pronominales no reflexivos de tercera persona en España e Hispanoamérica (CORPES XXI) [¿Los atlas la aburren o Los atlas le aburren? Third-person unstressed nonreflexive pronouns distribution in Spain and Latin America (CORPES XXI)]. In Isabel Molina Martos, Esther Hernández, Pedro Martín Butragueño & Eva Mendieta (eds.), *Caminos y palabras. Estudios de variación lingüística dedicados a Pilar García Mouton*. Valencia: Tirant lo Blanch.

Index

A
advergence 140–141
Arabic 73 *See also* Cairene
  Arabic, Moroccan Arabic

B
Baudouin de Courtenay, Jan 7,
  15, 18, 21–22, 24–25, 29, 31–35
broad focus. *See under* focus
Bybee, Joan 19, 20, 22–24, 27–29,
  31, 108, 116

C
Cairene Arabic 64 *See also*
  Arabic
Canarian Spanish 9, 100, 103,
  106
central Mexican Spanish. *See*
  under Mexican Spanish
centre of gravity (CoG or COG)
  56, 67–68, 82, 86, 89–90, 94 *See*
  also spectral moments, discrete
  cosine transformation
clitics 140–141, 145, 148, 150,
  152–162
coastal Spanish. *See under*
  Mexican Spanish
cognitivism 15, 16, 19, 21–24,
  27–30
    proto-cognitivism 29
composite varieties 8, 174, 182
contrastive focus. *See under*
  focus
convergence 4, 10–11, 13–14, 39,
  52–53, 159–160, 162, 164–165,
  167–168, 173, 178–182, 184–186,
  190
coronalisation 9, 79–84, 86,
  91–92, 94–96, 98
Cypriot Greek 10, 140–143, 145,
  147, 150–154, 156–159, 161–163

D
de-dialectalisation. *See under*
  dialectalisation

demerger. *See under* merger
destandardisation. *See under*
  standardisation
diaglossia 140, 154 *See also*
  diglossia
dialect contact 54, 100–101
dialect divergence 187
dialectalisation 95, 164, 165
  de-dialectalisation 135, 168,
  169, 173
diglossia 140, 164 *See also*
  diaglossia
discrete cosine transformation
  (DCT) 82, 86–94, 98 *See also*
  centre of gravity, spectral
  moments
dorsal fricatives 79, 80, 82, 94–95
Dutch. *See under* ethnolect:
  ethnolectal Dutch

E
enclisis 141–142, 144–145,
  147–152, 156, 158, 160
ethnolect 56, 58, 60, 61, 72
  ethnolectal Dutch 56
  Moroccan (ethnolectal)
    Dutch 56, 57, 60, 61, 62,
    64, 66, 68, 73, 74, 76, 77
  multi-ethnolect 58
  multi-ethnolect (German)
    79–81, 83–84, 94–95
  regional differentiation (in
    multi-ethnolects) 79–80,
    95, 178
  Turkish (ethnolectal)
    Dutch 56, 57, 60, 61, 62,
    66, 68, 69, 72, 73, 74, 75,
    77
  Turkish/German 81
exceptional clitic placement 145,
  147, 151–153, 156–157, 161

F
first language acquisition. *See*
  under language acquisition

Firth, John 17, 18, 27, 31, 34
focus
  broad focus (BF) 121, 129,
    130, 132, 133, 135, 136, 138
  contrastive focus (CF)
    129–130, 132, 135–136,
    149–150
  narrow focus (NF) 129, 130,
    132–133, 135–136
frequency. *See* word frequency

G
gender 9, 37–38, 40–41, 45–46,
  50, 53–54, 60, 65, 76–78, 85, 88,
  91–92, 94, 96, 100, 106, 108,
  111–114, 116, 119, 122, 130,
  132–133, 134, 150, 183–185
German. *See under* ethnolect:
  (German) multiethnolect
Greek. *See* Cypriot Greek,
  Standard Greek

H
Hjelmslev, Louis 17, 26, 32
hybrid variant 9, 104–105,
  107–108, 110–111, 115
hybrid grammar 149
hybridism 115

I
implicational scale 168–171
information structure 119,
  132–133, 135–136, 157
interdialectalism 100–102, 114
Italian 10, 81, 164–182
Italo-Romance dialects 10,
  164–167, 172–173, 178–179, 181

J
Jones, Daniel 16, 17, 32

K
koine 6, 10, 140–141, 147, 157,
  161–162, 187
koineisation 160, 163

L

Langacker, Ronald Wayne 19, 22–23, 28, 33
language acquisition
  first and second language acquisition 56
  second language acquisition 8, 58, 60, 72, 118, 157, 163
language change 14, 32, 100–101, 118, 157, 163
language contact 8, 12, 56, 58, 77, 101, 138, 160, 180
language variation vii-viii, 3, 56, 77, 100, 160, 163, 180
levelling 51, 135, 140, 163, 179, 189
lowland Spanish. *See under* Mexican Spanish

M

mental representation 7, 15–16, 20, 23, 26, 29
merger 5, 8, 36–39, 43, 46–47, 49, 50, 52–55, 79, 82–83, 89, 95, 97, 190
  demerger 191
  near-merger 39, 51, 53–54
  (quasi-) merger 80, 94
Mexican Spanish 9, 119–120, 138
  central Mexican Spanish 135–136, 139
  coastal (Mexican Spanish) 121, 133–136
  lowland (Mexican Spanish) 119, 121, 133, 135
Moroccan Arabic 72, 73, 76, 77 *See also* Arabic, ethnolect: Moroccan (ethnolectal) Dutch
multi-ethnolect. *See under* ethnolect
multi-ethnolect (German). *See under* ethnolect

N

narrow focus (NF). *See under* focus
near-merger. *See under* merger
neo-standard 167, 173, 179
nuclear pitch accent. *See under* pitch accent

P

palatalisation 2, 8, 56–57, 61–71, 73–78, 85
peak alignment 122 *See also* tonal peak
perception 8, 16, 19, 21, 23–24, 26–28, 32–33, 36, 38–39, 44–50, 52, 53, 58, 78, 82, 94, 98, 117–118, 134, 190
phoneme 7, 15–19, 21–36
  diphoneme 27
  triphoneme 27
phonetics 15, 17, 24, 26, 30–34, 36
phonology 7, 15–23, 25–35, 53, 116
pitch accent 10, 119–136
  nuclear pitch accent 119–132, 135–136
proclisis 141, 143–145, 147–153, 156, 158, 160
production 8, 16, 23, 27–28, 36, 38–41, 43, 47–52

Q

(quasi-) merger. *See under* merger

R

regional differentiation (in multi-ethnolects). *See under* ethnolect
regional features 39, 54, 109, 166, 168–169, 178–179
regional varieties 10, 164–167, 169, 173–174, 178, 180
restandardisation. *See under* standardisation

S

Sapir, Edward 7, 15, 16, 25, 26, 27, 29, 30, 34
Saussure, Ferdinand 16, 17, 18, 26, 32, 34
second language acquisition. *See under* language acquisition
semi-standardisation. *See under* standardisation
social meaning 56, 58, 65–66, 77, 83, 99, 115
socioprosody 119, 121–122
Spanish. *See* Canarian Spanish, Mexican Spanish

spectral moments 86, 89–94, 98
  See also centre of gravity, discrete cosine transformation
Standard Greek 10, 140–141, 147, 152–153, 155, 157
standardisation 100–101, 103, 110, 117, 187
  destandardisation 179
  restandardisation 167, 169, 173
  semi-standardisation 103
  See also neo-standard
Stankiewicz, Edward 18, 21, 23, 24, 25, 26, 31, 34
stratification by age 135–136
structuralism 16–20, 29–30
Swedish 8, 36–55 *See also* Uppland (region of), Uppland Swedish
syllable duration 119

T

Tobler-Mussafia (law) 142, 155–156
tonal peak 119, 122, 124–136 *See also* peak alignment
Turkish 72, 73, 76, 81, 97 *See also* ethnolect: Turkish (ethnolectal) Dutch, Turkish/German
Twaddell, William 17, 18, 21, 25, 26, 35

U

Uppland (region of) 7, 36, 37, 50. *See also* Swedish
Uppland Swedish 55 *See also* Swedish
usage-based phonology 20
usage-based cognitive linguistics 24
usage-based model 25, 28

V

vowel change 37–38, 40, 55
word frequency 7, 15, 20–21, 24, 28–29, 43, 46, 67, 80, 106–108, 111–113, 116